The author is a graduate engineer, who rapidly progressed up the ranks in each of the several manufacturing companies that he worked for, becoming Director of Engineering at the age of 33 and promoted to Plant Operations Manager of 1200 employees at 35. At 44, the author started his own business and used that as a springboard to purchase and successfully run several more businesses and commercial properties. Over the years, the author has gained an incredible knowledge of how to negotiate, fund, purchase and operate a vast array of businesses.

Antoine Ferducci

THE GROCER

AUSTIN MACAULEY PUBLISHERS™

LONDON ★ CAMBRIDGE ★ NEW YORK ★ SHARJAH

Ordering Information
Quantity sales: Special discounts are available on quantity purchases by corporations, associations, and others. For details, contact the publisher at the address below.

Publisher's Cataloging-in-Publication data
Ferducci, Antoine
The Grocer

ISBN 9798889102779 (Paperback)
ISBN 9798889102786 (Hardback)
ISBN 9798889102793 (ePub e-book)

Library of Congress Control Number: 2023918629

www.austinmacauley.com/us

First Published 2024
Austin Macauley Publishers LLC
40 Wall Street, 33rd Floor, Suite 3302
New York, NY 10005
USA

mail-usa@austinmacauley.com
+1 (646) 5125767

Author's Note

Other than Tony, there are no names; of cities or individuals. The men are referred to by capital letters. All of the women, men and places are a figment of Tony's imagination, yet the realism in the story is incredibly believable.

Introduction

WOW! Here I am sitting in the conference room of the largest bank in town, waiting for the bank's attorney, so that we can conduct the 'closing' of the purchase of the only grocery store in town … from the present elderly owners, to me, a 21-year-old, first-time businessman.

When the bank's attorney arrived, with a large folder in his hand, he sat at the head of the large conference room table and apologized for the delay. To his left were the three elderly brothers that owned the grocery store (Mr. X, the store manager, Mr. Y, the grocery manager and Mr. Z, the frozen food manager) and their attorney. To his right sat the bank manager, then me and my attorney.

The bank manager introduced me and my attorney. Then the bank's attorney opened his thick file folder and began the proceedings.

The first order of business was to review and approve the inventory (which we had taken the day before). The store's accountant had prepared a formal summary report showing the inventory of goods and another report showing the equipment inventory … our earlier estimates weren't far off.

Mr. X (the president of the grocery store) passed copies of the inventories to everyone.

I explained that I had participated in the inventory, and I agreed with the totals.

The remainder of the purchase was detailed in the formal Purchase and Sale agreement that we all (me and the three brothers) had previously signed.

Then, we each signed the appropriate documents and checks were prepared for each of the brothers.

Finally … it was DONE!

I owed sooo much money … it was unbelievable. I had never had a loan of any nature in the past. While I act fairly mature, I am thinking that the bank is taking a big chance with me.

How did all of this get started?
You will have to read on.

Chapter 1

When it came to my twenty-first birthday this year, my folks made a big deal out of it!

Of course, my sister, her husband and all of the aunts and uncles were there … it was a beautiful day … we played horse shoes, barbequed Hamburg's, Hot Dogs, Steaks and a wide variety of Italian dishes. I even had a beer … to satisfy everyone that I had an alcoholic drink!

I got several golf shirts (all black … I wear only black clothes, black socks and black shoes or black sneakers), several ties, some aftershave and my Uncle T gave me $200 to put towards my next car (Uncle T was my godfather and always was very generous to me).

My mother had three older brothers, all married. Uncle J was the oldest and he owned a gas station/garage; he had one daughter, who was older, married and they moved away. My Uncle T owned a large construction company and my uncle A, the youngest brother, owned a painting company.

My father had only one brother, Uncle R and he owned a carpet and tile store, he had one daughter and she worked in the store with him. All of my relatives lived within 20 miles of us.

I was the only boy in our immediate family; Uncle J had a daughter, Uncle R had a daughter, but Uncle T and Uncle A had no children and were always interested in what and how I was doing.

All of my relatives were impressed to hear that I had been made assistant manager at the grocery store … I was very proud and somewhat embarrassed.

How did I get here? Well, I live in a very small town. The son of Italian immigrants. I have a sister, four years older than me (married and both her and her husband work as graduate pharmacists).

I am 6'2" inches tall, thin, with jet black hair and olive skin. My mane is Antoine Ferducci … but everyone calls me Tony.

At work: now, I was able legally, to order, receive and handle any or all of the alcoholic beverages for the store. I did a lot of work for Mr. Z.

One day back (when I was 17 years old), when I got to work, Mr. Z had his arm in a sling, he had evidentially hurt it the day before and went to the emergency room that evening. He pulled me aside and said that I would need to help him out for a few days (Mr. Y had approved). First thing, I needed to drive the company pick-up truck to the grocery warehouse to pick-up our mid-week order. He gave me directions and off I went.

When I got to the warehouse, I had to find a certain bay (which was for pick-up trucks) and back in between two large 18 wheelers. As I backed in, a man came out and had me back in close to the dock.

I told him that Mr. Z had sent me to pick up our weekly order.

He asked, "Where is Mr. Z?"

I told him that Mr. Z had injured his arm the day before and was unable to use it for several days.

The guy said, "You know, he is too old to be slugging around all of these heavy boxes?"

I just nodded in agreement.

The guy then said that he would go into the office, find my paperwork and pull my order. Fifteen minutes later he was delivering a skid of merchandise, to the dock behind my truck. As he drove away, he informed me that he had two more skids. When he came back, (I had taken several cases from the first skid and put them on the floor of the truck, all the way back against the cab), he asked me if I had ever loaded a truck before … so I told him that I hadn't. He came down onto the pickup and showed me that I should put two cases on the floor, one on top of the other, next I should put a carton, partially on/over the sidewall of the truck, resting on the cases on the floor, slightly below … leaving the carton on an angle. This way, I could load cartons well over the side of the truck, without them falling off as I traveled. Great!

I continued to load all of the rest of the cases from the three skids, finishing with a stack which was well over my head. I was physically beat, and I was wondering how Mr. Z could do this every week.

Before I left, I took a long rope from the truck and strapped down my load. The guy gave me all the paperwork and I signed for the product and left for home.

The back of my truck was weighted down so badly I wondered if the front tires were still on the ground. In any event, I drove back to the store slowly, watching my side view mirrors, to see if anything fell off … nothing fell!

When I got back to the store, Mr. Z and Mr. X were waiting for me.

Mr. Z asked me, "Where the hell have you been?"

My reply was that I had been busting my butt, loading the truck and driving back.

Mr. Z had me back up to the door we used for deliveries … I hooked up the roller conveyor and loaded the entire load onto the conveyor … while Mr. Z checked each item off the list of the paperwork, I had gotten from the warehouse guy. When I finished unloading the truck, I was really exhausted … Mr. Z looked up and down his inventory list and remarked, "That was everything on the list!"

I was thinking, *Great, I didn't lose anything,* but Mr. Z said, "It usually takes me two trips to pick up all of that stuff … no wonder you took so long!" Then he said, "You must be tired … take a break … I am going to tell Mr. X that you picked up the entire order in half the time it takes me … when I come back, we (me) can unload the conveyor, downstairs."

I sat for 10 minutes and then I went down to the basement and started to unload the conveyor. After 10 to 15 minutes Messrs. X, Y and Z came down to the basement to tell me what a wonderful job I was doing and to ask if I would mind picking up the mid-week orders in the future. I was flattered that they were happy with my performance and of course I would be pleased to pick up the mid-week orders in the future.

Mr. Z stayed and watched me unloading the conveyor.

After a while, I said, "I don't know how you have done this … it is an exhausting job."

Mr. Z agreed and said that usually, he picks up the mid-week order on my day off … but since he had hurt his arm, they waited for me to come in and pick the order up. He continued to tell me that he usually picked up half the load, came back to the store, unloaded the cases onto the conveyor and while he was going back to pick up the next load, Mr. Y would take the inventory and start to unload the conveyor. When he came back with the second order, he again unloaded the cases onto the conveyor, while Mr. Y inventoried the load. Then they would both go down to the basement and unload the conveyor. Then, Mr. Z said, even though it was mid-day he would go home, take a nap and sleep until dinner time.

He was amazed at the ease that I appeared to be performing the same job that would wear him out.

He said, "I am not as young as I used to be!"

So, from that day forward, I picked up the mid-week order. When I was in school, I would go immediately, to pick up the order, unload it onto the conveyor and while Messrs. Y and Z inventoried and put it away, I would do the deliveries for the day. When I returned, I would help the two managers to put any remaining cases from the order away.

In the middle of the summer, after my 21st birthday, Mr. X invited me to lunch, on my day off, at noon, at a real good steak restaurant down the street.

He said, "We park in the back of the building so that we can't be found!"

So, I showed up at 12:00 pm promptly to find all three brothers at a table and they had been there a while, given their almost empty martini glasses.

They seemed overly pleased to see me (of course they had been drinking). When I sat down, Mr. X called the waitress over and ordered another round.

It was my first martini, fortunately, I took a small sip … it burned all the way down to my belly.

"Well," Mr. X said, "I have decided that it is time for me to retire … sometime between now and the end of the year … and my brothers will retire at the same time!"

"WOW!" I replied, and I took a drink of the martini, "Good for you guys … but what will happen to the store?"

The three smiled at me and Mr. X said, "We plan to sell the store to you!"

"ME!" I exclaimed … and all three nodded their heads up and down. "Holy Cow … but I do not have the kind of money it would take to buy the store."

Mr. X replied, "We know … I have already spoken to the manager of the bank that handles the store's finances … he is very interested in meeting you on Friday."

Mr. X continued, "You will need a down payment … which my brothers' and I will split three ways and loan to you … you will pay us back monthly, over five years. You will purchase the building, all fixtures, coolers, counters, cash registers, desks … plus, all of the product, produce, meats … in other words, everything in the store … one exception … Mr. Z will keep the pickup truck … you will have to buy a new one."

My head was spinning! I called the waitress over and ordered a large iced tea … the brothers all ordered another martini … I don't know how they could handle it.

Mr. X went on, "Stop by my office this afternoon … I have had my accountant prepare a Proforma, for the bank … you will need to present it to the Bank Manager on Friday. My accountant has even calculated how you will handle all of the payments … even the 'side payments' to me and my brothers."

"WOW … I was shocked … you could push me over with a feather … never in my wildest dreams did I think I would ever have the chance to own the store!"

Mr. X then said, "WELL … do you want to purchase the store from us?"

"Yes … but I would like to bounce it off my folks, first."

"Of course," Mr. X replied, "just give me your final answer, tomorrow … in the meantime, do not mention this to anyone … and I mean anyone!"

"Okay, I will see you in about an hour," I said and I headed for the door.

I was floating on a cloud all the way home. When I got there, Mom was home, alone.

I said, "Today, is the greatest day of my life! Mr. X and his brothers all want to retire before the end of the year and they want to sell the store, to me! Can you believe that?"

"But you don't have any money," Mom replied.

"I am going back to the store for Mr. X to show me how it can happen … each of the brothers are going to loan me one third of the down payment … don't mention this to anyone … please."

When I got back to the store, all three brothers met me in the office, Mr. X opened a booklet on his desk and said, "Our accountant prepared this 'Proforma' for us, so that Tony can present it to the bank tomorrow."

He pulled out a very long sheet of paper and said, "This shows our itemized income and expenses for the past five years, and projected for the next 10 years … it does not show any 'side expenses' (in other words … Tony's repayments to the three of us). Expenses will rise and so will income … but the biggest change is Tony and a new Frozen Goods Manager, will make half of what we make now … plus there is a savings in taxes and insurance benefits for the three of us … so the difference, which is two of our salaries, plus benefits can be put toward the bank loans … and of course there will be enough to cover our 'side payment'." He continued, "Also, in this booklet is Tony's offer to buy the business … that is so much for the building, property, equipment (fixtures, coolers, counters, freezers, registers, etc.), inventory and goodwill."

Each of the brothers and I opened their booklet and followed very closely, what Mr. X was saying.

Then he went on, "To show his estimate for what the building is worth, is a page showing the tax value and another page showing the value of the building that our Insurance Carrier came up with … also, he used the Insurance Carriers' estimate for the value of the equipment and the inventory … lastly, he came up with a 'fair' value for goodwill. I worked with the accountant to put this together and I feel it is a fair offer for all of us … of course the bank will have to get their appraiser to verify these numbers … and a complete inventory will have to be done, just prior to closing to establish the exact value of the inventory … what do you guys think?"

I said, "While there are a ton of numbers, it all boils down to how can I payback all of the loans … and the answer is the savings in payroll, associated taxes and insurance premiums from not having to pay the three of you!"

Mr. X was impressed, he said, "Tony, you got it!" Then he gave me a separate, long sheet, showing the impact of the payments to the three brothers, over the first five years.

The other brothers felt it was fair as well. They were all in agreement, but I hadn't given my final approval.

So, Mr. X said, "Please give us your decision in the morning."

He then told me to take home the booklet and review all of the numbers for our meeting with the Bank Manager the next day at 1:00 pm … and to make my decision!

That evening, after dinner, I showed Mom and Dad the Performa and I explained the numbers … they agreed that it looked very 'doable' but felt I should bounce it of my Uncle T, since he had a lot of experience with these types of things … great idea. My Uncle T was my godfather, and he owned a large contracting business. So, I called my Uncle T and he was available to see me.

In Uncle T's office, I presented the Performa … he reviewed the package and agreed that the offer appeared to be doable and fair. Of course, he asked me how much I needed from him … I was embarrassed … and said, I didn't feel I would need his help financially … I needed his experience more than anything. My uncle was impressed and told me that my presentation was excellent and when I needed the pickup truck, he would buy it for me, as a 'new business' gift … gee how generous!

———————

The next day, when I showed up for work, I told Mr. X and his brothers, that I was delighted to purchase the store (I think they were delighted, as well). Again, I had to say how thankful I was that they would trust me, with their 'baby'.

At noon, I shot home to change into my suit and then, I met Mr. X at the bank.

Mr. X and the Bank Manager appeared to be very friendly … they had worked together for a long time. So, Mr. X introduced me and explained that I had worked at the store for over five years and that I had an excellent feel for the business. He went on to say that he and his brothers were getting on in age and that they each wanted to retire before the end of the year. Fortunately, Tony made an offer that he and his brothers felt was very fair … but Tony needs funding.

With that said, I told the Bank Manager that I had my accountant prepare a 'Performa' and I handed each of them a booklet. I opened the booklet, turned to the offer page and explained what I was offering for the business. Then, I showed how I came up with the offer numbers. Next, I pulled out the long sheet of paper and went over the Income and Expense Report, to show how I expected to pay for the business. Finally, I said what I wanted to put down, as a down payment.

The Bank Manager said that he was impressed with my presentation … he asked several questions, which Mr. X or I answered. Then he said he was very knowledgeable regarding the profitability of the store, but he would like some time to review my plan and to come up with how the bank would fund it.

I said that I would wait for the Bank Manager's call.

We all shook hands and when Mr. X and I left the bank, he asked me to meet him at the steak house for a drink.

At the steak house, I met Mr. X at a table (he had a martini, and I had an iced tea) … he told me that I had just made an excellent presentation! He did not feel that there would be any major issues that we could not overcome. Then I went home, changed and went back to work.

How did I come to be a grocer?

When I was younger, I worked on a farm, which my mom hated, because when I came home my clothes were filthy and smelly. Then, when I was 15, I went to work on tobacco, with my older friends … same filthy clothes, not as smelly but it paid better. I was always a hard worker and didn't give a care how hard the work was.

Well, on the afternoon that I turned 16, my mom told me to go up to the local grocery store, to apply for a job. There were three Italian brothers that owned the store, and the oldest brother was the Store Manager, another brother was the Grocery Manager, and the third brother was the Frozen Food and Refrigerated Food Manager. Mom told me repeatedly, to tell the Manager (Mr. X), I was HER son. So, I walked to the store (about six blocks) and I went up to the Manager Mr. X and I said to the Manager, "You know my mom, Mary Ferducci … right?"

He said, "Yes of course."

So, I asked him for a job. He smiled at me and had me walk with him to his office, where he pulled out a file from his desk drawer, opened it up, turned over several pages and said, "You can add your name to the list … next to number 185."

I was flabbergasted … so I said, "I am not looking for a job when I retire … I am looking for a job now."

The manager laughed heartily and replied, "No, you won't need to wait that long, since many of the fellas will have already found a job by the time, I give them a call … plus many of these names are girls and they just work on the cash register (remember this was in the olden days)." So, I reluctantly wrote my name and phone number on line number 185.

When I got home, my mom asked me what day I was going to start, and I told her on my 75th birthday! Mom did not think my reply was funny. No, she scowled at me and asked why? I told her that I was number 185 on the list for new hires.

Mom said sternly, "Did you tell the manager that you were my son?"

"Yes, I did."

Mom was in the process of making supper, so she said, "Tomorrow you and I are going to that store, and I am going to tell that manager, When I send my son to this store for a job, you are supposed to give him a job."

You know Italian women are very possessive … but I am thinking, *what did my mom ever do for the grocery store … she can't be buying lots more groceries than the other moms.* So, I was befuddled.

The next day right after lunch, Mom said, "Let's go," and the two of us walked to the store (my mom didn't have a license to drive).

When we walked into the store, Mom walked right toward the store manager, who said, as soon as he saw her, "Marie!"

Then he put out his arms wide to give her a hug … which as I remembered he and the other two managers would do every time my mom went to the store (I never gave it a thought).

Before he got to Mom, she stopped and said sternly, "Don't you Marie me, when I send my son to this store for a job, you are supposed to give him a job."

Mr. X looked right at me and said, "He didn't say he was your son!" Then he asked me, "What time do you get out of school tomorrow?"

I replied, "2:45."

He then asked, "Can you be here by 3:15?"

I replied, "Sure."

Mr. X then told me to come in the back door and to the right was a clock to punch in. Next to the clock are the timecards and there will be one with my name on it, in the adjacent rack.

"You will be working for Mr. Y (his brother), the grocery manager, as a stock boy."

Then he turned his attention to my mother and said, "I am soooo sorry for the confusion, I just don't think of you by your married name."

Just then, Mr. Y was walking near us, and Mr. X called him over, to say, "This is your new stock boy, he starts tomorrow."

Mr. Y had a confused look on his face … and said, "I didn't know I needed another stock boy?"

Mr. X replied, "This is Marie's son … Tony."

At that point, Mr. Y noticed my mom standing behind Mr. X … and he immediately threw out his arms, put a huge smile on his face and as he gave my mom a big hug he said (very loudly), "Marieee!"

Then, he put his arm around my shoulders and escorted me to the back of the store, where we found his brother, Mr. Z, the Frozen Food Manager … "Look who I have here … my newest hire … Marie's son, Tony … he starts tomorrow!"

Mr. Z, the smallest of the brothers, put a wide smile on his face, gave me a big hug and said, "Welcome, Tony … soooo glad to meet you!"

It was a very warm gesture, because I could tell that Mr. X and Mr. Y were not necessarily enamored with my hiring.

Next, Mr. Y brought me in back and introduced me to the head butcher and the other butchers. Finally, we went back out on the floor and Mr. Y introduced me to the other stock boy, whom he said had worked there for three years and he told him to work with me, for a few days, to break me in.

I had seen him at school, but I had never met him before. He was a senior and just graduated from high school.

I guess that was it for introductions, my mom was headed down the aisle, so Mr. Y said, "Okay, then … we'll see you tomorrow," and he left.

Mom and I finished the shopping and went to check out. The two lady cashiers had, evidently, heard of my hiring and they, very congenially, welcomed me to the crew … very nice.

Mom didn't buy a lot, but it filled up a bag, which I picked up and carried home.

On the way home, I asked my mom, "What the heck did you ever do for those grocery guys … for them to drop everything and hire me?"

She smiled and said, "Back when me and my family moved here from Italy, their family, also just moved here from Italy, and they moved in right next door to us. They have a much younger sister, and she was my best friend. We all lived in the Italian section of the large city to the north."

Okay, now I understand!

———

So, the following day I shot over to the store, right after school and actually got to the store a little early. I punched in and then met the other stock boy. A senior, that I knew since we played on the same little league team … years ago. He had one year of experience. The other stock boy came in and we all spoke for a few minutes then Mr. Y came in and gave each of the other stock boys a list of groceries that needed to be refilled on the shelves.

My trainer showed me where the aprons were kept and got me a price stamper and a holster for my stamp. After putting on the bright white apron and holster, I started to feel like I was then, an employee.

Next, we went down a flight of stairs to the basement, where skids and skids of groceries were stored. We went up and down the aisles, picking up one or two cases of canned goods that were on my trainers list (me picking up the cases) and carrying them over to a roller conveyor (me carrying the cases to the conveyor), that ran along the wall.

When we retrieved all the items on the list, we pushed them along the conveyor to a powered conveyor, that went up next to the stairs to the main floor. Where we (me) took the cases off the conveyor and stacked them on a pushcart. We (me) then pushed the cart out to the first aisle, to the first item, that needed to be replenished. My trainer then informed me that I needed to cut off the top of the cardboard box with my case cutter (razor knife) … which I didn't have, so we went to the back room where he showed me where to get a brand-new case cutter … plus he showed me where the ink was and how to ink up the stamp, neat!

Then, he showed me, that the price per can, was on a label attached to the shelf, below where the cans went. Next, he took me up to the front, register #3, and showed me a booklet that contains the price of every item in the store (so if I came upon a new item to the store, I could find the price).

Eventually, we got back to the item that we needed to price … he showed me how to put the price into my stamp and how to stamp each can legibly. I put the cans on the shelf, broke down (flattened) the empty cardboard box and we moved on to the next item. Although it was fairly repetitive, I really enjoyed the work.

You see before computers came into the grocery store, we had to mark each item with its price. Then the cashier would 'type' the price into the register, for each item separately. There was no scanning.

After a while, Mr. X came to get me and take me to the office. I needed to fill out a bunch of 'new hire' forms. He asked me if I could work 3:15 to closing; Monday, Tuesday, Thursday and Friday, and Saturday from 8:00am to closing at 6:00 pm, while in school and 8:00am to closing when school is out.

"WOW," I said, "That's a lot of hours … I had the feeling that you guys didn't need me, but gave me a job because of my mother."

"Oh no," Mr. X replied, "we have big plans for you!"

"Well, thank you," I said.

Then we talked for a few minutes, before he asked, "How is everything going so far?" I told him that I had a lot to learn, but it was going great so far and I enjoyed the work.

Next, he gave me a sheet of paper with the 'Rules of the Store':

1. No swearing, no yelling, no horsing around on the market floor.
2. When you hear the cashier ring the bell, go immediately to the front and help bag groceries.
3. If a man purchases one bag of groceries, he can carry it to his car or if he chooses the Stock Boy can carry the bag to his car. The same is true if a woman purchases a small bag of groceries. BUT, if a man or a woman purchases more than one bag of groceries the Stock Boy MUST bring all of the groceries to the customers car (the same if a woman purchases one full bag of groceries).
4. Always address the customer as – Ma'am or Sir … and be polite.
5. Always come to work with clean clothes and be well groomed.
6. NEVER come to work under the influence, or with alcohol on your breath.
7. If you are unable to work your shift or if you are coming in late, give us as much notice as possible.
8. If you are injured – come to the office or contact the office as soon as possible.
9. NO SMOKING!

When I finished reading the rules, I looked up and Mr. X said, "We are a small-town store, but we offer the best meat that you can buy and the best hometown service … always remember that we must provide the best service to our customers … look at the butchers, when they see a customer at the counter, they come out and help that customer, so does my brother down in frozen goods, as well as me and my brother in the grocery area … you need to always realize that we need to provide the customer with the best professional service that we and you can provide."

With that said, I went back to work. My trainer was about half done with the shelf stocking and he looked amazed to see me. "Where have you been," he asked.

"I had to fill out all the new employee paperwork with Mr. X," I replied … just then, we heard the cashier's bell ring. So, we hustled up to the front to bag groceries. My trainer said, "Watch me," as he snapped open a brown paper bag, "put the heavy items on the bottom … start with cans and bottles first, then boxes and bread, rolls and any items that will crush goes on top," which is what he was doing as he spoke. "If you have a lot of cans, open more bags and cover the bottoms with the cans … if there are lots and lots of cans, ask the customer if they would like a box." After he put all the items in bags, the trainer put the bags in the customer's empty cart and he pushed the cart into the parking lot and asked the customer where she preferred to put the bags … she said, "In the back seat," which is where he put her groceries … I watched, paid attention and followed him around like a puppy dog.

When we went back into the store, it was starting to get busy and both cash registers were checking out customers. So, we separated … I went to one counter and my trainer went to the other counter and he kept his eye on me, so he could give me a heads up, as certain things occurred … like when a gallon of ice cream came down the conveyor, he said, "Put that in a smaller, separate bag."

I really enjoyed bagging groceries … I noticed, it was like putting together the pieces of a puzzle and the more I did it the faster I became.

So, I bagged up until closing time. Then my trainer brought me into the back room, to show me where to hang my apron and holster … then we punched out for the day.

When I got home, Mom had put aside a dish for my supper. She and my dad wanted to know how my first day went. I was ecstatic … I told them I learned to; find, mark product and stock shelves and bag groceries … Mom was ecstatic as well, my clothes were clean, and I didn't smell!

As the days passed, I became more and more proficient in bagging groceries and stocking shelves. Also, over time, I became Mr. Z's right-hand man. I could see Mr. Z struggling when he received a large order of beer or wine … so I asked him if I could help. When we received deliveries, the truck would back up to a garage door which lined up with our powered conveyor … we would hook up a roller conveyor from the truck to the powered conveyor and the cases would roll from the truck, onto the powered conveyor, down to the basement. Mr. Z would do an inventory as the cases came by (Mr. Y would do the inventory if we received groceries). To handle alcoholic items, you had to be 21 years old, but I worked under Mr. Z's supervision.

We had a locked cooler (and a freezer) in the basement and all of the beer and wine had to be moved, by hand, from the conveyor into the cooler … it was a workout for me to move all the heavy cases … I don't know how Mr. Z could do it, he seemed to struggle moving the cases, although he had been doing it for many years. As time went by, Mr. Z would borrow me, to move anything heavy (alcoholic or frozen) from the basement to the main floor coolers, or from the main floor to the basement coolers, always under his supervision. Mr. Z was always very appreciative of the work that I did for him.

During this period of time (after I turned 16) my dad started to teach me to drive … I got my Driver's permit, read a book of rules and drove around with my dad as the instructor. By the end of the summer, Dad felt I was ready to take the test. So, we scheduled an appointment in the afternoon and Dad had me practice driving around and around all the roads near the Motor Vehicle

Office. I breezed right through the written and easily passed the driving test … and we left with my license … Hip, Hip, Hoorah! Getting your driver's license is one of the major achievements in everyone's life and I was proud to have gotten it.

Next would be a car. I had been stashing away a bunch of money each week, when I got paid. The first $10.00 went to my mom, a few bucks went into my pocket for spending money and the remainder went into an envelope for a car.

Dad and I found an old Ford sedan, that was in decent condition; no dents and it ran well. So, we took a chance on it, and it turned out to be a pretty good purchase.

Toward the end of my senior year. After being asked, a jillion times, "What are you going to do when you graduate?" I decided to go into the office and ask Mr. X if they would bring me on 'full time' once I graduated. I told him that I wanted to be a 'Grocer'. I could tell he was pleased, and he told me they would be delighted to have me. So, I went to work for them, full-time, after I graduated.

Not long after my 18th birthday, Mr. X called the entire store together to announce that I was being promoted to Assistant Manager! Of what? I would assist Mr. Y, Mr. Z and Mr. X, WOW!

Later in the day Mr. X called me aside to inform me, that since I was working full time, they were significantly increasing my pay and I would receive company paid health and life insurance and … I would get paid vacation time, after a year … Fantastic!

The following week, I met with the Bank Manager, and he explained that the bank would give me one loan for the building and the land, another loan for the equipment and another loan for the inventory. Each of these loans would be for 80% of the appraised value. Plus, I would need a Line of Credit, which I would need to even out expenses … working capital.

Fortunately, my down payment would cover the remaining 20%! So, I told the Bank Manager that I would like to go forward with the loans. He explained the various expenses that I would incur (for the appraiser, the bank's lawyer and for the bank's expenses, etc.), which would be collected at Closing. He asked me for my lawyer's name, and I said that I wasn't sure which lawyer I would be using, but I would get back to him in a few days. I also, expressed my appreciation for the bank to be lending me the money (given my age). The Bank Manager told me that they had handled the store's funds for a very long time, and they felt that the store would continue to be profitable and that I came with very high praise from the present owners.

That afternoon I called my Uncle T, to ask what lawyer he would recommend to make a Purchase and Sale agreement for me? He told me to use a specific lawyer, that he said was young … but very good. This was the lawyer he used all the time.

Next, I called the lawyer, and we made an appointment for the next day.

When I met with the lawyer, I explained that I was purchasing the store, the owners had agreed to my terms and I have met with the bank, and they have agreed to fund the purchase. I needed him to prepare a Purchase and Sale agreement and to represent me … and I also mentioned that my Uncle T had recommended him.

He was amazed that such a young person would be so 'entrepreneurial'. I told him that I was a grocer … it was in my blood … I had worked in the store for over five years … the owners wanted to retire, and they chose me to purchase the store.

The lawyer laid out what he would charge (plus expenses) … he needed a retainer to get started and he would bill me as he goes along. I wrote him a check and asked that he wait a day to deposit it, while I transfer funds from my savings. Fortunately, I had enough in my savings to cover the check … but it left me with very little in my savings account.

That evening Uncle T called to say that he heard from the lawyer that I had hired him. I told my Uncle That I was impressed with the lawyer, but his retainer pretty much wiped out my savings account. My Uncle T told me that I would come across various expenses over the next few months and that I would need more funds. He suggested that I incorporate my business and create a corporate savings and checking account … and he would 'loan' me enough money to make it to the closing. WOW … how generous … I told him that I wasn't looking to take his money, but he told me not to worry and to pay him back after my business got up and running.

The next morning, I called my lawyer to say that I needed to incorporate. He told me what it would cost and asked what I wanted to name the corporation. Tony's Super Markets, Inc. was my suggestion … he said he would check to see if the name was available and get back to me … the name was available.

———————

At lunch, I went to the bank and set up a business savings and checking account, under my corporate name … I transferred funds from my personal savings account into my business account … it just about wiped me out!

———————

At the end of August, I went to the college (about 20 miles north) and enrolled in an Introductory to Accounting course. It would run for 16 weeks, one night per week. I could have gone to college but chose not to because I felt my vocation was as a grocer and evidently, I was correct, since somehow, I now plan on owning the grocery store.

There were two older women (in their 30s), in the class, one was pretty and the other … not so pretty … and a dozen teenage students. The instructor was excellent.

After class, the two older women and I would go to the local pub for a drink … they were bookkeepers and would talk about their boss and bitch about how much work he expected of them and then he would take credit for what they had done … I told them that I loved my job and was taking the course to better understand accounting. They were working on getting an accounting degree.

While I was 20, I noticed that my bosses were showing me more and more of their jobs … even to the point of Mr. Z, near the end of the year, signed me up to take Liquor License courses … which I enjoyed. Once I turned 21, the Liquor License Bureau issued me a Liquor License.

I am, like, doing the job of Mr. Z and when I am free, I am doing Mr. Y's job. I guess that is what an Assistant Manager does! And I loved every minute of it!

––––––––––

Back at work, the three brothers took turns teaching me everything I should know about their jobs.

Eventually, the Closing was set for mid-November.

Therefore, we needed to hire someone to manage the frozen food and alcohol area. Fortunately, one night when I was out with my friends. I met a fella in a bar that worked in frozen foods for a store 40 miles north of my store … this guy (about 27 years old) was wearing a shirt with the store name on it … so, we got to talking and he was complaining that he was under paid and over worked … he wasn't a 'bar fly' … he was in a dart league there. So, on my day off, I went to his store, found him in the frozen food section and told him that I needed someone to manage my frozen food and alcohol section. He was interested. So, I asked him to come to my store the next day for an interview.

Mr. X and I interviewed the guy, and we were both in agreement that he would be a fine candidate for the job. I made him an offer and he agreed to start mid-October, for Mr. Z to train. The new guy had to get his 'Liquor License', as well … we really didn't offer much of a variety of beer or wine … just the three most common beers and wines.

––––––––––

Time seemed to fly by. I was busy preparing for my BIG purchase.

My attorney completed the Purchase and Sale agreement and one day, the three brothers signed it. Also, my attorney had prepared a loan agreement (side agreement) that the three of them and I signed.

A couple of weeks before the Closing, Uncle T and I went to the dealer, where he bought his trucks from. Uncle T introduced me to the Owner and the three of us looked around the lot for a pick-up truck … I wasn't fussy … just a/c and a radio were the only options that I wanted. We found a pretty green truck and Uncle T bought it for me … thank the Lord!

As agreed, the first of the month the three brothers made their deposits to my corporate account.

We closed the store the second Sunday of the month (and the store stayed closed on Monday) all of the employees (and our Accountant) came in at 7:00 am and Mr. X explained that he and his brothers were retiring and that they were selling the store to me, on Monday. So, we needed to take a very accurate inventory of everything in the store and we needed to keep at it until everything was accounted for.

Each Manager was responsible for their own area and the Cashiers were responsible to take the inventory sheets, look up the most recent cost of each item from a massive printout and put it next to the quantity. Then the Accountant would multiply the quantity times the cost, on his calculator, for each item and total the value of each sheet. As each area was completed the accountant would total all of the sheets from that area and put the total in a master Inventory Report.

I inventoried all of the shelves, counters, coolers, hand trucks, conveyer and office equipment. Then I sat down with Mr. X to determine what we should use for the value of each item … it was a long day!

The next morning, the accountant prepared a formal summary report showing … the inventory of goods and the equipment inventory … our estimates were not far off.

After lunch, the three brothers, their attorney, the bank manager, their attorney, me and my attorney met in the bank's conference room to consummate the sale. I was now, officially, THE GROCER. I was incredibly proud, but felt I had the weight of the world on my shoulders … I owed so much money … it was unbelievable!

As we left the bank, Mr. X invited me to join him and his brothers for a 'celebration' drink, at the steak house. When I got there, I found that the three guys had invited their wives, as well. Mr. X asked me to invite my mom and dad to join us. Dad had taken the day off and was at home, so, I called and asked them to come to the party … they did, and a great time was had by all (we even had dinner there).

During the celebration Mr. X informed me that he would suggest that we meet once per month at the restaurant to discuss how the business was going and any issues that may arise … of course he was always available on the telephone for more immediate problems … great! We agreed to meet at noon, on the first Tuesday of each month.

―――――――――

The next day, first thing, before we unlocked the doors, I called all of the employees, up to the front of the store.

I said, "It is hard to believe, even for me, that I bought this store yesterday. All of you have been very supportive of the three brothers in the past and I hope you will be just as supportive of me … probably even more supportive (a few chuckles). I do not plan on changing anything going forward … just do your job!"

Then I explained that I would be the store manager and the new guy would be the frozen food and beverage manager … with that said we opened the store, and we all went to work.

One of the few changes I made was to order two black golf shirts for each employee, with Tony's embroidered in white on the left chest area. My personal color choice in clothes was black shirt, black pants (preferably jeans), with black socks and black shoes (preferably sneakers).

―――――――――

Nothing seemed to change, except I was working every day and often until 9:00 pm. I would also, go in to do 'paperwork' on Sunday mornings, after church … I loved my job.

I met with the three brothers once per month … for lunch, of course, they would get to the restaurant early and stay later than me, and now, I, paid for the lunch … there weren't many issues that I couldn't handle, but sometimes, someone would come to me and say that one of the brothers had promised them something … I would tell them that I would get back to them, with an answer after I talked to the brother that made the promise … 99% of the time, the brothers' story was different and he had not made the promise in that way, usually when I understood what was said, I could, easily solve those issues.

―――――――――

We went through the holidays and the new year without many problems. I had settled into the job … there was, generally, enough money to pay all the bills, but a few times I needed to borrow from my line of credit … which I paid back as quickly as I could.

When I took over the store, I bought my parents a fax machine and asked my mom to just call or fax her weekly shopping order to me and I would have someone do the shopping, I would pay for it, less my 5% employee discount, (there is not a lot of mark-ups on groceries) and I would bring it home, at supper time.

Once Mom got the knack of faxing, she loved it!

So, I decided to offer the same service to our customers. I put up a sign on the wall, in front of the cashiers and I put it in my weekly flyer … fax in your order by noon and we will deliver it between 3:00 pm to 5:00 pm, to your home … free of charge.

Well, we would get about seven orders per week … five of them from new customers. In addition to the three to six deliveries from customers that shopped in the store daily.

Then on a Tuesday in January, we got a fairly large order with a request that it be delivered at 7:00 pm, from an unfamiliar customer, in the next town north of us. I allowed the order and said I would deliver it.

———————

When I got to the house, it was in a fairly nice neighborhood, it was a fairly new raised ranch design, with the lights on outside and inside. I carried the first box up to the front door and was met by a young girl (about 23 or 24), attractive, short (about 5' 3" tall), with short brown curly hair and a very nice smile. She told me to put the box in the kitchen, where I found another pretty gal, with medium length blond hair, short (about 5' 3" tall, as well), cooking what appeared to be supper.

This girl asked me to put the box of groceries on the kitchen table (which was set for dinner) … so, I put the box on one of the side chairs and told the girl that I had another box. When I came in with the second box, both girls met me in the kitchen, so that they could pay me. They both seemed interested in me … so they asked me my name …

I smiled and said, "Tony."

They both giggled and noticed the name on my jacket read Tony's.

So, giggling they facetiously asked if I owned the store … when I said, "Yes, I own the store," we all laughed … I could tell, they didn't believe me.

When I left, I stopped at a local bar that offered a special, on a steak and a baked potato dinner.

In any event, I watched the fax machine all day the following Tuesday, looking for an order from the two girls … no order … darn … I thought they were happy with the order. Well, the following Tuesday at 10:00 am we received another order from the two girls, it looked very similar to their last order.

So, that night, when I made their delivery, the two girls asked if I had dinner and when I said I hadn't, they invited me to join them for dinner … and they wouldn't take no for an answer.

While, the one with the long hair cooked, the other poured wine and brought me into the living room, where: the lights were turned down low, there were candles burning and the gas fireplace was aglow … very seductive!

As we spoke, I found out their names, that they worked in a women's wear store in the mall (the one with the short hair was the store manager and the one with the long hair was a store clerk). When the one with the short hair went into the kitchen to refill our drinks, the one with the long hair came back into the living room … the one with short hair was in the kitchen finishing the preparations for the meal.

The girl with the long hair was just as delightful to talk to … she told me that they both had Wednesday off and could 'let loose' on Tuesday evening. I told her that I started to work for the grocery store when I was 16, and I have worked there ever since … I just left off the part where I purchased the store.

In no time, dinner was served in the dining room. The house and the furniture were very nice and very clean. Dinner was excellent (Veal Scallopini). Again, the lights were turned down low and several candles produced most of the light.

When we were done with dinner, we all carried our dishes into the kitchen and put them in the sink. The one with short hair asked if I would like to see the rest of the house. Of course, I would!

The gal with short hair led the way out of the kitchen and into a hallway, to show me the bathroom, on the right and a bedroom (they used as an office) on the left … the girl with long hair said, "Oh no, I got a spot on my blouse …

I'm going to change." With that said, she ran down the hallway to their bedroom and I could hear her opening her closet door in the master bathroom, to change. We continued down the hallway … to another bedroom to the left and a large master bedroom to the right. When we entered the master bedroom, I noticed there were no lights on, just candle lights … it was very romantic … in the center of the room was a four-poster bed, with a whispery white canopy over the top, which came down along the posts … very delicate and very pretty!

When we got to the middle of the room, the girl with the long hair came out of the bathroom, with a pair of sheer, white, flimsy, almost see through baby doll pajamas on … in the dim light I could see just about everything and what I could see, I liked. The bed had been turned down and the girl with the long hair, sort of jumped into the bed (body parts jiggling everywhere) and asked me to join her … the one with the short hair said, "I'm going to take a shower." I had the feeling that this had all been rehearsed.

When I sat on the bed, which was extremely plush, the gal with the long hair pushed me flat on my back and started to kiss me … softly, to start, then more and more aggressively … I got a chance to try the condom with the ridges … and she loooooved it!

When we were done, on que, the girl with the short hair came out of the master bathroom, with a bath towel wrapped around her and a warm wet hand towel, in her hand. Without asking she did a more than professional job of washing me down … reached into a drawer and took out a condom, slipped out of her towel and started kissing me … the other girl was good, but this one was way better … in any event, we had a mutually satisfying time (her twice, me once). Sure enough, when we were done, the other girl came out of the bathroom with a towel wrapped around her. I then had the sense that they didn't just plan this … I think it had been performed before … so what!

After that night, I looked forward to making a delivery to their house, every other Tuesday … I wonder what or who, they did on their off Tuesday nights!

———————

Then in late April, just after opening, the old Pharmacist from across the street came into my store and asked me if he could speak to me in my office.

He informed me that he had been diagnosed with cancer, and the doctors gave him six months to live. This was devastating to me … I had known this man, all of my life. I asked, "What can I do for you?"

His reply was to purchase his pharmacy, just as fast as possible … he went on to say that he was asking for 50% for the land, building and inventory … in order to facilitate a quick sale. His building was split down the middle, with his pharmacy on one side and a candy store on the other side, run by a very old lady.

I said that I was very interested; given my sister and brother-in-law are both pharmacists. I asked if he could give me a day or two, to do my due diligence and to talk to the bank … he agreed. I also, asked him to have his accountant prepare, a 5-year history of expenses and income … he agreed.

I called my older sister, the pharmacist, and asked if I could take her to lunch, I had something very important to discuss. Of course, she agreed. Then I called Uncle T and asked if he could come over later in the afternoon, to look at a building that I was interested in purchasing … he chuckled, and we agreed to meet at 4:00 pm.

Back when I was 19 years old, my sister (four years older than me) had spent five long years of study to become a pharmacist. When my sister and her fiancé graduated, both got full time jobs in a pharmacy, 45 miles away. So, they got an apartment together close to work … and they were planning their wedding … for the next year. My parents were, 'lukewarm' regarding the upcoming marriage. My sister was very smart, fairly mature, but my folks didn't know if anyone was good enough for their 'little girl'.

I liked the guy. He really treated my sister well and he really seemed to care/love her … and vice versa.

Planning a wedding on the women's side was a lot of work for both my sister and my mom … and very expensive! Fortunately, I gave my mom $50 per week … I increased what I gave Mom, as my income increased … my sister never gave my parents any money when she worked … even though they paid a lot towards her education.

The wedding was FANTASTIC! I couldn't be happier for my sister … she looked so happy and so beautiful in her wedding gown. After the reception, my sister and her husband (I am not used to saying brother-in-law) flew to the islands for their honeymoon.

At lunch, I told my sister about the old pharmacist and that he wanted to sell his business … quickly. I asked if she and her husband would be interested in running it for me. I would pay them better than their present job, it would be closer to our parents, and I suggested, a 25% of the profit bonus. My sister was delighted and felt her husband would be as well … she was so excited it was difficult for her to go back to work!

When Uncle T showed up, I explained about the old pharmacist and how he offered me a deal to buy him out, quickly. Further, I said I wanted to take down the dividing wall in the middle of the building and to make it one large pharmaceutical store … which my sister would run.

When we got out to the street, I pointed out that I wanted to expand the tiny parking lot on the side of the building to the property line. At present, almost all customers parked in front of the store in the two available parking spots. Uncle T noticed the building exterior was a dark brick, not very appetizing … he said, "We are going to need to paint the exterior."

I said, "White."

Uncle T had brought a pad of paper for notes and a wheel, with a register, on the end of a long handle. He could roll the wheel along and measure whatever he needed to.

Inside, I waved to the old pharmacist to indicate we were looking over the building … Uncle T shook his head.

"Tan walls and brown tile floors, makes it dark and not very appetizing." He looked at the shelving and other fixtures and said, "The interior needs to be gutted and refurbished … we can remove the center wall, no problem … let's take a look at the other side."

The old pharmacist introduced us to the old lady next door and explained why we were there.

We only needed to take a few steps into the store, before Uncle T said, "Total refurbish here as well … let's go upstairs."

There were two, two-bedroom apartments on the second floor, both vacant for a few months. The old pharmacist explained that he felt it would be easier to sell the building if the apartments were empty … I was thinking the opposite. Again, the carpet, linoleum, bathroom and kitchen looked old, dark and worn … Uncle T said, "Total refurbish!"

Then we went down to the basement, which was loaded with old broken shelving, fixtures and junk. There was some good product, which had to be hand carried up or down the stairs.

Uncle T said, "It's all got to go!"

I told the old pharmacist that I would give him an answer in a day or two. Before we left, I asked how much he had in inventory … it wasn't a lot, but he would take an inventory for me.

Back at my office, I made a sketch of how I wanted the store laid out (doors, windows, conveyor, etc.) while Uncle T made a list of what had to done. Uncle T told me that there wasn't enough room for a conveyor … instead, he offered to install a dumbwaiter elevator, which was an elevator, that was the size of a coat closet … it would accommodate up to six or eight cartons to go down to or up from the basement. On my sketch, I made a provision for a drive-up window in the pharmacy area, along the wall opposite the big parking lot. Of course, this would require the paving to go all around the building, which wouldn't be an issue (Uncle T had taken the measurements).

On my drive back after meeting with my sister, I had noticed a drive-up window at a bank that I passed. I thought that it would be a good idea to include it in our plans (of course, I would need to get my sister to agree). Uncle T told me he would go to his office, run the numbers (call Uncle A for the painting costs and call Uncle R for the cost of the carpet and linoleum) and get back to me first thing in the morning.

By then, the bank was closed. So, the next day I called the bank manager and asked him if he would like to meet me at the steak house for lunch, at noon (since I had the feeling that Mr. X would have done the same). He said he would be delighted to join me.

My uncle called and went over the cost to renovate the pharmacy and said that he could do it in 6–8 weeks … then he faxed over his detailed worksheet.

I made a 'plan'. I put together a sheet showing what I needed; a mortgage loan for the building and land, an inventory loan, a line of credit and a construction loan. How much would I need for a down payment?

At lunch, the bank manager and I started with a martini … we made small talk for a while and discussed how my store was doing (which was great). Then, the bank manager asked why I had invited him for lunch, since that is what Mr. X would do when he wanted to soften him up for a loan. I told him that I didn't know what Mr. X would do, but that was exactly what I was doing. I think he liked my honesty. We ordered a second drink. Iced tea for me and a martini for him. I told him what the old pharmacist told me the day before. He said that was too bad. He had known him for ages. I then explained, that the old pharmacist wanted to sell me his building, business, etc., at a discounted price, to expedite the sale. I took out the sheet that I had prepared showing the loans that I needed. Then, I showed him the detailed cost to renovate the building and I showed him the sketch I had made of the 'new pharmacy'. I pointed out the Drive-up window and the expanded parking lot … also, I told him how we would renovate the two apartments and how I would be able to rent them for more than in the past. I went on to explain that my sister and brother-in-law were both pharmacists and that my sister had agreed to manage the store.

The bank manager asked me, "You put this together in one day?"

I replied, "Yes."

After we ordered lunch, I went on to say that I was just looking to see if he felt that this was doable, from the financial side. If it was, then I would have my attorney prepare a Purchase and Sale agreement. I would prepare a Performa document showing the income, expense and hopefully profitability, and I would look to expedite the sale and the renovation.

The bank manager said he was impressed. He felt based on the fact that I was only paying 50% of market value (which the bank would need to verify), that it sounded like a great idea. He liked my plans to expand the parking lot, renovate and basically double the foot print of the pharmacy.

He felt it was something the bank would be interested in funding, but he reminded me that the bank cannot get started without a signed purchase and sale document. I told him I would get right on it after lunch. Then, I asked him to get an appraisal, hopefully in the next day or two … I promised to pay for the appraisal, even if I didn't purchase the property.

When I got back to my store office, I called my accountant and told him I was looking at buying the pharmacy across the street. He said he was informed by the old pharmacist … he didn't know about the cancer … it was too bad! I explained my plan to double the size of the pharmacy, expand the parking lot, add a drive-up window and completely renovate the two apartments. I told him, I felt on the pharmacy side, we should see an increase of 10% in month one, 15% in month two and 20% in month three and going forward. On the new 'side' of the store, I would put coolers for milk, cheese, etc. and racks for grocery type products, like chips, dips candy, etc. Also, we would feature beauty products for men and women … therefore, he could use a grocery factor for the square footage for sales and expenses on that side of the store. Finally, I said that I was going to charge an additional $100 per month, per apartment for rent. I asked how quickly he could prepare a Performa for me and he said to give him a few days … great!

Next, I called my attorney … I explained about the old pharmacist and that I wanted to purchase the building and the land, and his inventory … there wouldn't be anything for goodwill. I explained, that I needed the quickest, fastest Purchase & Sale agreement possible and I needed it this week. He assured me that he could do it and asked, "Who is representing the old pharmacist?"

Good question.

"I'll get back to you."

Also, I asked the attorney to set-up a corporation for; 'Tony's Pharmacy, Inc.' He said he would check to see if the name was available and get back to me.

When I called the old pharmacist, he said, "I will represent myself."

Okay, not a good idea … but no one was out to 'hurt' him. I asked him if we could get together Friday afternoon, in my office, with my attorney, to sign the formal Purchase & Sale agreement which I would need to bring to the bank to get a loan. He was delighted to hear how quickly I was moving … I explained that we would then need to wait for the bank, possibly 4–6 weeks.

I called my attorney and explained that the old pharmacist would represent himself … he agreed with me … not a good idea.

I asked if he could meet with the old pharmacist and me, on Friday, in my office … he said, "No problem."

When I went home for supper, my mom said that my sister had called and was all excited, because I was going to buy the pharmacy across the street from my store and let her run it!

I explained that it wasn't a done deal but I thought it was a very good idea. Then I explained about the old pharmacist and that he didn't have long to live … I told my folks that the old pharmacist was giving me a great deal for a quick sale … my mom and dad were very sorry to hear about the old pharmacist but my mom was concerned about me … I was already working long hours, seven days a week.

I assured my mom that I shouldn't need to be too involved, since my sister would be the store manager.

Mom mentioned that her friend, the Italian lady was looking for a job. The lady had her own Italian bakery in a town to the north and the city foreclosed on her landlord for taxes. They were going to level the building and sell the land. She had a few months to close up, remove all of her coolers, ovens and displays. I said maybe Uncle T knew of a storefront that was available, but Mom said that the lady didn't want to relocate … she just wanted a job. I got it! So, I asked Mom to call the lady and have her come for an interview the next day … she could start next week. Mom, was happy with me, so she called the lady and the lady was delighted to come and see me.

The next day, the postmaster came into my office, to hand deliver a 30-day notice to vacate the building. This wasn't a big surprise, since the new, much larger, post office building had been under construction a block up the street.

When I went to the bank, with the store deposit, I stuck my head in the bank manager's office to say, "I got the 30-day notice to vacate from the post office this morning."

He said, "That was expected … right."

I replied, "Yes."

He asked, "What are your plans, for the space?"

I said, "I plan on expanding my store into that space … can we meet a week from Friday, for me to make a formal request for a construction loan, a loan for equipment and inventory?" Then, I asked if we could meet, sometime Monday, for me to make a formal request for loans to purchase and renovate the pharmacy across the street from my store. We agreed on Monday at 11:00 am.

The bank manager said, "You are very industrious!"

I blushed and replied, "I am just trying to help out an old man and fill the vacant storefront next to me."

That afternoon, I met with my frozen food manager and the head butcher, to inform them that I was planning on purchasing the pharmacy across the street. Also, I planned to move into the space next door … when the post office moves out, in 30 days. They were both surprised and asked more about our expansion. I started to make a sketch to show them my ideas, and asked for their input, as well. My 'concept' was taking down the wall between the post office and my store to add an aisle behind the wall of existing coolers (the aisle would run perpendicular to our existing aisles) and to expand our wine and beer offerings. Wine racks would run down one side of the aisle against the back of the existing cooler/freezers. On the other side of the aisle would be a row of coolers for beer and one cooler with cold wine and champagne. I explained that I would like, if it was possible, to have a large room size cooler installed that would form the back of the beer and wine coolers … so that the beer and wine coolers could be refilled from the back. This would be a very wide cooler that would allow for skids of product to be stored … the frozen food manager would be able to take the skids from the delivery truck and to load them into the cooler with a hand-pump truck. The frozen food manager loved the idea … we wouldn't need to schlep all the heavy cases onto the conveyor and then off in the basement anymore!

Then, I focused my attention, to the main aisle. At the present time, the meat coolers stopped where the entrance to the back room was … I suggested that we put a dedicated 'sea food' section on the other side of the walk-through (where the bread used to be) and add a 'Fryolator' behind the counter, where we could do Fried Fish and Chips or Fried Clams or Fried Scallops. Further, I added a 'Lobster Pond' at the end of the cooler … this left a big space getting to the corner … we could move the bread there, or, it just dawned on me, we could put a bakery in that spot … we could make birthday cakes, and put people's names on the top to order … like 'Happy Birthday Mary'! Both guys liked my ideas and gave me some of their suggestions, which I added to the sketch.

When we broke up the meeting, the butcher lingered behind and said, "You are going to be awful busy preparing and building these two projects … you are already working night and day … how can you add more to your plate without missing things … why don't you make me the temporary store manager, while you finish your two projects … that way someone will be here, overseeing the store."

"WOW, what a great suggestion," I said. "Let's do it!"

As I said that, I could feel the pressure subsiding in my body.

Then I called my Uncle T to tell him that the post office, next to me, was moving out and that I wanted to expand into that area. Could he come over and take a look at what needs to be done. When he came over, I showed him my sketch. Then, we went over to the post office and the postmaster took us for a tour of the area.

When we got back to my store, my Uncle T told me that it wouldn't be a big deal to remove the wall dividing the store from the post office and that he could put up a thick plastic wall from the ceiling down to the top of the coolers and to the floor … it would keep dust and dirt out of the store during construction. Removing everything in the post office, also, would not be a big project either. He felt it would take some time to get the equipment like the coolers, the Fryolator and the ovens. During that period of time, the interior could be painted, the old vinyl tile could be removed and new floor tile (that matched the existing floor tiles, as closely as possible) could be laid. In addition, the electrical work could be done.

I explained that my best friend B, worked as a salesman for a beer and wine distributor. I felt that he would be instrumental in designing the new area and in getting the proper coolers and racks.

I told my Uncle T that I would like to do both projects (the pharmacy and the store expansion) simultaneously … so that I could open both, on the same day.

Uncle T told me he would get back to me in the morning, with his estimate for the construction.

I called my best buddy, B, from school and told him his dream had come true … that I was expanding my store and I was going to have a Wine and Beer aisle … could he meet with me in my store office at 7:00 pm. He was delighted.

B worked as a salesman for a huge beer and wine distributor and had been bugging me to expand my beer and wine offerings (from the three brands of beer and embarrassingly the three types of wine).

When B showed up, we reviewed my sketch and I showed him my concept of an aisle, with wine racks on one side and coolers with doors for beer on the other side. Further, I showed him my concept of having a huge (room size) cooler, which would form the backside of the beer coolers, so that the beer could be stored on skids, inside the large cooler and the coolers could be refiled from the backside. B told me, he had seen that done and it should not be a problem. Great!

The big question was how fast could we get the wine rack and the coolers … oh yeah, how much would this all cost and who would build the big coolers? B assured me that he could have an estimate of costs and a detailed sketch for me by lunchtime the next day. He would check on the availability of the racks and components for the backloaded coolers and the equipment to build the big storage room. He felt that my Uncle T could build the room size cooler. Great!

The next day bright and early I called my architect, and made an appointment in the afternoon, to meet with him. He said he was just about done with the renderings and blueprints for the new pharmacy. Super!

Soon after I hung up with the architect, the Italian bakery lady showed up. She was just about five feet tall, in her early 40s and very pretty. Her demeanor was 'bubbly' and she was a delight to speak to.

She told me of her plight … the old building her bakery was in had been taken for taxes, by the city, and was going to be demolished and replaced by some type of municipal building. She and all of her equipment had to be out by the end of the month. She had no plans to ever start another bakery and she could not afford to store her equipment until it could be sold. So, she and her husband had to find jobs, to support themselves.

I told her she was in luck! I explained that I was expanding my store and I intended to include a bakery as part of the expansion. She was excited to hear about the expansion. I showed her my sketch and she started to say this is where the pastry and cake coolers should be, this is where the ovens should be, this is where the work tables should go, this is where we will put the portable racks of trays … to go to or from the ovens and this is where the pizza oven should go … pizza oven, I never thought about offering pizza … what a wonderful idea! As she spoke, I sketched in the various pieces of equipment.

The Italian lady said, "I make-the best-a cookie, Italian pastries and the best-a outa this world-a doughnuts." … of course, she's Italian … they're always the best!

I asked about cakes for like birthdays and special occasions, she said, "That's-a my hus-a-bans specialty, he make-a the best-a cakes, I-a-talian bread, rolls-a and pizza in-a the whole world-a."

I asked, "Is he Italian."

She replied, "Of course-a."

I was impressed and said that I would be delighted to have her work for me. She could start in two weeks and her husband (I would need to interview him as well) could start once their bakery is closed.

Before she left, I put in a call to my Uncle T, it was almost lunch time but I caught him. I told him about the Italian lady's bakery problem … they had to vacate their building by the end of the month and they hadn't sold their equipment. I explained that I had just hired the lady and her husband and their equipment was just what I needed in my bakery area … would it be possible for his guys to remove everything from her bakery and store it, until it could be installed in my new bakery area.

He said, "Of course! I will need to stop over there to see how big of a job it will be."

The Italian lady was very pleased … she gave me a big hug and a kiss on the cheek!

When I went home for lunch, I told my mom that I had hired her friend the Italian lady and that she was starting in two weeks. I went on to say that I had to interview the husband, but I expected to hire him as well. Mom was very happy with her son … I learned well!

When I got back to work from lunch, I found that B had faxed over an estimate for the wine racks, the coolers and the room sized storage cooler (that would attach to the back of the aisle of beer coolers). He felt that my uncle's construction guys could install everything but the refrigeration part and he gave me the name of a refrigeration installation company that they would use. He also estimated what my uncle's company would charge and what the refrigeration company would charge. Then he answered the big question … how long would it take to get the equipment.

They had the wine racks in their warehouse and they also had way more than enough of the coolers, panels and cooling equipment in their warehouse waiting to go into a huge facility down south, but there was some hold up and the building had not even started construction, yet. So, his plan was to grab what I needed from what was on hand and replace it in his warehouse before it was needed … WOW … what a great deal!

He also estimated how much wine and beer I would need to get started with … he estimated over 1,000 bottles of wine, in the wine aisle, alone!

I sent the fax over to my uncle and asked what he thought about it.

He sent me back a fax with his estimate for construction … he was happy to have gotten B's labor estimates, which he felt would be more accurate than his would be.

Mid-afternoon my architect showed up. He brought four copies of the blueprints for my new pharmacy. WOW!

We reviewed the blueprints, which were perfect!

Then I explained that my next-door neighbor, the post office, was moving to their new facility within a month and that I wanted to expand into the vacated area. I made a copy of my detailed sketch showing the wine and beer aisle, the room sized storage cooler, behind the row of beer coolers, the new bakery area and the new seafood section.

I called the postmaster and asked if we could give my architect a quick tour and he agreed. After the tour, I gave my architect a copy of the existing blueprints of the building that were left over from the previous owners. My architect asked me when I would like to see the new blueprints for the store and I said, this coming Monday, by noon. He felt he could have them prepared by then … he needed to stop by the Italian bakery, to get precise measurements, that afternoon. So, I called, and the husband said there would be no problem.

Later, my attorney, faxed over the Purchase and Sale agreement to purchase the pharmacy … I read through it and made a couple of very minor changes. Then I made a copy for the old pharmacist and ran across the street to give him a chance to read it and see if he wanted to change anything, he said he would take it home and read it after supper.

Since I was out, I stopped at the bank to see the bank manager. I told him that the Purchase and Sale agreement was all set, and I was wondering if we could do the closing on Friday.

He said, "You know that you never made a formal written request for funds … but that may be in your favor." Then he continued with a big smile, "I just received the appraisal for the pharmacy building and land, and the value of the property is far more than what you are planning to pay … so much more that you could get a mortgage on the property for 80% of the value and it would exceed what you plan to spend on the renovation … of course, you would need to purchase the majority of the new inventory, with your funds."

HOLY COW!!!

The bank manager then told me, "You will need to make a formal request for the mortgage, and we can most likely Close at our Monday meeting."

When I got my breath back, I said, "As soon as I get back to my store, I will prepare the letter … is there anything else I need to do?"

The bank manager answered, "If you want to Close on your new expansion, I will need a formal request, stating what you plan on borrowing."

I told the bank manager that I had all the estimates and the blueprints would be ready Monday morning … I could work on the request letter, as soon as I complete the pharmacy letter … would it be possible to Close on Monday, after we complete the pharmacy Closing? I went on to explain that I would like to have the Grand Opening of both simultaneously.

He said, "I will try."

Back at the store, I prepared the two request letters, as quickly as possible and then delivered both copies to the bank manager before the end of the day.

I was exhausted!

On Friday morning, just after we opened, a very muscular man, about 5 foot eight inches tall, with a skin tight blue, V-neck T-shirt, came into the store asking for me. It was the Italian lady's husband. He had a very wide, engaging smile and I felt at ease speaking to him.

He told me that he was very appreciative that I had hired his wife, the day before and that he was hoping he could get a job in my store, as well. I explained that our intent was to be open 80 hours per week and that for the most part, he would need to be working, when his wife is off … but we would try to adjust their schedules so that they could both be off, one or two days per week.

The Italian fella laughed and told me that was basically how they had worked for the past several years … it wouldn't be a problem. Great!

I went on to explain that his wife would be in charge of the bakery and he would work for her … no problem.

I mentioned that we were interested in moving his bakery equipment to my store and he said that he and his wife were delighted. He said that my uncle had called and they made an appointment for that afternoon, to review what needed to be moved.

I told the man that once everything was moved out of his bakery, he could start working for us, in some capacity. He agreed, we shook hands and he left.

I called my Uncle T and said I would like to go with him to the bakery … so, we met at my uncle's favorite Italian restaurant for lunch and I filled him in, regarding how my bank loans were going to be configured … he was amazed. I also informed him that I would like to complete the pharmacy and the store expansion, simultaneously.

My uncle was impressed with my ability to get all of the various individuals involved, to all work so quickly to pull these two projects together. I was proud of myself!

When we got to the bakery, we found a bright, very clean store. Both the Italian lady and her husband were there and extremely proud to show us around. My Uncle T took measurements and made a list of each and every item. He asked when they had to be out and when he could get started … my uncle only spoke Italian to them which seemed to put them more at ease … they got along very well!

When we left, my Uncle T told me that he was impressed with the husband, the wife and the condition of the equipment. He wouldn't need to store the equipment for very long, before it could be installed in my store. I liked the sound of that!

I went back to my store, to meet with my managers and to review any issues.

Sunday, at lunch with my parents, my sister and brother-in-law, I was explaining that by Monday afternoon I planned to own the pharmacy and to have the funds to expand my store. I told them that I hoped to go with my Uncle T on Tuesday to pull building permits for both projects.

My sister interrupted me to ask, "You don't plan on closing the pharmacy during construction, do you?"

"Yes, that was my plan … hopefully we can get the reno done in four to six weeks."

My sister, yelled, "NOOOOOO! You will lose all of your prescription customers in that time."

She explained that the prescription business would represent 75% to 80% of the profits for the store.

She said, "We must keep the pharmacy open during renovation."

I suggested that we meet with Uncle T, to work out how we could do both renovate and keep the pharmacy open at the same time. I called Uncle T, explained the problem and asked if he could come over to my folks' house that afternoon, so we could discuss what we could do … he said, "Yes, of course."

When my sister, my bother-in-law, my uncle and I met, I explained that we needed to stay open during renovation and that we needed to create a plan. My sister said that she could put in her two-week notice that she was quitting … on Monday (the next day). Therefore, we would need to ask the old pharmacist if he would work the next two weeks. Uncle T informed us that he wouldn't be able to remove the wall separating the two stores, while customers are coming and going in the pharmacy. I asked how quickly we could get the drive-up window installed.

Uncle T saw where I was going and he said, "I believe I can get and install the window in the next two weeks … I would have to put up a plastic wall to keep the dust out of the pharmacist's way when we cut the hole in the wall. Then, we would need the driveway and the parking lot paved, over the weekend … on that Saturday the customers will need to park in the street and the paver will need to finish on Sunday."

Starting the following Monday, the store will be closed to all customers and my sister will service the pharmacy customers using the drive-up window, only, until the store construction is complete.

We came to the conclusion that large signs would be required in the front windows. Then everyone shared their opinion regarding what should be put on the signs. When we came to a consensus, I said I would order the signs first thing on Monday (good thing my sister knew that we would lose the pharmacy business, if we closed for renovation).

I called the old pharmacist and explained that we might lose all of his pharmacy customers if we closed-up during renovation and my sister would not be available for two weeks, so I asked him if he would stay and work for the next two weeks. He said that he would be happy to help in any way! He asked if he could have his 'part-time' pharmacist help out, as well, of course I agreed.

I asked if he had read the Purchase and Sale agreement and if he had any issues. He told me that he had no issues and that he felt it had been 'professionally' done. Very good!

On Monday morning, I went to the sign store and ordered the signs for the front windows. When I got back to my store, my architect was waiting for me in my office, with the blueprints of the expansion of my store. Perfect!

My attorney showed up at my office with my corporation paperwork and we went directly to the bank.

We went into the conference room and the old pharmacist; the bank's attorney and the bank manager were there.

After a few pleasantries, we got down to business. The old pharmacist and I signed my copy and his copy of the Purchase and Sale agreement … then I signed the Loan agreement and the bank manager passed out the checks to the old pharmacist and me.

Then, the bank's attorney went over the documents for my Construction Loan for the expansion. I agreed to the terms and the bank manager explained how I could 'draw' out the funds as construction progressed … only paying monthly interest on the portion that had been taken out … great!

While I was at the bank, I set-up a savings and checking account for my pharmacy and deposited the bank's check, that I had just received (they gave me starter checks that I planned on using, right away).

When I left the bank, I went directly to the steakhouse, to meet my mom, dad, sister, brother-in-law, my Uncle T and my aunt (his wife), for a 'New Business Party'. By the time I arrived, everyone had partaken of at least one alcoholic beverage … so they were all in a very good mood!

Mom asked, "How did it go?"

"It went great, I have never owed this much money in my life," was my reply …

Everyone laughed.

My Uncle T came over and put his big arm around my shoulders and reassured me, "By the time you're done, that will probably be a drop in the bucket!"

Somehow, that made me feel so much better. So, I ordered a drink: a rum and coke.

The party could not have been better or more fun. It broke up at 5:00 pm and I went back to my grocery store (my sister went over to the pharmacy, to spend some time with the old pharmacist).

————————

At the grocery store, I met with the guys and reviewed how the day went … I approved orders and I paid invoices before heading home.

————————

The next morning, I brought all of the paperwork required for a 'new employee' over to the pharmacy, for the old pharmacist and the part-time pharmacist to complete. I explained that I intended to pay both of them what they had been making, previously. The old pharmacist again told me how impressed he was at how fast and how easy I made the purchase happen. He praised me as a great entrepreneur. WOW!

I explained to the old pharmacist, that we were pulling permits that day and intended to start construction the next day but we were leaving the wall up, for now. This weekend, the paving company will expand the side parking lot, pave across the back of the building and create a lane for cars to drive around the building, to access the Drive-up window. Next weekend the paving company will install white arrows and printing, directing the customers to the Drive-up window. Also, next week we intend on cutting a hole in the wall in the pharmaceutical area, to install the Drive-up window. I went on to explain that we would install a heavy plastic cover, on the inside wall, which should prevent any dust or debris, from getting into the pharmaceutical area. Over the next two weeks the customers will all come into the pharmacy from the front, no change. Then two weeks from now, we will lock the front door, put large signs in the windows to direct all pharmaceutical customers to use our Drive-up window for drop-offs and pick-ups. In that way, we feel we can continue to serve our customers during our construction phase.

The old pharmacist told me I was a genius and that I think of everything. I was proud of my accomplishments but I explained that I had plenty of help.

That afternoon, my Uncle T and I took both sets of blueprints and went over to the Town Hall to meet with the building inspector to get permits, so we could start construction (the building inspector spent the morning checking on jobs and was in his office only in the afternoon).

The building inspector said that he had heard of my purchase of the pharmacy the previous day, when my attorney applied and received, a 'Permit to do Business', in town. He went on to say that he was wondering what would go into the space that the post office was vacating.

Well, we showed the building inspector the renderings and the blueprints of what I proposed for the expansion into the vacated area. He was impressed, had a few questions and issued us a permit.

The work on the pharmacy was far more expansive but for the most part was inside the building and there was no 'structural' work to be done. He spent more time reviewing the new parking lot … to ensure that we were not encroaching on any property lines … we weren't. So, the building inspector issued us the permit. I paid the required fees and my uncle and I went back to my office to review our plans for getting started.

Back at my office, I explained that we needed the paving company to do the paving this coming weekend and put the arrows on the following weekend. My uncle said he would take care of that. I asked him if he had sourced the Drive-up window … he had found a distributor locally and he was planning on checking them out, after our meeting (I asked if I could go with him and he agreed, of course).

My uncle explained, that he would have two big dumpsters delivered to the pharmacy parking lot the next day, first thing (one dumpster for construction materials and one for metals). Also, he would send three crews over to start the clean-up. One crew upstairs in the apartments, one crew in the old candy shop and one crew in the basement … to get rid of all the old racks, etc.

My uncle explained he would have the crew working in the apartments put the old refrigerators, stoves, kitchen sinks, bathroom sinks and toilets in the back of his pickup and he would bring them to an organization that would provide them free to those in need. Nice!

Then, the upstairs crew would remove the kitchen cabinets, linoleum flooring, carpet, doors and the old antique bathroom tub.

His plan was to accomplish all of this, in a week, so that he could remove the dumpsters on Friday afternoon, to be out of the way of the pavers.

Next week he planned on having his crews rip up the old vinyl floor in the candy shop, install the Drive-up window, cut the hole in the wall on the right side of the building up front and install the new automatic opening/closing double doors. While the upstairs crew were to remove the old dilapidated windows on the second floor and replace them with modern, double-pane vinyl coated windows. The crews would need to store everything they tore up, or out, in boxes or wheel barrows, until we could drive on the new pavement, again.

My uncle mostly and I continued to discuss the construction plan moving forward as we drove over to the distributor of the Drive-up Windows.

The distributor had a number of Drive-up windows on display ... both my uncle and I picked the same window for the pharmacy ... they had the window we chose in stock so I purchased it and we had them put it in my uncle's pickup truck (along with the directions on how to install it).

When we left, my uncle said that it was almost dinner time ... he lived fairly close ... would I like to join him and my aunt for dinner ... how could I refuse? When we got to his house, I called my mom to say that I was eating supper with Uncle T. Then I called my grocery store to ask the guys if there were any problems or issues? Not really, everything is going well, they informed me ... I hoped that was true.

My aunt's dinner was fabulous ... my uncle assured me that she cooks enough food for four people every night.

After dinner, my uncle and I drove to his 'construction yard' where we put the new window in a safe and secure spot until it would be installed.

The next morning, I posted the construction permits on the front doors.

On her day off, my sister went to the pharmacy, met with her husband and the part-time pharmacist and made a schedule for the construction period.

When the new pharmacy opens the hours would be extended to 8:00 am to 8:00 pm Monday true Saturday and 10:00 am to 6:00 pm on Sunday ... my grocery store hours would also be changed to match the pharmacy hours!

When I met with the three brothers for our monthly lunch, I brought the blueprints for my expansion but before I could say anything, they said they were shocked to hear that I had purchased the pharmacy across the street. So, I told them about the old pharmacist's medical issues and that he wanted a quick sale ... so that he could enjoy what life he had left. They all knew him well and were very sorry to hear of his medical problems (in retrospect, isn't that what these three brothers are doing? Only, hopefully, they have a lot more time!).

Next, I explained that the post office finally gave me a notice to vacate by the end of the month and my plan was to expand the grocery store into the vacated space. I rolled out the blueprints and showed my ideas for the new areas … the brothers were somewhat surprised that I wasn't expanding the grocery into the new space but they understood my reasoning. Mr. Z said that he loved the idea of building a large cooler behind the beer coolers … there wouldn't be all the hauling of heavy cases down to a basement cooler then upstairs to a main floor cooler.

I went on to explain that we would be offering deep-fried fish and chips, deep-fried shrimp and deep-fried scallops, in the evening and for lunch we would offer made to order grinders and pizza by the piece (or whole).

I would greatly expand our seafood offerings … including a lobster pool!

Next to the seafood area would be a bakery offering cakes, cookies, pastries, homemade Italian bread and pizza, packaged to take home and eat, or hot from the oven pizza, to take out.

Across from the seafood and bakery, would be an entire row on the left of wine racks. Where we will have over 1,000 bottles of wine on display (inexpensive to expensive). On the right, will be coolers for all types and kinds of beer and one cooler, just for the most popular wines.

I think the brothers' heads were spinning … they all ordered another martini … Mr. X whom I felt had the most business savvy said, "That's what happens when you get 'new blood' in a business … we are all proud of you and wish you great success!"

Sure, he just wants to make sure that I continue to make his monthly payments.

Throughout the lunch, I went on to explain what my plans were for my new pharmacy. They each thought my ideas were very good. I explained how we had to modify our construction schedule since we couldn't close the pharmacy to make improvements without losing all of our pharmacy customers … they were flabbergasted!

Before I left, Mr. X asked me how I could get all this done without losing sight of how the grocery store was running? I explained that I had temporarily made the head butcher the store manager … plus I met with him and the frozen food manager each day. Mr. X winked at me and told me that he felt I had everything under control and if I needed him just to call. I assured him that I would and I appreciated the offer.

———————

Once my sister started, my uncle's crew walled off the pharmaceutical area (with heavy sheets of plastic) and installed a very large construction fan to blow clean air from the outside into the pharmaceutical area, which had vents, so that would allow the fresh air to blow back into the store, which would prevent dust or debris from getting into the pharmaceutical area. It worked out very well!

Inducing our customers to use the Drive-up window worked fairly well. We had huge signs in the front windows, arrows on the pavement, in the parking lot and the local paper had interviewed me regarding the change in ownership and we made a special point that during construction we would service all of our customers through our new Drive-up window.

Then, we could remove the wall that had, previously, divided the two stores, remove all of the racks, rip up the tile flooring and for disposal they had brought a couple of small (low) dump trucks … which they had to dump often.

My sister called me to say, "HOLY COW! This store is enormous!"

My reply was, "GREAT!"

She went on to ask if we could have a fax line installed, for prescription orders from doctors … she would save a lot of time, not having to answer the telephone … it was how they received orders in her last job.

I said, "Sure, remember you are the manager … if you need a fax line just order it … if you need me to help you, just ask me."

I asked how she was doing with the new layout. She assured me, she was doing well and it would be complete … shortly. I explained that I needed to order the racks, displays, counters, cash registers, etc. Also, we need to order signage and the product to fill all of the shelves.

I suggested that she have the part-time pharmacist come in to cover while she finished the layout and to have me work with her regarding the grocery items and frozen/cooler foods. She liked that idea. I explained that she should start with the architect's blueprint, which was to scale. He had left space on the aisles along the walls, for some type of displays on the walls. Once you have the general layout then you need to determine what will be on each rack or display … when you get to grocery, I will fill those aisles in. She felt I had simplified the job for her and said it would be ready in a few days.

While I was waiting for my sister's layout on a Tuesday, I had to make a run to the pharmacy where I had been buying condoms. Buying condoms is the most difficult task that a male, especially a teenager has to do. I, fortunately, have become a maven at buying condoms (for me and my cowardly buddies).

It all started when I was 15 and was planning (hoping) on becoming sexually active. I had three best friends, two my age and one a year older. So, I asked them where they got their condoms from? Only one had ever gotten a condom, which he had stolen from his brother's drawer and when the brother found out, he was furious and after being threatened, my friend promised not to take any more.

All three of my buddies were 'desperate' to get some condoms … but they were all scared to go into a store to buy them. I was determined to buy some. I couldn't go to the pharmacy across from the grocery store because the pharmacist knew me and my mom and dad, very well. So, I took a bike ride, about ten miles, up the main road to the shopping center, with a small pharmacy.

There were six to eight adults mulling around in the store. I walked around, here and there, until there wasn't anyone at the pharmaceutical counter. Then, I scooted over to the counter and asked the old pharmacist (he looked like Albert Einstein, by the way) for a box of three condoms … he studied my face for a beat or two, smiled and asked, loudly, "Will Trojans do?"

Blushing, intensely, I replied, "Yes … Great!"

The old codger turned around and opened the drawer behind him, took out a small box which he put on the counter and asked, "Will that be all?"

"Yes sir," I replied.

Then, as quickly as possible, I paid as he put my box into a small white bag.

At that point, I was sweating profusely, so I turned around to make my escape from the store … and when I did, there were several ladies in line, directly behind me. OH NO! I was sure that they had heard about my purchase … this further embarrassed me. Now, there were about ten people in the store and as I walked all the way to the front door, I could feel everyone's eyes on me. I got onto my bike and took off for the main road … I have played soccer and basketball, but never in my life did my heart beat as fast as it was beating when I made my exit from that pharmacy.

It was by far, the most embarrassing and the most humiliating event of my life.

As I rode my bike and the excitement of buying my first condoms subsided, I became proud of the fact that I had accomplished this monumental task … a 'Right of Passage' for a young man.

When I got home, I went directly to my room, closed the door and I hid the condoms in my backpack (so my mom wouldn't find them).

The next day, when I got together with my three buddies, I told them of my harrowing experience the afternoon before … as I explained, step by step, we were all laughing.

They asked, "How many did you buy?"

When I said, "A box of three," they each asked for one.

I told them that I needed two, as backup, but the next time I buy condoms I will buy some for them.

What a disgusting thought!

Just by chance, on a Saturday, about a week later, I accompanied my dad, as he went to a doctor's appointment, in the next town north of us. The doctor prescribed a prescription, so Dad drove to a pharmacy in the center town. There were no open parking places in the lot in front of the store, so Dad drove around to the parking lot in back of the store. When we walked in, the pharmaceutical counter was directly to our right, interesting! Pop gave the pharmacist (a big burly, fairly young guy) his prescription and we walked around the store for 10 to 15 minutes, before the pharmacist called Dad's name.

All the way home, all I could think about was how much easier it would be to buy condoms at that store … it would be a much longer bike ride … but a much shorter embarrassing exit.

So, on Monday morning, I rode my bike to the pharmacy that Dad went to and on the way, I went over and over what I would say to the pharmacist. When I arrived, at the back parking lot of the store, I went in through the back door and as I walked in, I could see there wasn't anyone at the counter … great … so I made a quick right and walked to the middle of the counter, where I was met by, undoubtedly, the most beautiful, young pharmacist, EVER! She was short, blond, had pale white skin, with the reddest lipstick I have ever seen … Magnificent!

She asked, "How can I help you?"

As much as I had prepared on the way, I was speechless. I never saw a female pharmacist … didn't think they existed … nonetheless, I was in front of the most beautiful girl I had ever seen, I think my heart stopped and I turned red.

The pharmacist very kindly asked, "Is there something I can help you with?"

I wanted to run!

Finally, I took a deep breath and said, "Two boxes of Trojans, please."

She smiled, widely, exposing her perfect white teeth, behind those succulent red lips. She turned around, opened the drawer and took out two boxes, which she put on the counter.

"Will that be all?" she asked.

"Yes ma'am," I mumbled out.

She put the boxes in a bag, I paid and turned to walk out … there wasn't anyone behind me in line … so I pushed back my shoulders, stuck out my chest and walked out of the store as proudly as the man I had become.

Later that afternoon, I rendezvoused with my three buddies and gave them two Trojan condoms each. They were delighted and happy to pay me for thinking of them.

From that day forward, I was the guy that bought all of the condoms.

Each time I went, the lady pharmacist was there. We became friendly and I became less and less embarrassed with every purchase. One time, I had to buy three boxes, one for me and one each for two of my buddies. The lady pharmacist said that I could buy a box of nine and it would be a lot cheaper … without thinking ahead I said, "I can't hide a box that big."

The pharmacist blushed and so did I. But that was a good idea for when I get a car.

In any event, we became friendlier and friendlier each time I made a buy.

———

So, now, years later, I brought my camera. The lady pharmacist appeared happy to see me, as usual. I was no longer shy or ashamed to speak with her and she always seemed to be amazed at how many condoms I purchased. I think she thought I was some kind of stud.

I noticed that she reached into her smock and secretly put a note into the bag with the condoms.

I took out my camera and took her picture, then asked if I could take some pictures of her store, she said, "Sure, why not?"

Then she whispered, "Don't forget to read my note."

I nodded my head up and down and noticed her husband looking down on us from where he filled prescriptions So, I took off to take pictures of what was on the racks and walls … and how much room to devote to each product. I left and took the roll of film to another store to have it developed, overnight.

To my surprise (and amazement), when I read the note from the gorgeous pharmacist, she asked for me to meet her at her house on Wednesday, at 10:00 am and she gave me her address. WOW!

Since I am so good at following orders, I cleared my very busy schedule and drove over to the lady pharmacist's house at precisely 10:00 am. She was sitting on her front steps wearing a bright red blouse, white shorts and the biggest red smile that you could imagine!

She was delighted that I showed up and spirited me into her house. A three-bedroom ranch … very nice … very neat.

She showed me around, in the kitchen she took two beers from the refrigerator and offered me one (I usually wouldn't drink in the middle of the day … but I was nervous … so, I took the ice cold bottle and gulped down a drink), next she showed me the dining room, living room, their office down the hall (I noticed in the hallway, that my host's nipples were protruding through her blouse … my guess was that she was not wearing a bra … oh my), across from a bathroom, at the end of the hall was another bedroom, outfitted with workout equipment … finally she took me into the master bedroom … the lights were off, the shades were closed and the only light was from the dozen or so candles burning around her king-sized bed.

My host said, "I thought we could lay down and discuss a few things."

I replied, "Why not." I couldn't believe my good fortune!

When I laid down in the bed, I found it to be extremely plush, as were the pillows, but the best part was when the most beautiful pharmacist, I could ever imagine rolled on top of me and started to give me the wettest, most aggressive kiss of my life. Her tongue didn't just dart into my mouth, it poked and prodded like it was looking for something … our tongues played with each other for a while until I slid my hand up on the back of her head and pressed her face toward mine and then I inhaled in, sucking the air from her lungs … I held it a while then exhaled back into her lungs … it was a very sexy move on my part. When we ended the kiss, she said, "Let's take off all of our clothes and make love!" Then she said, "I can't wait!" Neither could I.

As she was undressing, she took a package of condoms from a drawer next to the bed and threw it onto the bed.

"This is my favorite," she said.

When she was done undressing, I was looking at the most beautiful girl imaginable … her skin was milky white … perfect … except she had dark black and blue bruises on her arms, side and butt.

I asked, "What happened to you?"

The smile left her face and she replied, "Those are from my husband … he is a bit rough."

That's an understatement!

Over the next hour I got to use two types of condoms: one with raised rings and one with raised bumps … I think both of us preferred the raised rings, but the bumps were great as well. We then showered together and almost needed a third condom but we didn't go that far.

Before I left, she told me that she had imagined, in her mind, how great our sex would be … but it actually far exceeded her expectations! Now that's a compliment.

I said, "The feeling is mutual!"

Then I kissed her and said goodbye. WOW! I couldn't get her out of my mind.

Next, I drove over to the photo shop to get the prints of her pharmacy racks as a reference. I drove back to my grocery store office and reviewed the photos. I have been driving around, with very few exceptions, in my car for the past month, so that the pickup truck would be available for pick-ups or deliveries.

The new post office officially opened. The entire staff had relocated over to the new facility but they had not completely moved out of my building yet. They still had a few weeks but I couldn't wait to get started!

My Uncle T called to inform me that my Uncle A planned to bring his entire crew and a couple of scissor jacks this coming Sunday to paint the exterior of the pharmacy … Great!

That Sunday, I watched from my office in the grocery store as one crew taped and covered the top floor windows, and the second crew came right behind them spraying the white paint over the brown bricks … it was obvious that a second coat would be required but it looked better already. When the first crew finished covering the upper windows, they parked their scissor lift and started to cover the ground floor windows and doors. The first crew continued around the building again, applying the second coat of paint to the top floor … what a difference. When the top floor crew was finished painting, they went around the building again to remove the coverings from the top windows … then both crews completed painting the ground floor walls and then they removed the first-floor window coverings … WOW! The building looked fantastic! It looked like a new, crisp, clean building. They finished just in time because it was starting to get dark … I ran across the street to thank my uncle and his guys for doing such a great job and for working on a Sunday.

My Uncle A said that the paint covered very well but, in his opinion, we needed something on the side walls to break up the flatness of having the whole side all white … he suggested painting an eight-inch border of some color where the first and second floors meet. He said he could come back the next Sunday and finish in a half day. I agreed given his expertise and told him the border would have to be black, preferably shiny black … to match the sign.

When my sister came in to work on Monday, she called me to say how nice the exterior looked … I told her about the border and she agreed it sounded like a good idea. I asked how she was doing on the layout … she was close to complete … so I asked her to have the part-time guy fill in for her that afternoon so we could complete it in my office.

I made a copy of the blueprint so that we could write all over the copy … until we got it right. Then I took out my pictures … my sense was that the first couple of racks toward the prescription counter should be loaded with medical stuff … then transition into shampoos, razor blades, hair spray and hair coloring stuff … on the right side of the store there were more aisles because the pharmaceutical area jutted out on the left side … therefore, I was thinking of putting the greeting cards on the extra two aisles and along the adjacent walls … then, starting on the front racks on the right I would suggest candies, next side would have potato chips, pretzels, etc., then, candies in a bag, next canned juices, then, canned goods, next a detergent aisle, both sizes (small to large containers), next a feminine hygiene aisle, both sides. On the right hand, side wall, I envisioned a rack of umbrellas to the left of the front doors, then a number of coolers for milk (gallons and half gallons), for individual bottles of soda (large and small), another for 'sport' drinks, one for sliced cheese packages (American white and yellow), cottage cheese, Parmesan cheese and other packaged cheeses which could be sliced and finally a freezer for ice cream (gallons, pints, ice cream sandwiches and ice cream on sticks).

Between the freezer and the gift cards, I would suggest school/office supplies (which I got from my pictures that I took of the other pharmacy).

In the front of the store my plan was to have two cashier stations, on a long front counter, with all types of candy and gum displayed on the front side of the counter and behind the counter, I would suggest a long row of cabinets beneath the windows, for cigarette cartons, the front of which would be clear plex-glass sliding doors.

Then I lined up my pictures with what I thought should go on the racks. I took the pictures of what I felt should go on the first rack and I paper clipped them back-to-back to the pictures for what would on the other side of the rack.

By then it was lunch time, so I went home for lunch. I kind of wondered what took my sister so long to make a layout, when I did it in a few hours.

On the way back, I stopped at the pharmacy to see how the guys were doing. On the first floor; one crew was pulling up the tiles on the pharmacy side, two guys were framing a shaft down to the basement, for the dumbwaiter (should be completed in a day or two) and upstairs I found my Uncle A; determining how much paint he would need to paint the two apartments … I had pinned up a swatch of the color gray that I wanted on the bedroom wall … he planned to paint the apartments the beginning of the following week, the cabinets were installed in the kitchen, which was waiting for the counter to be installed and one crew was installing all of the new doors, while another crew was installing the new fiber-glass bathtub and fiber-glass walls around it. The bathroom vanity was in the hallway waiting for the counter guy, as well. I was impressed that my uncle's guys were moving along so quickly. I would guess that the apartments could be rented out in a month.

When I got back down stairs, my sister was waiting for me with her paperwork to go over to my grocery store office.

In my office, I had a photo copy of the store layout from the architect. My sister took out a sheet of paper from a manilla folder … it was a detailed copy of how she wanted the pharmaceutical area configured … she extended the back storage wall five feet, plus she made it wider, adding a row … also, she added a third work space for filling prescriptions, finally she would move some counters and cabinets around. That was it for the pharmaceutical area … no big problem.

I asked how the new Drive-up window was working out and my sister told me that it was a major distraction when she was busy … I asked her if it would be wise to hire someone part-time, just to cover the window at the busy times of the day (I have a hundred something names on a list in my office). My sister felt it would be a good idea so I gave her the list and told her to make the calls and interviews … it's her job.

When it came to the racks, my sister's ideas were similar to mine except, she had much more detail. Along the left wall my sister proposed lipsticks and cosmetics (she said the mark-up was terrific). Great!

Next, was my turn to show what I was suggesting. I showed on the drawing what I planned for the right side and I showed my sister the photos I took of the pharmacy. She could not believe I had taken the pictures … she was laughing. Then, she saw the picture of the lady pharmacist.

She said, "I know that girl. I went to college with her. She was so nice but she married a big oaf of an asshole for a husband. I think he used to beat her up!"

WOW!

Once we agreed to the layout. I told my sister that I needed to order the new racks, counters, cash registers and displays … ASAP … also, we both needed to make a list of all the items (and the quantities required, for each) that will be on the shelves, so we can start ordering all of it. In addition, I asked my sister to inventory and list all pharmaceutical items, on hand. Also, did she know where to order each item and what the lead times would be … possibly the old pharmacist could help with all of that.

Next, I drove over to my Uncle T's office and I showed him our finalized print/sketch. I went over the items that he needed to order … ASAP … since we now knew the exact size and quantity of the racks, counters, cash registers the peg board, the coolers and the freezer … and my uncle's guys could build all of the storage cupboards below the pegboard, in front of the register counter and on the front wall (for cigarettes) … also, his guys could build the front counter, as well as, the customer counter around the pharmaceutical area and the Formica guy would cover each counter and the cupboards.

I listened as my uncle ordered each item … he would ask me what exact item we needed, the size and the quantity … then he would call the supplier and place the order … it appeared to me that he knew each person that he called … fortunately, everything that we ordered was in stock and my uncle asked for deliver in seven to ten days. Great!

The next several days at the grocery store I gave a 'heads up' to the soda guy, the milk guy, the ice cream guy, the snack guy (candy, gum and breath mints), the chip/pretzel and nuts guy and the cigarette guy. I ordered everything for delivery in 20 days … in many cases, the supplier would have to calculate what we needed to fill the coolers, racks and cupboards. I went over the space which was allotted for them … they had no problem running with the ball. I reminded everyone that they would be charging Tony's Pharmacy Inc. for all of the products.

I had to determine and make an order for all of the grocery items required … since it would be time consuming to calculate just how much of each item would be required, I just ordered more cases than I estimated were needed and didn't worry since we had so much storage in the basement.

When the gift card lady showed up, I explained what we needed at the pharmacy … she said no problem she would handle everything including signage. Great!

Then, I called the sign shop to inquire about my exterior signs … she told me that the signs and metal structures were all made and waiting in their storage room.

The next day I went to the pharmacy to inform my sister that I had ordered all of the cash registers, racks, counters, coolers and freezer, plus all of the products we would need for my side (the right side) of the store. Noting, that all of the product was due in 20 days. My sister laughed and told me I was efficient.

Nothing had been ordered for the left side of the store but my sister had spoken to the cosmetic lady who was coming in to see what she needed … she would supply all of the product and signage we needed (much like the gift card lady). All of the pharmaceuticals were supplied by several companies, she was putting together an order. All of the band aids, tape, ointments, etc. came from one distributor, and he was coming in that day. She hadn't gotten to the shampoos, hair coloring, soaps, tooth brushes and razor blades … I carry these same items in my store, so I said I would order them … also, I suggested, I should order signage for the aisles, so that customers could find things easier … we discussed how big the signs should be, the color and the printing … then I was prepared to order the in-store signs.

Back at my office, I took out our 'pricing booklet' that had all of the items the warehouse offered and the list price of each. Referring to my pictures I made a long list of what I needed to order, noting that we didn't carry many of the higher priced items in the grocery store. I called my sister and asked her about the 'specialty' shampoos and soaps … she said she would ask the cosmetics lady when she spoke to her.

That Sunday, my uncle painted the black border around the building where the first and second floors met. I think it made a huge improvement and I told my Uncle A that … he sure knows his business.

The next day, as soon as she got to work, my sister called me to say how much of a difference the border made … we were both delighted!

My Uncle A's guys painted the interior walls on Monday. WOW! What a difference the white paint made … the store looked 25% bigger and 100% cleaner! While, my Uncle R's crew laid the linoleum in the kitchen and bathroom apartments.

Tuesday, my Uncle R had his crew tiling the main floor, while Uncle A's guys painted the apartments.

Wednesday, the guys continued to tile the main floor and another crew installed the carpets in the apartments.

Thursday, the crew completed the tile on the main floor and took down the plastic around the pharmaceutical area. My Uncle T, my sister and I discussed the modifications to the pharmaceutical area, since the guys planned on starting to frame that area out the next day. Then my uncle and I went upstairs to check out the apartments. My uncle was impressed and asked how much I planned to ask for rents … I told him that I had added $100 dollars to what the old pharmacist was getting and my uncle laughed … he felt I should ask at least $150 more and he should know, since, he had a lot of rental properties.

We made a plan to go the next morning to buy the refrigerators and stoves.

When I got back to my grocery store, I created an ad for the two apartments, I called the paper and placed the ads every day for the next two weeks.

On Friday, my Uncle T and I drove to the contractor's appliance store and purchased two white refrigerators and two white stoves … which they loaded onto his truck … and my uncle's guys took them off of the truck and installed them in the apartments.

On Monday, a large crew of electricians came and installed the overhead lights and all of the ceiling tiles. WOW! The store looked terrific!

They also installed the lights in the rest rooms and in the apartments. They installed lights over the kitchen and bathroom sinks as well as installing ceiling fixtures in the center of each bedroom.

I mentioned to my sister that she should hire a stock handler, since the racks and products were being delivered in a week or two. She had a big, strong fella ready to go the following week!

After three days of adds, I rented both apartments … one to a physician's assistant and the other to a recently married couple (both had jobs). The PA wanted to move right in and negotiated a partial payment for the first month

… I offered the same deal to the young couple and they jumped right on it … so, just like that I had both apartments rented. Great!

Later in the week, the guys finished the expansion of the pharmaceutical area and then we waited for the racks, etc.

As the school year was coming to a close, I realized that with all of the items in the pharmacy added to those in the grocery store, that it would be a monster task for me to verify every invoice to a packing list and to pay all of the invoices on time. Therefore, I would need help, so I offered my friend the bookkeeper in my class (who aced all of the tests) a job. She accepted immediately but said she wanted to give her boss, a four-week notice … fine, that worked for me!

Fortunately, the postmaster stopped in to tell me that they were completely out of the space next door, and he dropped off the keys. I immediately called my Uncle T to tell him the good news. He said he would send his crews over the next day to start clearing out the vacated space … the next day the guys showed up with the two dumpsters and went to town removing all of the walls, counters, offices, etc.

Then, on Sunday the guys put up a thick plastic material wall on the grocery store side of the dividing wall, to prevent dust, dirt and debris from getting into the grocery store once they removed the wall dividing the store from the post office.

Monday, Uncle R's guys showed up to lay the tile floor and the racks were delivered to the pharmacy.

My sister and I had to identify how many new hires we would need to stay open given the new hours once we had our Grand Opening … we went through the list of job applicants almost completely. Over the next two weeks, we had to interview and hire a good number of people and then train them.

My Uncle T's crew put the racks together and positioned them as they were drawn on the blueprint. Another crew was just about done building the front counter and the cupboards.

By Wednesday, all of the racks were put together and the cupboards and counters were complete and ready for the Formica guy. The coolers and the freezer were delivered and installed.

Come Thursday, the Formica guy arrived and stated covering the counters, while the carpenters installed the white peg board, put in the cupboard shelves and made and installed the sliding doors (some Plexi-glass and some from a white plywood).

By the end of the week at my grocery store, the entire area was clear and the tile floors were completed.

The next week was very busy checking in all of the new products and loading each product onto the right shelves. The cosmetic and gift card ladies came in and loaded in their stuff, along with attractive displays with pictures and header signs. The medical supply guy did the same with his myriad of products … he even had what I considered feminine hygiene type products! Plus, my brother-in-law picked-up and installed the signs identifying what was in each aisle. WOW! It really looked great!

My Uncle T's guys constructed the huge, 'walk-in cooler', while another crew positioned and hooked up the bakery and seafood equipment (they even filled the lobster pool with sea water).

By mid-week the soda, water and ice tea guys, loaded in their products (the dairy guy had to wait until the last minute … next Thursday) … our Grand Opening was scheduled for the next Friday! Yikes!

I ordered signs for the front windows and tons of balloons. For next Thursday afternoon.

Chapter 2

Now that I am 22, we celebrated my birthday with just my close family (Mom, Dad, sister, brother-in-law, and my Uncle T and my aunt, since they were my godparents). After we ate, we sat outside in a circle discussing our plans for the next few weeks.

The following week was a blur … except for the food! The bakery was baking cakes and pastries, for display … the bakery lady would bring me a different grinder, for lunch, each day … magnific! I think the seafood girl was jealous so she made me deep fried Fish and Chips … also, terrific!

B showed up with the wine … cases and cases of wine. He and I loaded the wine into racks. He had determined where each bottle of wine would go … he had header signs for each category of wine (like Chardonnay, Riesling and Burgundy), there were 'Best Buy' signs and a big wine mural for above the racks. Still, it took forever for us to load all of the wine bottles into the racks.

Fortunately, the frozen food manager, could load the big cooler with skids of beer, then load the coolers … except for the very last cooler, which B filled with the bestselling wines and of course champagne!!

On Wednesday, the sign shop erected the new signs on the top of the buildings but didn't turn the lights on yet.

By Thursday, we were all set on both sides of the street! The full-page ads broke that evening … describing the Grand Openings of the brand new … TONY'S PHARMACY … and TONY'S SUPER-SUPER MARKET. With cigarette prices 20% off! First prescription FREE! Cosmetics and gift cards, 10% off at the Pharmacy. The Grocery Store offered 3 FREE doughnuts, 50% off Fish & Chips and 10% off all beer and wine!

Also, so that all the employees would be dressed the same … I had ordered and distributed, two black golf shirts, with Tony's embroidered on the front, left breast to each employee … with instructions to wear them during the Grand Opening; Friday, Saturday and Sunday.

I invited the three brothers for lunch but asked them to stop by the store first … previously, I asked the seafood girl to fry up two orders of Fish & Chips whenever she saw me escorting someone up the main aisle … additionally, I asked the bakery lady to make a whole roast beef grinder and slice each half, in half again, making four small grinders, each time she saw me escorting someone up the main aisle.

When the brothers came into the store, they immediately asked me about the new sign and the new name! I explained that with the new additions I felt that the store was taking on more of my personality. We walked up the aisle toward the new expansion, I was proud! Of course, the brothers had to say hello to everyone, employees and customers. When we got to the new seafood area, they were surprised at the bright new addition … the seafood gal offered each of them a half order of Fish & Chips … WOW!

They said, "This melts in your mouth!"

Exactly!

They each looked closely at the lobsters in the Lobster Pool but when they got to the bakery counter, the bakery lady let out a very loud yelp! She, evidently knew Mr. Y (from her bakery days) … she came around the counter and gave him a big kiss and an emphatic hug … of course they were speaking fluent Italian ("How have you been … it's so good to see you … I am surprised to see you here!") … then, the other two brothers chimed in and it was a cacophony of noise, everyone in the store had to look at them … finally the bakery lady said, "I am goina to make a you the best a grinder … you hold ona"! She went back behind the counter and made two, whole 'Italian Grinders', with everything on them, including mozzarella cheese … then she put them in the oven, until the cheese melted down the sides … she took out the grinders, cut them in half and handed them to the three brothers and myself with a big smile and said, "Monga!"

The grinders were magnificent! I changed my directions … "Next time you see me escorting someone up the aisle, make a hole grinder just like this and cut it into four pieces."

Next, we toured the beer and wine aisle and finally the walk-in cooler. That was Mr. Z's highlight of the tour … seeing how easy it was to bring beer into the cooler and then how easy it was to load the coolers … he said, "That almost tempts me to come back!"

When we were done, I took them across the street to view my new pharmacy. Magnificent, spectacular and outstanding were some of the terms they used to describe my new expanded and renovated store.

At the steak house, the brothers were not very hungry … but they were thirsty! Each of the brothers at one time or another told me how proud they were of me and how good they felt that I was carrying on the tradition that they had started … they said that their wives would be delighted to see and shop in the new store when they come in to shop.

Back at the grocery store, I met up with my parents and my Uncle T, to give them a tour of my new store. Mom was amazed at how much larger my store appeared. When we reached the seafood area, the girl per my original request handed each of us a half order of Fish & Chips … which everyone said, "Melts in your mouth!"

Then as we passed the new lobster pool the bakery lady came around the counter screaming with delight as she kissed and hugged my mom … of course the two of them started to blabber in Italian … my mom was saying how nice it was to see her and the bakery lady was saying how thankful she was for the job, what a wonderful son she had and what a genius I was … Mom was glowing with pride … then the bakery lady's husband came around the counter and he lifted Mom up and gave her multiple kisses and hugs … as the bakery lady gave my Uncle T a hug and a kiss … what a nice reunion … all spouting Italian as well … then the bakery lady handed each of us a plate with her special grinder on it … and said, "Just for you … Monga!" …

Each of us told the bakery lady just how good the grinder was! My folks were just as astonished with the size and the quantity of my new 'alcohol aisle' … they had heard about it but seeing it was another thing.

Next, we went across the street to my new pharmacy and to see my sister.

Getting across the street wasn't easy given the traffic at that time of day.

My Uncle T said, "You better call the police department and ask for an officer to direct traffic, over the next three days."

When we went into the pharmacy, my sister was standing at the front counter to welcome Mom, Dad and Uncle T. As she gave them a tour of the store, I made a call to the chief of police requesting officers to direct traffic in front of my store's during my Grand Opening … he said he would line up some off-duty officers.

My folks had frequented the old pharmacy for many, many years and could not believe the transformation. It was so much brighter, it was sooo much larger and it offered soooo many more items! WOW! I was happy to see how impressed my folks were … as they were showering me with praise … I told them that Uncle T was responsible for at least 50% of what they see … my uncle wouldn't have it, he put his arm around my shoulders and said, "I build things every day, but this kid had the vision to see all of this way ahead of time … he is really special!"

Then he said, "We make a hell of a team!"

I was proud, embarrassed and encouraged all at the same time.

After my folks left, I went out to pick up the balloons and signs I had ordered for the Grand Opening. I dropped off half of the balloons and signs with my brother-in-law with instructions of where to put them. Then, I went back to my grocery store where the managers and I festooned the store after closing … all that was left was to hopefully have a successful Grand Opening!

I got to work early the next day and was encouraged to see all of the employees coming to work wearing their new Tony's shirts.

A lot more people came for the Grand Opening than I had expected … even the mayor stopped by to thank me for improving and expanding what our city provides. Great!

Good thing I had requested police officers to direct traffic, since many of our customers parked in the front lot of the grocery and crossed the street to the pharmacy.

I called my sister to ask how it was going and she said her store was packed … I asked if she needed any help … she said that they had it handled … there were four cashiers at the front counter … two were ringing and two were bagging, and they still had a line! Cigarettes were a hot commodity!

I called the cigarette guy and asked if he would stop by later in the day, to make sure we wouldn't run out of cigarettes … he assured me that he would make sure we wouldn't run out.

At the end of the day, when I totaled up the receipts, I realized that we had the largest single day since I purchased the grocery store. When I went across the street, they still had customers in the store … I asked the cashiers to lock the doors … my sister was worn out but excited about the enthusiasm and the quantity of the customers … once all of the customers had left the store, we totaled the receipts and I was amazed at just how much we had received in one day!

The next day was even busier … we had lines everywhere. Because of the size of the deposit, I asked the head butcher (who was a major body builder and looked like a body guard) to accompany me to make the daily deposit at the bank. When we arrived at the bank, I realized that I had not given the bank manager an invitation to tour my two stores. So, I ducked into his office and invited him to come over at lunch time … and bring a good appetite.

Then, we went over to the pharmacy to get and make their deposit.

Back at my grocery store I informed the seafood lady and the bakery lady that when they saw me escorting a gentleman up the aisle to make a half order of Fish & Chips and a special whole grinder cut in half … this guy is a big eater!

Later when the bank manager arrived, he commented on how good it looked to see all of my employees wearing the same shirt … he said, "It looks professional!"

When we got to the new seafood counter, the lady gave us a dish with Fish & Chips … the bank manager said, "It melts in your mouth!"

Then, as we passed the lobster pool, the bakery lady came around the counter with two dishes of her special Italian grinders … hot out of the oven … as we ate the grinders in the busy aisle the bank manager said, "That's the best grinder, I have ever had!"

Great! Then he was amazed at the quantity and the variety of our beer and wine selections.

As we were walking out of my grocery store, I told the bank manager that I had made the largest deposit for each store earlier and I expected to beat that with that day's deposit. I think he was impressed.

When we entered my pharmacy, he was like everyone else, amazed at the transformation from an old fashion pharmacy to a modern pharmaceutical store. We didn't stay long because the store was so crowded … Great!

At the end of the day as I expected, we had the biggest day of receipts ever … for both stores. I noticed that a lot of the shelves were almost empty so I asked all of the stock handlers to come in an hour early on Sunday … I gave each one (and myself) the responsibility for an aisle and asked them to try to finish before we opened … some guys had a lot more to do than the others but as those of us finished early we went and helped the other guys … and we finished everything before the rush of customers … great team work everybody!

Without a doubt, we had the best Sunday ever!

————————

On Monday, my new bookkeeper started. Great!

After we completed the new hire paperwork, I explained that I had overlooked creating a work area for her but I would rectify that, that day.

Next, I had the head butcher and the frozen food manager come to the office to meet the new bookkeeper … then, I asked the frozen food manager to show the bookkeeper around and introduce her to everyone (while the head butcher and I went to the office supply store to get her a desk, a chair, a file cabinet and two, two button telephones, so that we could both be on the telephone, simultaneously … and yeah, we needed to get telephone wires to interconnect the telephones).

When we got back, I had the new bookkeeper observe the cashiers while we rearranged the office, assembled the desk and chair and connected up the telephones … it went fairly quickly.

Finally, I had time to go over a few things with the new bookkeeper, like how we prepared the deposit and how we faxed the numbers over to the accountant.

Then, I had the head butcher accompany me as I made the very large deposits for the weekend for both stores.

When I got back to my grocery store, I had the bookkeeper work with me as I placed the biggest order for groceries, I had ever made … It felt good! Then, I did the same for the pharmacy. I explained how she should verify each item on an invoice to what we had received on a packing list.

She spent the rest of the day setting up her desk and going through the files.

————————

As time went by, the bookkeeper took on more and more responsibility and I found more time to devote to my managerial duties plus, I could go home at an earlier hour.

When I met with the three brothers, they were all interested in how the grocery store was doing, and Mr. X had a proposition for me … he wanted to sell his rental properties to me. He owned five, three family apartment buildings in the town to our north. The buildings were ten years old, brick exteriors, all in excellent condition and all apartments were occupied. He felt, the local bank in that town would be pleased to give me a mortgage for the buildings.

Mr. X went on to say that he was trying to liquidate his holdings and put the money in the bank for his wife as he gets older. I thanked him for thinking of me and asked him to give me a few days to think it over. He gave me the addresses and directions to go over and look at them.

Later I called my Uncle T and told him about the apartments and Mr. X's offer for me to purchase them. My Uncle Thought it sounded like a good idea … he owned lots of rental properties and he felt these units were in a good area.

I asked my uncle if he would be available to take a ride by in the afternoon … he told me to swing by and pick him up at his office.

When we got to the apartments, we noticed that all five were in a row next to each other. My uncle asked me to drive into the parking lot behind the buildings … to see what the condition of the asphalt and the back of the buildings looked like … everything was as Mr. X had said … it all appeared to be in excellent condition. My Uncle T thought it was a good idea for me to invest in rental property … so did I.

The next morning, I called Mr. X and told him that I was interested in purchasing his apartment buildings but I wasn't sure if the bank would lend me the money after spending/borrowing so much money for my pharmacy and my grocery. He asked if I knew where his bank (a branch of a large bank in the city to our north), near the apartments was and I said I knew … he told me to meet him there at 1:00 pm.

At the bank, Mr. X introduced me to the very pretty, very single bank branch manager. She brought us into the conference room and was very interested in my grocery store and my pharmacy. She had attended my Grand Opening and was amazed at the transformation of the old pharmacy building. Finally, Mr. X interrupted to say that I was interested in purchasing his five apartment buildings. She said that I would need to complete a mortgage loan application … she left the room and came back with the application … I thought I would take the application back to my office and fill it out there but when I looked up, I noticed that they were both looking at me expecting that I would fill the application out then and there.

Mr. X and the branch manager made small talk as I worked on completing the form. It was a good idea to have them there so when I had a question, they could give me an answer. For example, when it came to how much my existing loans where … I said I didn't know exactly … the branch manager said not to worry … it was important for me to list all of the loans, with approximate balances and they would verify everything. When the paperwork was complete, I wrote a check to the bank, to start the bank's process of qualifying me and appraising the buildings. The branch manager told us, that it would take about a month for the bank to do its due diligence.

When I made my daily deposit, I stopped into the bank manager's office to inform him that I was intending on purchasing five, three family apartment buildings from Mr. X and that we were going through Mr. X's bank to the north. He understood and wished me well.

Back at my office I called my attorney to have him draw up a simple Purchase & Sale agreement. Also, we will need to establish another corporation … I would suggest: Tony's Rental Properties, Inc.

The following Tuesday, we received an odd order from the two girls. Just two bottles of wine and a cold bottle of champagne … for delivery at 6:00 pm.

When I got to the house with the delivery, I asked why there were no groceries. The girls opened the champagne, poured three glasses and we all went into the living room … where the short haired girl informed me that they both had been promoted to new jobs in the mid-west and they were moving out there at the end of the week …

I said, "HURRAH!" And offered a toast. Both girls were excited … the short hair girl got a huge job as the manager of all the stores in the mid-west and the blond was promoted to store manager of a store in the town that they were going to live in.

I was very excited for them even though I was going to miss our bi-weekly trysts.

The blond re-filled our glasses and then the short hair girl said, "The company will buy our house for the appraised value … but we would rather sell it to you at the same price … plus we will leave all of the furniture for you and we will just pack up our things when we leave." … the short hair girl continued … "My sense is that you can assume our mortgage which should be quick and easy and you will just pay us the difference."

The blond told me that the lady branch manager was a delight to work with … I asked what bank she was talking about and when she told me, I laughed and said, "I just asked for a jumbo loan there the other day!"

I told them that I would be delighted to purchase their house and that I always was impressed with it! So, the girl with the short hair asked if I would meet her at the bank at 10:00 am the next day. Of course, I agreed.

Then, the short haired girl went in the kitchen to finish making dinner and the blond said she was going to take a shower (since she was sweaty from packing stuff, all day). I just sat in the living room looking around, drinking my champagne and wondering if I would own this beautiful home one day?

During dinner, we all drank more wine than we probably should have but we were all feeling very happy. The short haired girl said she would clean-up and the blond, wearing a bathrobe, took my hand and said she was going to take me into the bedroom and give me a real good look at the ceiling!

When we went into the master bedroom, the blond closed the door and took off her bathrobe … she was completely naked … she was also a bit tipsy … maybe a lot tipsy … then she hurriedly helped me out of my clothes before we made love with reckless abandon … when we were done, we both took a shower and I was revived … as I came out of the bathroom wearing only a towel wrapped around my lower section the gal with the short hair entered the bedroom and said, "Let's do it … for the last time!"

The blond put on her robe and said she would finish cleaning up in the kitchen.

Well, the short haired gal was a girl of her word … we tried every position that I knew and a few more before we were exhausted.

I always wondered but didn't ask why we never had both girls in the bed at the same time?

————————

I met both girls at the bank the next day at 10:00 am, sharp. The lady branch manager gave each of the girls a hearty, "Good to see you," but when she got to me, she smiled and said, "you again?"

The girl with the short hair appeared to me to be very smart as she explained to the branch manager that they were both being promoted to big jobs in the mid-west. They were leaving by the end of the week and they wanted to sell their home to me … actually they would like me to 'assume their mortgage' … the branch manager said she felt that could be done fairly quickly since they had just verified my assets and liabilities … hopefully we could have the Closing on Friday!

As we walked out of the bank, I told the gals that I would have my attorney write-up a Bill of Sale and said that when the bills come in for the telephone, electricity and gas, I would pay the bills, change the name on the bills, to my name and send the girls a note for repayment. We were all in agreement … HOLY COW! I am going to be a HOME OWNER!

I stopped by my attorney's office on the way back to work. I explained that I wanted to buy a house from my two friends and I needed a Bill of Sale by Friday. I explained how soon they were moving … that I was assuming their mortgage paying them the balance and our agreement regarding the telephone, electrical and gas bills. My attorney asked how we were going to handle the taxes? We hadn't discussed that. My attorney told me he would stop by City Hall to see what was owed for taxes (and he would check to see if there were any liens on the property) and we would subtract that amount from the balance that I was paying to the girls. Great! That is why I go to an attorney.

When I got back to work, I called the girls and they agreed about how we would handle the taxes.

That night at dinner, I broke the news to my parents that I was buying a beautiful three-bedroom home on Friday and I would be out of their hair by the end of the week! My mother was sad her youngest was leaving the nest. She said to me that I should learn to be more frugal with my money … good advice.

Then I told them that I was negotiating to buy five apartment buildings from Mr. X. Mom almost fainted … then she said, "Do you know the problems you will have? People calling at all hours with complaints!" My reply was, "I will have them call my business phone … and I will handle the problems from there."

My mom was just concerned for me … she thought I was not spending wisely and that I should be saving. I told her that I showed my Uncle T the apartment buildings and he thought it was a good idea for me to be investing in real estate … that sort of soothed my mother's feelings.

I was excited and so were my folks … I asked them if they would like to see my new house … right then.

They simultaneously said, "Yes!"

I called the girls to ask if I could bring my folks over to see what I was buying … they said, "Sure."

I think they just wanted to meet my parents.

We piled into my truck, and I drove over to the house. When we got there, the girls were very pleasant toward my parents. They took us through the entire house (I noticed the girls blushed when we got to the master bedroom … but I think I was the only one that noticed it). Then we went downstairs. I hadn't seen this area before. There was: a bathroom/laundry room, a finished family room (with a fireplace and a sliding glass door to the fenced, backyard). Finally, they showed us the two-car garage (you could eat off the floor).

When we got back into my truck, my mom and dad said that they could not be more impressed with how clean and how pretty the house was … that was before I told them that all of the furniture was included … it blew their mind … they wondered how I keep coming up with such good deals … I told them, "So do I."

Friday afternoon we had the Closing which went off without a hitch … I kissed the girl's goodbye and wished them both good luck … then they left for the airport and their new lives out west.

That night, I bought a tube of tooth paste and a tooth brush, at work … went home got a change of clothes, my underwear and gave both my mom and dad a big, big hug and a kiss and left for MY HOUSE.

———

On Sunday, I went home for our weekly family luncheon. The main topic of conversation was my new house … my parents told my sister and her husband how nice it was. After we ate, I packed up my stuff and dad and my brother-in-law helped me load it all into my truck. Then I invited them all to follow me over to my new place.

When we got there, they were all, 'WOW and look at that', from the outside (my folks had never seen my house in the daylight) and it continued when we went inside … I couldn't be prouder … after we took the Grand Tour my dad, brother-in-law and I unloaded my truck … I then took out a special bottle of champagne from the refrigerator and we had a toast to my new house! Eventually, we all took a walk into my backyard while we finished the bottle of champagne.

When my folks left, I rode home with them so I could drive my car over to my new house.

After a couple of weeks, my mom started to come to my home mid-week and clean it … and she wouldn't take anything for it!

In addition, she would bring a large pan of lasagna or stuffed shells or manicotti … she wouldn't want me to go hungry.

I felt that I should do something nice for my parents … so when I was making my daily deposit at the bank, I told the bank manager that I wanted to pay off my parent's mortgage on their house … once I had paid off the mortgage the bank manager gave me a (standard) letter from the bank thanking my parents for their business and stating that their mortgage was paid in full.

I joined my parents for dinner that night and when I presented them with the letter from the bank, they were overjoyed and so appreciative.

My mom kept saying, "Tony … you can't afford this!"

I could see that my dad had a tear in his eye when he hugged me and said, "You can come over for dinner more often!"

Both stores appeared to be doing well. I checked with my accountant and he said we were significantly ahead of our forecast and more profitable than expected! Great!

He also gave my new bookkeeper a glowing report!

After a couple of weeks, I received a letter from the bank up north stating that my loan application was approved and that the Closing would be the following Tuesday. Another letter would follow with what the Closing costs would be. I called Mr. X and he had received a similar letter.

Then, I called my attorney he was copied on the letter as well. He reminded me to take a 'walk through and around', the buildings on the morning of the Closing … to ensure there were no surprises. Mr. X would be responsible for the accumulated taxes up to the Closing date.

I called Mr. X and invited just him, to lunch.

I said, "The Closing date is so close to the end of the month, why don't we 'finalize' everything, as of, the end of the month (the taxes, electricity and gas)."

He would collect this month's rents. He would be responsible to pay to me out of the proceeds from the bank for one month's rent for every tenant to cover the last month's rent each tenant paid when they paid 'First and Last' month's rent. Also, he agreed to join me for the walk through before the Closing.

After lunch, I called my attorney to tell him what my agreement was with Mr. X.

The Closing went very smoothly. I keep taking on more and more debt. It is mind boggling to me that these banks would ever consider loaning all of this money to what I consider myself as a young kid. It really bothered me to owe so much to the bank when I purchased my grocery store but now I look at it as the price of doing business.

On the first of the month, I sent a letter to each of my tenants informing them that I had purchased their apartment building and that any future problems or issues should be directed to me (and I gave them the telephone number in my office). Also, I directed them to mail all future rental payments to: Tony's Rental Properties, Inc. at my post office box.

I realized that I needed another pickup truck … I am in and out of the store often and there needs to be a pickup truck available.

I called my Uncle T to say that I was headed over to see his truck guy … my uncle said he would meet me there.

When I arrived at the Dealership, I asked for the owner … he came right out and didn't recognize me. I had to remind him, who I was.

Then he said, "Oh yeah, you're Tony's boy."

Good enough. I told him I needed to buy another pickup truck … he asked if I was trading in the last one that I bought … I said, "No trade … I just need another truck for my business."

About that time, Uncle T showed up and he and the owner exchanged pleasantries. I told the owner that I needed a basic pickup truck with a radio, AC and power windows … color black.

The owner checked his inventory and said, "I have a black pickup, in stock, but it has the Electronics Package and real nice wheels on it."

Uncle T said, "No problem … just throw that in!"

The guy chuckled but you could tell by his voice that my uncle was not kidding.

The truck was great … it had leather seats, a top-of-the-line radio and speakers (a sound system), real nice-looking side-view mirrors and a little bit bigger engine than what I had in the last truck … I loved it! Uncle T negotiated the guy down to well below the MSRP on the truck and I purchased it. The owner told us the truck would be serviced, titled and ready to go in two days … I said, "Oh yeah … I want TONY'S on the driver's door, below the window, in white."

The owner said, "The detail guy will be here tomorrow, I'll have him do it then."

Uncle T took a twenty-dollar bill out of his pocket, gave it to the owner and said, "That should cover it!"

The owner agreed.

I bought Uncle T lunch at his favorite Italian restaurant and told him how much I appreciated his help.

When I got back to work, I called my insurance agent to inform him that I bought a new truck.

When I picked up, my new truck it shined … the owner said, "I had the guy's clear coat the truck so it will look like you just washed it all the time … and dirt and dust won't stick to it … I threw it in."

WOW!

"Thanks!"

It sure looked good and the detail guy did a great job putting the TONY's on the door.

Over the next several months, everyone seemed to settle into their jobs. Both stores continued to do better than originally estimated … and I could tell by the amount of our deposit's. Great!

In the fall, I went back to college to take the advertising class that I had signed up for. The first night the instructor (a real pretty girl) about 30 years old, had each student come up to her desk so that she could meet them … personally. There were several students in front of me in a line. I was the last student to come into the room because I usually run late. When I gave her my name, she looked at my shirt and asked if I worked at the grocery store, I said, "Yes."

See paused, smiled and asked demurely, "Do you own the grocery store?"

I replied, "Yes, I do."

She asked, "Who does your advertising?"

I replied, "I do."

The professor pushed away from her desk stood right in front of me and said loudly, "Well … you have just ruined my lesson plan for this semester!"

I said, "How?"

She said, "I have saved your ads, and I planned on demonstrating what was wrong with them … I think it would be quite embarrassing for you to sit through it."

I blushed, then I said, "No, I won't be embarrassed … because I don't know anything about advertising … and apparently it shows!"

"Okay," she said. "Sit down and we will get started."

I am so glad that I took the course, for I learned a lot!

———————

Come December, I went bowling one Sunday afternoon … after our family lunch with my three best buddies; A, B and C. When we were done bowling, the guys all wanted to stop at the pizza shop next to the entrance to the bowling alley's parking lot.

We all ordered beers and an extra-large cheese pizza. As we were all babbling, a guy I thought to be the owner, came out from the kitchen to close the venetian blinds (to prevent the sun from shining in our eyes). He looked like a Mister Muscle guy … with a white V-neck T shirt, stretched around his mammoth arms and bulging chest. He evidently must have heard the guys saying, Tony this and Tony that. Then, I noticed him looking at my shirt … not because of my muscles but to read the name on my shirt. He came over and asked me to speak with him in the other room … a room used for the overflow when they were very busy.

He introduced himself and asked me if I was the guy who owned Tony's grocery store … I replied in the affirmative … he told me that he wanted to sell his building across the street … he felt it would make a great grocery store … it was presently vacant … there was a little market, at one time … there was a tropical fish store … and there was a hobby shop, all were gone now! He said that he wanted to sell the building so that he could build a big Italian restaurant with a large banquet facility in the back … on the very large plot of land that he owned next door … I asked about the parking lot and the roof of the building he was selling … he said the parking lot had just been resurfaced and the roof was replaced five years ago … he assured me that the building was in excellent condition and he would give me a great price for a quick sale. I told him I was interested and I would like to come back the next day to take a tour of the building and the grounds … he was delighted.

When I got back to the table, the guys had devoured half of the pizza … no problem I just wanted two pieces. My friends were inquisitive regarding me and the pizza shop owner. So, I told them that he wants me to buy the building across the street … I said I would take a look at it the next day. When we left, I took a ride around the building across the street … it looked pretty good to me.

When I got home, I called my Uncle T to tell him that I had a chance to purchase a real nice building about 12 miles south of my present store. I would turn it into another Tony's Super-Super Market.

Uncle T asked, "When does it stop?"

My reply was that, "You told me that I would come across deals that were too good to be true and that I should be prepared to jump on them … I think this is one of them!"

"Okay, then … when do you want to go and look at it," my uncle asked?

I said, "How about you pick me up at 9:30 tomorrow morning and we'll drive over together."

I hadn't told my uncle anything about the owner of the building, so the next morning when we got to the pizza shop as soon as my uncle saw the owner, he started to speak Italian to him. It was interesting how comfortable both were when speaking their original language … my uncle and the pizza shop owner really hit it off well.

I heard my uncle ask the guy, "You aren't trying to cheat my nephew, are you?"

The pizza shop owner told him, in Italian, "No, I'm trying to give him a good deal!"

So, we took a walk across the street (my uncle carried his measuring wheel and a pad of paper) … first we took a walk around the building while my uncle measured the length and the width … when we went inside my uncle looked at the dividing walls (no big deal to remove), the tile floors, the exterior doors and the windows. Next, we looked at the basements, most had a lot of junk in them (left over from previous renters) … then we went up onto the roof … which my uncle felt looked good! It was very evident that my uncle knew what he was talking about. My uncle asked the pizza guy how much are the taxes, what does the city appraise the building at, what has the building independently been appraised at, what was the property size and what price did he expect to get.

When the pizza guy told my Uncle T the selling price, my uncle roared laughing out loud and said, "That … will never happen … I thought you wanted a quick sale … if we wanted to, we could write you out a check for the building right now … for the right price!"

Of course, all of this was spoken in Italian … my uncle was one tough cookie when he was negotiating.

The pizza shop owner invited us back to his shop for a beer and a grinder … while he had time to come up with a number … my uncle explained that he only had one shot and my uncle was not going to let his nephew get screwed. They both agreed and we went back across the street to break bread.

I was so happy that I brought my uncle … he was really beating up the guy over the price.

While we were eating, my uncle asked the pizza shop owner what his intensions were when he moved next door? He said he would need to sell the pizza shop. My uncle indicated that we might be interested in it. This peaked the pizza shop owner's attention even more. My uncle inquired about the second floor. The guy said that there were two apartments … both unoccupied … occasionally he would take a lady customer upstairs for a dalliance and he would sleep there on occasion if he was extra tired … the other apartment was vacant … he had a guy in there that stopped paying the rent so he physically threw him out and had not had a chance to re-rent it.

Uncle T asked, "So what do you think you could sell this building for."

When the pizza shop owner answered, my uncle said, "No way! You're not selling the pizza shop … you're just selling an empty building! You better sharpen your pencil!"

Then, we all ordered another beer and Uncle T asked the guy what he expected to build next door?

The pizza shop guy exploded with enthusiasm as he explained his vision in detail. A huge very ornate restaurant … like they have in Italy … a large kitchen in the middle of the building and a banquet hall in the back, to hold at least 250 guests … and a huge waterfall on the back wall … he wanted to call it: The Falls of Napoli.

My uncle, piped in, "I am from Naples!"

"So am I," replied the guy.

They both stood up and hugged each other. Then Uncle T told him that he, Uncle T, could build the restaurant for him … that he had over 100 men, working for him doing construction … it blew the guy's mind!

The pizza guy asked how long do you think it would take to build his new restaurant … my uncle asked him what type of building it would be (block, or stick construction), would there be a basement and what he regarded as ornate. The pizza guy answered all of my uncle's questions then my uncle quoted six months … after receipt of blueprints and permits. I said, in Italian to the surprise of the pizza shop owner (meaning, I understood everything they had spoken about), "I can attest that my uncle's guys are fast and very good!"

"So," my uncle bellowed out, "What do you really want for the building across the street … and what do you want for this building?"

The guy ordered another round and said, "Hold on … I don't want to sell both buildings now … I want to keep the pizza shop running, while you build my new restaurant … then I would move my ovens and kitchen over there and open up my new restaurant!"

My uncle replied, with enthusiasm, "The Falls of Napoli!"

The guy was so excited, that he stood up with both arms stretched into the air (like a prize fighter that had just one a 15-round fight), he danced around and around in a circle, yelling, "YES … YES … YES!"

When he calmed down, we all took a drink and my Uncle T told him that his plan would be for me to purchase the store across the street, the proceeds of which the pizza guy could use for the downpayment of his new restaurant then my uncle would start the renovation for my new store across the street while his architect drew up the plans and they pulled permits for the new restaurant. Then, my uncle would construct the restaurant and once the pizza guy closed the pizza shop, I would buy the building which would pay for the remaining work on the new restaurant. Then, my uncle would renovate the old pizza building to my plans.

If I thought the pizza guy was excited before he was even more excited now saying, "You got a deal," and shaking our hands. My Uncle T told him, "We don't have a deal … we don't even have a price!"

The pizza shop guy got very serious, sat down next to my uncle and leaned close to his ear and whispered something, I guessed it was a number, my uncle grunted, "Okay."

The pizza guy smiled, leaned back in and whispered in my uncle's ear again, I'd guess he was quoting a number for the pizza building, my uncle shook his head, several times, "No!" … the pizza guy sat back and pondered the number then he leaned in again and whispered another number into my uncle's ear … this time my uncle smiled and said, "We've got a deal!"

The pizza guy, also with a big smile jumped up and ran to the bar in the adjacent room and came back with a bottle of Ouzo and three glasses. As he filled up the glasses he made a toast, "To my new best friends, and to … The Falls of Napoli!"

Uncle T and I picked up our glasses and said, simultaneously, "To the Falls of Napoli!"

On the ride back to my grocery store, my Uncle T told me, "That is how you negotiate in Italy."

Then before he left, he gave me the dimensions for each building and told me to contact the architect and the bank.

When I checked the dimensions of the buildings I planned to purchase, I found that the buildings were almost identical in size to my Grocery Store and Pharmacy … GREAT!

My architect told me that it was common for buildings to be built in sort of standard sizes. I asked him to create a set of blueprints for my expected new grocery store … since he had to have exact measurements, he asked if he could contact the seller to get in and take measurements … I gave him the telephone number and asked him to … go for it!

Next, I called my attorney to notify him that I wanted to purchase an existing building and turn it into another grocery store … I gave him the address and the purchase price and asked him to create a Purchase & Sale agreement. I asked if he felt I would need to create another corporation and he said we could but he felt that since it is another grocery store … we should just add it into the existing corporation.

Then, when I took the daily deposit to the bank, I stopped into the bank manager's office to explain how I was looking to purchase the two buildings probably 8–10 months apart and turning them into identical grocery and pharmacy stores to my existing stores.

He chuckled and told me to make up a sheet showing how much was required for each loan and then we would fill out the loan applications for each one. In the meantime, he would have the properties appraised.

The next day, I called the head butcher and the bookkeeper into the office to inform them of my plans. I asked the butcher to cover the store as store manager for the next few days and I asked him if he would like to be the store manager for our new 'South End' grocery store. He said he would be delighted! Then I asked the bookkeeper if she could help me pull together what our costs would be for a new store. Of course, she was happy to help.

I started to create a summary sheet of all the costs involved. We knew the purchase price. Next, we needed to calculate what the construction costs, the equipment costs and the inventory costs would be. Since we recently expanded the grocery store and completely renovated the pharmacy, I asked the bookkeeper to go through the invoices and breakdown what the costs were, item by item.

Then, I took out the present blueprints for my grocery store. I went from one end of the print to the other end, making a list of each item we would need to duplicate in the store how many racks, coolers, etc. The inventory was easy … we had an exact inventory, in dollars, of what was on the floor and in storage … I would just duplicate that (a huge number).

As my bookkeeper fed me the numbers, I would extrapolate the cost. Finally, we were done! My bookkeeper was a huge help … and I told her so.

I called my Uncle T to set up a time we could get together to finalize what the costs would be. He was a pro at estimating construction costs. We settled on Friday morning, at 10:00 am.

At our meeting, I showed my uncle how I had estimated what the costs would be and asked him for his input. He asked what I intended to do with the exterior of the building … would we leave it as is, or paint it, like we did with the pharmacy. My sense was that we should paint it. Then, my uncle added 20% to the entire number, just to be safe … we were talking big money!

Over the weekend, I massaged the numbers and created a summary sheet of funds required.

Monday, mid-morning, when I took my deposit over to the bank, I met with the bank manager, to review how much I needed to create my new grocery store.

First, the bank manager told me that his appraisal was significantly, more than the purchase price … so they would loan me the entire amount, I would have to compete a loan application (but I only needed certain applicable information … because they had all of my other information) … they would give me only 75% of the construction costs, in the form of a construction loan (another application to partially fill out). Finally, they could only give me 50% of what I requested on an Inventory Loan (I negotiated it up to 65%) … of course, all of these loans had to be approved by their Lending Board but when the bank manager approved of a loan, the committee usually followed suit.

Given that this was the Christmas time of the year, everything moved a lot slower, but the Purchase & Sale agreement was signed and the loans were approved as I had requested, by the end of the year.

Just after the start of the year, Uncle T pulled the permits and construction begun!

Prior to the end of the year, my three buddies wanted to stock up for the holydays, giving me their orders. As usual, on Tuesday I went to the pharmacy up north, to see my beautiful friend the pharmacist … she always seemed happy to see me and I noticed that she put another note into my bag as she filled my order … she asked me if I had big plans for the holidays and I said, "Very big! … I will see you tomorrow!" She smiled and I left.

The next morning, she was at the door when I arrived, wearing just a bathrobe, why waste time taking off your clothes? I now lived only two blocks away, but I never mentioned it.

When we made love, it was a thing of beauty … an experienced woman knew what she liked/wanted and how to ask for it. I often had a date on Friday or Saturday and when I made love to my date, I would have to guess, what she liked or wanted … but I enjoyed that too … the hunt!

In any event, as we laid there, catching our breath, I told this beautiful pharmacist, that I planned on building another pharmacy, and I wondered if she would like to manage it for me. She was more than delighted and showed me her appreciation, in several ways!!! I told her that it wouldn't be opening for about 9–10 months, and there would be an apartment for her above the pharmacy. GREAT!

Also, at Christmas time, at our family party at my Uncle A's house, everyone was talking about the new stores I was building. My Uncle JJ, the oldest uncle, pulled me aside, to say that he wanted to retire and would I be interested in buying his gas station … it was a surprise to me, I told him I would think about it and said I would get back to him in a few days.

After thinking about my Uncle JJ's offer, for a few days, I told him, I decided I was interested in the gasoline part but not in the garage/car repair part … I am a grocer. I asked if I could convert the garage building into a store … my Uncle JJ thought that was a good idea, but I would need to get approval from the big gasoline corporation, since he only had a 99-year lease on the land.

Also, my uncle said he had a friend that had a gas station and wanted to get out of it because he was allergic to the grease and oils ... and he was very knowledgeable regarding the rules and regulations of the gasoline corporation, since he formerly worked in the headquarters.

When I met my uncle's friend, the gas station guy, I was amazed that he appeared to be in his 50s. Yes, he was also looking to sell his station and he knew of several other guys that were getting on in age, looking to sell. I told him my idea of converting the garage into a store and letting the customers pay first, then allow them to pump their own gas ... he liked the idea ... he told me of the issues that I would face, negotiating with corporate ... but if I would like, he could help ... Great!

I set up a meeting with my attorney, the gasoline guy and myself, to discuss the possibility of my purchasing and converting the garages. My attorney explained that I may face a huge environmental issue with pollution from the Petro-chemicals ... the gas guy felt we could negotiate a 'Hold Harmless' clause ... as a matter of fact the gas guy had all the answers to the attorney's issues (because he had worked in the corporate office) ... so after our meeting I asked the gas guy if he would manage these gasoline stores that I was proposing ... he said it would be a pleasure to do the job and to work for me.

I told the gas guy what I was offering for each station and asked him to speak with the others to see if they were interested or not ... he came back to me with three other stations ... good, a total of five gas stations.

I had my attorney make an appointment with the appropriate people at the main gasoline corporation's office for the attorney the gas guy and myself.

At the meeting, my attorney laid out my plan to convert these five (old fashion) gasolines stations, into self-serving gasoline and commercial store stations. The corporate people were not averse to the suggested conversion ... so we discussed our issues and their issues ... coming to the agreement that they would maintain ownership of the property, I would get a 99-year lease (for a monthly fee), I would be responsible for the renovation of the pumps and the garages, and they would give me a Hold Harmless agreement to cover past or present environmental issues ... perfect!

My Uncle T loved the idea, but he suggested that I use a company that is experienced in renovating gasoline stations, and he gave me the name of a local company. I showed them my plans and they gave me an estimate for the renovation and a discount for doing 5 stations within 15 miles, all at the same time.

I hired the gas guy and put him in charge of the project (he was a very sharp guy).

We met with my architect to give him our vision of the new gasoline stores.

Finally, I met with my attorney to have him create a new corporation TONY'S GAS & GO, INC. and once the corporation was created, I set up checking and savings accounts.

Once I had my Letter of Agreement from the gasoline corporation, I went to see the bank manager, with a request for funds and five signed Purchase & Sale agreements. It didn't take long for the loans to be approved and I called the gas station renovators and gave them the go ahead to start the renovations.

The first thing they asked me was where they should put the garage doors, the car lifts and all of the supplies (oil and belts and pulleys)? I called my Uncle T to ask his opinion … he knew a fella that had a warehouse that I could rent space from … I met the man at the warehouse and the space looked safe and clean, so I rented a section.

There also were desks and file cabinets, but they all smelled like gasoline/oil … so we junked them. Once everything was removed, the crews closed up the holes left from the door removals with concrete blocks and large attractive windows. They also installed new gas pumps on the islands that we could control from inside the store and they poured a new concrete floor so that we had one even surface (formerly there was a step down from the office to the garage area). Finally, they covered the old asphalt with a thick sealcoat and painted white lines for where cars could park.

Then, Uncle A came in and painted the exteriors and the islands, bright white … plus he painted the floors, with a gray paint, to seal them … the stores really looked good, refreshed.

Next, my uncle's crew built an enclosure for the cashier while the coolers and freezers where being installed, along one end and across half of the back wall.

Two rows of our standard racks down the middle of the store completed the installation.

While the food, groceries, soda and ice cream were being loaded in, the sign company erected my new Tony's Gas & Go signs.

It had been the gas guy's job to hire the staff, to run the stations from 6:00 am to 8:00 pm. Which he did, in fact, several of the hires were guys that had run or had worked in the stations before.

This all took until the beginning of November and fortunately, we had one of our most successful Grand Openings ever! Opening all five stations simultaneously with rock bottom pricing on our gas and 10% off on cigarettes (cartons or singles).

Chapter 3

Back in early June, at my family, birthday party, my mom was very concerned about how I could manage so many different projects and businesses at the same time without screwing up somewhere or becoming ill from all the tension.

I consoled her by saying that I had managers for each of my various businesses and I oversaw what they were doing. Plus, my bookkeeper was keeping a close eye on my finances.

My bookkeeper informed me that she did not feel that she would be able to handle the increased workload that would come with the additional grocery store and five gas and goes. I told her to hire another bookkeeper and have her work from my desk … reluctantly I moved my desk to my home office for the time being.

Also, after my last advertising class I hung back to ask the professor if she would like to do my advertising for me and what she would charge. She was interested and said that she had plenty of spare time to do it. GREAT!

So, we would forward the items on special each week and she would create the ad and forward it to the newspaper … for a reasonable fee.

In the summer, when I met with the three brothers, they were astounded by how many new ventures I was into … Mr. Y and Mr. Z said that they were going to ask me to buy their apartment buildings … they each owned five, three-family apartment buildings, on the street behind the apartments that I had purchased from Mr. X the previous year … their buildings were several years newer, but virtually the same as the ones that I owned … they were asking 20% more than what I paid Mr. X, they must have thought I was an easy mark … I said I wasn't interested … unless they would settle on an increase of 5% … they agreed!

I stopped in to see the pretty branch manager and explained that I wanted to buy more investment properties … so, she had me fill out a mortgage request, make out a check for the appropriate fee and she would start the process of getting me approved … she told me it shouldn't take long but they would need to get the buildings appraised first.

In the meantime, I contacted my attorney to prepare Purchase & Sale documents for the apartment buildings I planned to acquire.

A month later I received an approval letter from the bank. I met with the two brothers to sign the Purchase & Sale documents and two weeks later we had the Closing at the bank.

It took about five months for the pizza guy to get his restaurant designed and to get a building permit. Finally, Uncle T could get started.

Meanwhile, my South-end grocery store was getting close to completion … I ordered everything for the grocery part of the store to come in three different deliveries … so we could bring it directly to the floor to load onto the shelves … which was a big job when starting from scratch!

I decided to promote the frozen food manager from my original store to store manager of the new store. Of course, I promoted the head butcher to store manager of my original store and he promoted the lady butcher that was filling in for him to head butcher.

We had to advertise for; butchers a Frozen Food Manager, cashiers and stock handlers … fortunately, we got lots of applicants … one man had been the head butcher in a store out west and had moved back east with his wife to take care of her mother who was quite ill … we took a chance on another middle-aged fella with years of frozen food experience as the frozen food manager … and we had to send him and the new guy in my original store to get their liquor license.

We also needed someone to run the bakery but fortunately early on, the Italian guy from our bakery came to me to ask if he could manage our new bakery … he said that he wanted to be able to work the same hours as his wife so they could have more time together … how sweet … and how fortunate … he was an expert in the bakery!

Another great find had been for the sea food area. A girl came into my original store to apply for the sea food manager position … she had worked in a sea food store for years, with nowhere to go since the owners were the only ones ahead of her … she answered all of our questions and when I asked if she ever cooked in a Fryolator she said come with me … she walked down to one of our freezers took out a package of chicken patties dropped two patties in the Fryolator, went into the bakery and selected two sour dough buns, went over to where the grinders were made, sliced the rolls, slathered them with mayo, put sliced tomato, lettuce and cheese on them, then retrieved the cooked patties, put them on the cheese, closed up the buns and handed them to me and the head butcher and said, "Try this!"

As my teeth sunk in, through the bun, the lettuce, the tomato, the cheese and the warm chicken patty, my taste buds said to me, "OH MY GOD!" It was deeeeeelisious! We hired her on the spot and we added the chicken sandwich to the menu!

It was all hands-on deck to load all of the groceries, meats, beer and wine on the racks and in the coolers and freezers at the new store.

Our Open House was another smashing success! Yippee! I am sure my new advertising helped immensely. By the way, I moved into the new grocery store office with the store manager … I needed to get back into a store and I felt it would be a good place for me to be to train the new store manager and the remainder of our new employees, in how I expected them to act and help our customers.

With a month left to finish my South-end grocery, Uncle T started to build the new restaurant for the pizza guy. It took until the end of the year to get the restaurant ready for the pizza ovens and kitchen from the pizza shop.

The pizza guy waited until the day after New Year's Day to close his pizza shop.

We scheduled the closing on the old pizza shop for the following week … almost immediately my Uncle T started the renovation: tearing down the interior walls, cutting the hole for the Drive-up window (which was working out amazingly well at my original pharmacy), re-paving the parking lot to go all around the building, while another crew worked on the apartments above.

I planned to decorate the apartments similar to the ones over my original pharmacy so, they tore out and replaced the kitchen cabinets and counter tops, bathroom vanity and tub (we added a fiber-glass tub and shower enclosure), and tore out the linoleum in the kitchen and all of the carpeting in the two apartments.

After the word got out that I was building another pharmacy, my brother-in-law came to me in secrecy to ask if he could run it … he felt that he and my sister were working too closely together and he felt it would be advantageous if they could work apart. It almost broke my heart to tell him that I had already offered the job to someone else but if I built another pharmacy, he would be the manager.

It took until the end of Spring for the majority of the work to be complete.

In the interim when the apartments were completed, I rented one apartment and, on her day off, I had my new pharmacy manager go with me to purchase all the furniture, curtains and niceties' she would need to live in the other apartment.

With two weeks to go before, we would be ready to open the new pharmacy … my new pharmacy manager needed to move out of her present home and into the apartment over the pharmacy … so on her day off, I helped her pack-up her belongings and everything of hers and load it into my truck … she left a note on the kitchen table that she was leaving him (her abusive husband) asking for a divorce and finally getting out from the years of beatings and torment she had endured. Further, she said … don't come looking for me!

Next, we went to the post office to change her mailing address to my PO Box … I could pick up her mail along with my own and give it to her. Then we were off to unload my truck and set-up her apartment and buy the basic necessities for food/groceries. I charged her $150 per month over the rent to re-pay me for the cost of her furniture.

My new pharmacy manager was like a new person … bubbly and energetic … and above all … very appreciative for the help I had given her.

At lunch, we would go next door to the new Italian restaurant. Whenever the owner saw us, he would come out and hug me (with his mammoth arms) and kiss me on both cheeks … he told my pharmacy manager that I was a genius … that I was the reason that he had this new restaurant … his dream!

I explained to the guy (in Italian) that the pharmacy manager had left her husband because he beat her and that we had to watch over her … to protect her … the smile left his face and he told me, "How could someone hurt such a beautify little flower?" Then he looked down at the beautiful pharmacy manager and said (in English), "If anyone-a comes to bother you, you call-a me and I beat-a the guy up-a!" That was emphatic!

I had hired all of the staff for her … another full-time pharmacist (a guy that worked a lot of part-time for my sister), as well as another part-time pharmacist, cashiers and stock boys.

We all worked long hours to get the store loaded with everything required … when I looked around, I couldn't tell what store I was in … except when I looked at the pharmacist!

The Open House was a big success … we offered one free prescription and 10% off on cigarettes again!

———

Of course, the subject at my family birthday party got around to what my next adventure was going to be. Surprisingly, I had no new plans.

———

Then one day I just happened to be at my first grocery store when this big hulk came in highly agitated and asked me go outside with him … when I got outside the beautiful pharmacist's husband grabbed my shirt with both hands and pushed me up against his pickup truck, "Where the hell is my wife?" he yelled.

He caught me by surprise!

I told him I didn't know … he said, "Yes you do … you get her mail!" I could smell alcohol on his breath.

I said calmly, "She comes in and picks it up, occasionally." Then I said, "Let go of me … now!"

He didn't and I think he was preparing to fight with me … but I didn't want to make a scene.

Then we heard, "Take your hands off him … or I will cut them off!" spoken from the new store manager holding a cleaver in one hand!

I said, "I would listen to him … he was a butcher for 30 years … he really knows how to use that thing!"

The guy let go reluctantly.

Then he said, "You tell her I want her to call me ASAP!"

Aggravated, he got into his truck and sped away.

Then I went into the office and called the beautiful pharmacist to tell her what had transpired. She said she had gotten a 'No Contact' order and her lawyer was working on the divorce. I told her to be on the lookout for her ex. Then, I called the pizza guy … to be on the lookout as well.

It took about six months before the divorce was final and she received the proceeds from her portion of the pharmacy that they had owned together.

I still got together with the three brothers, once a month even though they didn't have anything to sell me, any more … except for their condos in Florida. They were interested in my businesses but mostly they wanted to drink … and I paid for it … happily!

One of the things that I did each time I purchased a property was to have my picture taken in front of the property with me holding a white piece of paper with the closing date on it.

Chapter 4

I decided to display my pictures on the wall in my home office to the left as you walked in. There was nothing on this wall since the previous owners took whatever was displayed there.

I started in the middle of the wall. At the top with my picture standing in front of my new grocery store. Slightly below and to the left I put my picture in front of my first pharmacy … to the left of center I decided would be businesses other than grocery.

Even with the pharmacy picture, I put the picture of me standing in front of the new expansion of my grocery store. To the right, would be real estate. So, slightly down and to the right I put my picture in front of my new house and just below, I put the pictures of me in front of each apartment building … I put two pictures, centered over three pictures.

Next, I put the pictures of the five Gas & Goes, slightly down and to the left (using the two over three method). On the right again went the ten pictures of my apartments … using the two over three, then, two over three again. Slightly down and in the center went the picture of me in front of my South-end grocery and finally, down and to the left went the picture of me in front of my South-end pharmacy.

When I was done, I stepped back and looked at the graphic display I had created on the wall … it was impressive and I vowed at that moment that I was DONE! No more purchasing or buildings or renovating. I was going to be content with what I had!

Well, my vow didn't last long. About six months later once everyone settled into their new jobs a middle-aged man came into see me at my South-end grocery store … he owned and operated a small market that his late father had left to him about 15 miles to our west … the business didn't fit him and he just wanted to sell and get out ASAP. He said that there had been two businesses adjacent to his store, a billiard parlor and an ice cream shop but they had recently left and their store fronts were vacant. He seemed downtrodden and I felt sorry for him.

So, I took down his address and said I would come over to take a look the next day.

After he left, I called my Uncle T to see if he wanted to take a look at the man's property the next day … yes, he was interested.

We arrived around 10:30 am the next day to find a building much larger than what I had expected to find. My uncle measured it as usual and it was close in size to my two existing grocery stores. Plus, the building and parking lots were in very good shape.

Inside we found a dingy old-fashioned market … I wouldn't be interested in shopping there.

The man seemed to perk up when he saw us. He took us for a tour of his market and the two vacant storefronts, the basement and roof … all in good shape!

My uncle asked the man how much the building was accessed for and how much he was looking to sell for … his answer was, for a quick sale slightly below the assessment … very reasonable!

When we left, I noticed a building diagonally across the street … it was vacant … previously a shoe store.

I took my Uncle T to lunch at a nearby diner where we could discuss the market building and the one diagonally across the street. My uncle felt I should buy them both if the prices were right.

After lunch, we went over to the Town Hall to see what the two buildings were valued at. Also, we pumped them for information regarding the shoe store building. We found out that the manufacture of the shoes had gone out of business so they just closed the store and had the renters in the two apartments on the second floor move out. The City had recently taken the property for taxes and was willing to sell at a reduced price … that was music to my ears.

When we left the Town Hall, we drove over to the old shoe store with the building inspector who gave us a tour of the building. The first floor was still loaded with shoes. The basement had a bunch more shoes and extra racking. The two apartments were clean but outdated. The measurements were close enough to my other two pharmacies.

Back in the truck, my uncle asked what I wanted to do. I said that I thought both buildings were in very good shape and I wanted to buy them both.

My uncle said, "Then let's do it!"

So, we drove across the street to the market and went in to talk with the man in his office. My Uncle T told him that his construction crews were very busy but they had a small window of time open to work on this building but the man was going to have to make his decision today … my uncle made the man sort of a low-ball offer … he accepted! Yippee!

I told the man that my attorney would prepare a Purchase & Sale agreement quickly but we couldn't go any faster than what the bank required, probably a month. The man was delighted.

Then, we went back to the Town Hall to meet with the mayor, the head of finance and the building inspector. My uncle asked how much was owed in taxes … it was well below the assessed value … my uncle said we would take it off their hands for what was owed in taxes … they agreed immediately. My Uncle T told them we would return with a check that day.

They said, "Fine."

When we got back into the truck, I told my Uncle T that I was unsure that I had enough to buy the building that day. My Uncle T told me that he would get a check from the local branch of his bank and I could repay him when I had the money. So, we got a bank check and returned to the Town Hall to finalize the purchase … in the name of Tony's Pharmacy, Inc. … we received a receipt but we were told we would get an official letter from the Town's attorney stating that we now owned the building tax free.

On the ride back, I asked my uncle why he felt we needed to pay for the shoe building that day? His answer was that he had seen several times where someone from the Town offices would contact a friend and tell them what they could get the building for if they moved fast and when you showed up the next day you would be told that someone had already purchased the property. Smart, experienced and savvy, was my Uncle T.

Also, I asked, "What do we do with all those shoes?"

My uncle chuckled and said, "We will donate them to the Salvation Army!"

The next morning, I had my bookkeeper scrounge around in my accounts to see if we could put together enough money to repay my uncle. The bookkeeper said, "No problem … you have plenty."

Then I called my attorney to inform him that I needed a Purchase and Sale agreement for the market and asked his opinion on my purchase of the shoe store that my uncle paid the town for in my name (Tony's Pharmacy, Inc.) but now I am going to re-pay my uncle. He said he would contact the town's attorney for clarification.

Next, I called my architect and asked him to prepare blueprints for our new pharmacy. He could get the keys from my uncle. Of course, it would be similar to my other pharmacies and of course, I would like them ASAP. Then I asked him to prepare blueprints for the market building across the street which I intended to purchase.

I had to rough out the amounts I would need to borrow from my friend at the bank. Basically, other than the purchase price I could use what we recently spent to complete my South-end grocery and pharmacy.

So, after lunch I stopped into the bank to see the bank manager … as soon as he saw me, he said, "How much is this visit going to cost me?"

Actually, he was happy to see me since, I didn't handle the deposits any longer … I had hired an armored guard company to pick up and drop off the daily deposits.

I explained that I had purchased a building in the town to the west. Which I intended to turn into a pharmacy and I was in the process of purchasing the building across the street from it to turn it into … wait for it … a grocery store. The bank manager said, "What else is new?"

So, I told the bank manager that I would like to use the pharmacy building as collateral for the remainder of the loans that I require. First, I need a construction loan for the pharmacy building, then I would need a loan for inventory (or a line of credit). Second, I would need a mortgage loan for the grocery building, a construction loan and an inventory loan. I went on to say that I felt that the buildings would both be appraised at far more than what I was purchasing them for.

He said, "Let's get the two buildings appraised first, then we can decide how to fund everything."

Great!

Three weeks later, I met with the bank manager. He told me the appraisals came back at twice what I had offered for the grocery building and more than three times what I paid for the pharmacy building. Therefore, the bank manager suggested, that I take out mortgage loans, at 80% of the assessed value of the buildings and use that to fund inventory and to request construction loans for the renovation of the two buildings. Sounded great, so I filled out the loan paperwork and three weeks later we had the Closing.

My uncle wasn't waiting for any funding, it was the middle of December already so as soon as we received the plans for the pharmacy he sent over the two dumpsters, a box truck (for all of the shoes) and several crews. In a week, the place was emptied and the floors ripped up.

Uncle A came and painted the outside white, on a fairly warm day. Then he painted the inside … all white on the main floor, white in the kitchens and bathrooms and gray everywhere else.

Uncle T got another Drive-up window and his guys installed it all before the end of the year.

Uncle T was not worried about getting paid … he just said that when I got the construction loan then he would send me an invoice.

By the end of January, the apartments were ready to rent and fortunately I was able to get both apartments occupied by February 1! This is always a good sign since it means INCOME!

My uncle really liked having to work on the inside of buildings during the winter … it kept a lot of his guys occupied … and you know what they say about idle hands.

So, just after the first of the year my uncle put a number of crews to work on the new grocery store.

My brother-in-law was over the moon happy to be getting his own pharmacy … I let him hire his entire staff.

Fortunately, the asphalt parking lot was large and wrapped around the building (because the asphalt factories were closed for the winter) so, we had an aisle for the Drive-up window … all we needed to do was to have the lines painted on the asphalt. The crews built the pharmacy counters and store front counter and by the end of February all of the racks, coolers, cash registers and storage cupboards were ready.

The big question was should we have the Grand Opening before the new grocery is ready or should we wait and have both Grand Openings together?

So, I asked the advertising professor what she felt I should do. Her answer surprised me … she said to do the Pharmacy Grand Opening right away … and to run the Grand Opening Specials in all three pharmacies. Then when the grocery store is completed, run the Grand Opening Specials in all three grocery stores. Problem solved!

The Grand Opening was a great success; offering 10% off on cigarettes and 20% off on all prescriptions (20% off on all, new customer prescriptions in the existing pharmacies).

On the way home on Tuesday evening, I stopped in a local bar/cocktail lounge (about four blocks from my house) to partake of their Tuesday Night Special, 16 oz sirloin steak dinner with a baked potato, a side salad and a delicious roll. As I had done many times before, I ordered a beer from the tap in a frosted glass and when it was about half-way gone, the door opened and five young girls (in their early 20s) came in as a group. One girl stood out! She was about 6", taller than the other girls. She had long, incredibly light, blonde hair and she was off the chart of beautiful … it was like a beacon from above was shining down on her … I couldn't take my eyes off of her. As the girls took off their coats and sat at a high-top table, I asked the barkeep/owner to buy the blond a drink from me … only, I told him not to tell her that I was the one who bought the drink.

I watched as the bartender made his way over to the girls table to take their order … then when he brought their drinks, I watched the excitement from all of the girls as the bartender told the blond that someone had bought her the glass of wine that the bartender put down in front of her … there were eight men, of varying age, that could be paying for her drinks … I had planned on looking away but when the bartender made his little announcement … the girls made such a loud squeal that everyone in the bar looked over at the table … including me.

When the bartender came back, I spoke to him as he poured me another beer … I asked him to bring another drink to the blonde girl from me when he got a chance … and again not to tell her it was from me. I had never done this before and I was getting a kick out of it.

Well, an even louder roar came from the girls table when the bartender arrived at the table with another drink from the anonymous man and when the bartender came back, he asked me not to send him over with another drink because the girls were becoming very aggressive trying to get him to identify the guy that was buying the drinks.

Of course, I kept my eye on the blonde and when she had about one-third of a glass of wine left in her glass I ordered another drink for her and another for me. This time I delivered her drink. All of the girls looked at me with wide eyes.

I put the blond girl's drink down in front of her and said, "I hear that you have been wondering who was buying your drinks?"

All of the girls including the blond said emphatically, "Yeah!"

I said, "My name is Tony … would you like to join me at another table?"

The blonde said, "Yes!" Several of the other girls just moaned.

One girl evidentially saw the Tony's on my shirt and asked, "Your name is Tony and you work at Tony's?"

I said, "Yeah … how many people with the name Mc Donald, work at the Hamburg chain?" It seemed to answer the question and they all sort of laughed.

I carried the blonde's drink and my beer over to a table far enough away from the other girls, so they would not hear us talking.

When we were settled in, I asked, "What brings you girls to this bar tonight?"

She said, "We are all hair dressers and we work together for the meanest old bitch you can imagine. We come out every now and then when we are all frustrated with our boss and we have a huge bitch party, drink too much and when we leave, we all feel better!"

As I looked at her, I realized she was the most beautiful female I had ever laid my eyes on … even more beautiful than the beautiful pharmacist. She had shockingly beautiful blond hair, the whitest skin, beautiful blue, blue, blue eyes, a beautiful pert nose and the most beautiful lips that I had ever seen. I WAS SMITTEN!!!

Before we finished our drinks, I asked, "Have you eaten dinner yet?"

The blonde answered, "No … we came directly from work."

I said, "Why don't I order two steak dinners to go and we can take them back to my house and eat?"

She said, "Yes … you have a house?"

I put my hand up to get the bartender's attention then I put up two fingers and mouthed the words 'Two steaks … to go'. He smiled and nodded.

Then I replied to the blonde, "Yeah, I live about three to four blocks away."

I think she was impressed.

When the bartender came out and signaled to me that my two dinners were ready, we got up and as I was headed to the bar to pay my tab the blonde went to the girl's table to get her coat and pocketbook and to tell the girls she was headed to my house for dinner … I heard another roar come from that direction.

The blonde followed me in her car (a little, tiny, yellow, foreign car, convertible).

When we got to my house, the lights were on.

The blonde asked, "Who's home?"

I responded, "No one … I have timers to put on some of the lights, because I hate to come home to a dark house."

She smiled and followed me into the house, looking all around. I went directly to the kitchen with the two meals to put them on proper plates and get forks, knifes and napkins. While I was getting the meals ready, I asked the blonde to light the two candles on the dining room table with the lighter that was on the table. In just a few minutes, I had the meals ready for the table … when I brought them in, I put one plate at the end of the table and the other just to the right of it. Then, I held the chair at the end of the table for the blonde to sit in it, and I said that I would be right back with the salads, I asked, "What kind of salad dressing?"

"What do you have?"

I smiled, "Whatever you want but I would suggest the Blue Cheese."

Blue Cheese it was and in moments we were eating … I was famished … partly because it was so late and partially because I had been drinking … but wait … we didn't have anything to drink …

I said, "I'm sorry, what would you like to drink with your meal?"

"What do you have?"

"Honey," I said, "I have got, whatever you want!"

I had a whole wall of wine cases, turned on the sides (to keep the corks wet), in my office and I had four to six bottles of each type of wine … and I had the best stuff! My buddy B made sure of that.

She chose Riesling … a German wine … Great!

I poured us both a glass of wine and put the bottle on the table.

The steaks, as always, were excellent … the baked potatoes were loaded and equally superb … and the salads, loaded with the Blue Cheese dressing were terrific! But even better … was the conversation which just flowed from one subject to the next. When we were done with dinner, I asked the blonde if she would like to sit by the fireplace and have an after-dinner drink with me … she said, "NO!"

She wanted to see the rest of my house … so, we took the tour, first was my study … she could see all of the wine (over 100 bottles) … I told the blond that I had a friend who's a wine distributor … across from my office was a full bathroom, I turned on the light, so that she could see it better … further down the hall was my work-out room and finally, the master bedroom … I had to explain as we walked into the room that the six lights, that looked just like candles were turned on automatically by a timer (I had always been concerned of a fire when the previous owners used real candles). Halfway into the room the blonde very gently, touched my shoulder and when I turned around, she gave me a soft, almost gentle kiss … but before our lips separated, I felt her tongue pass my lips … this really turned me on so I pressed in and continued the kiss.

When we stopped, she said, "Thank you!"

I said, "For what?"

She replied, "For making my night better … I had a real shitty day!"

With that said, I put my arms around her, pulled her full body against mine and as we kissed passionately my hand slipped up to the back of her head to press her lips even more firmly against mine. Somehow in our passion we ended up laying on the bed … and somehow, I was undressing her, as she was undressing me … finally we made love (for me it really was LOVE) … for a thin girl she was very limber … I was on top, then she was on top, finally, I was on top … and when we were done and she was still quivering from her last orgasm she said, breathlessly, "WOW … that was the most outstanding sex I have ever had!"

Then we both went into the shower and I was surprised how many different ways we could do it … spurred on by the slipperiness of the soap.

Then, once we were dry, we snuggled up in bed and took our time giving each other as much pleasure as we could … when we were done, we were exhausted … and we fell asleep entwined in each other's arms.

We both had Wednesday off … so I got up early and made us both breakfast. I think the smell of the bacon cooking woke the blonde up.

She came into the kitchen wearing my bathrobe and said, "Something smells good!"

I said, "Good timing … I hope you are hungry … I made omelets (with tomatoes, bacon and broccoli) and home fries."

As we sat at the kitchen table, eating and talking, the blonde said, "Last night was the first and only night that I have ever done that … that is, meet a guy and sleep with him the same night … that is not the type of girl that I am … I have never slept overnight with a guy!"

I replied, "Last night was … magical for me. I have never bought a girl drinks like that and I have never seen anyone else do it either … but as soon as I saw you walk in the door … I was smitten … I had to meet you, I wanted to know you."

She blushed and smiled looking directly into my eyes.

I asked, "It is going to be a real nice day today … I was thinking we could go to the beach?"

She told me that she didn't have a bathing suit with her.

"No problem … there is a mall real close … we can stop there and buy you a swimsuit," I replied.

The blonde helped me clean up … even the dishes from the night before … all went into the dishwasher. Then, when we got to the bedroom and she took off my bathrobe I had another fantastic idea and I think she did too. I loved the way she orgasmed, every muscle in her body seemed to quiver … and I know she loved it too. Finally, we both took independent showers or we would never have gotten going. She grabbed a pair of slip in sneakers from her car and it was still early when we got on the road.

When we reached the mall, I told the blonde that I knew of a great store with beautiful clothes (it was the store that the two girls that sold me my house used to work at). Of course, the new manager knew me and was only too pleased to help me and the blonde. They had a super selection of bathing suits … the blonde picked a pink, a blue and white striped and a gold suit … with her figure anything would look great … well, they all did look great when she modeled them for us but the gold suit looked sensational! I told the blonde we also need to buy a sporty outfit to wear before and after the beach and I knew she was self-conscious about wearing yesterday's underwear for the second day so we found a yellow knitted top with a scoop neck or she could push the top over her shoulders and wear it straight across form her bicep to bicep. To finish the outfit, she selected a pair of white short, shorts. When she was headed to the dressing room, I handed her a bag of three underpants … she blushed but she took them. While she was getting dressed, the manager told me how beautiful my girlfriend was … I think I blushed.

When my girlfriend came out of the dressing room, she looked spectacular, I said, "I love it … let's get it all and get going."

Next stop the beach.

The drive was special … she slid right over against my side … I put one arm around her and we talked all the way to the beach. It was lunchtime when we arrived. So, I bought her a hot dog on-a-stick and two cheese burgers for me, fries and two sodas. We sat outside on the beach at an umbrella table and we looked into each other's eyes as we ate.

Then I took the beach umbrella, blanket and towels (from my truck) and set it all up on the beach … I was concerned about my new girlfriend's, delicate, almost white skin getting sunburnt and I guess so did she for as soon as she took off the clothes covering her bathing suit, she took out a bottle of suntan lotion and applied it all over her body. I didn't have to worry much about the sun and my skin since I was born with the Italian olive-skin. I took off my black T shirt and black jeans to expose my black silk bathing suit (what else?). When we both laid down on our backs on the blanket, we held hands, she intertwined her fingers with mine … it really was sexy and turned me on!

After baking in the sun for quite a while I said, "Let's take a dip."

There were not many people on the beach, it was very early in the season so when we got to the water, we found it was far too cold to go in … it sent shock waves of pain up our legs and we were only in up to our ankles. So, we walked back to an ice cream store and I bought her a lemon ice … it was very refreshing.

Then, we returned to our blanket. I laid down and she laid on her side against my body. When I turned my face toward her, she kissed me, very sexily! Then she said very softly and very gently and very, very sexy, "I think I am falling for you!"

My world stopped … I had fallen in love with this girl last night and I couldn't believe that she had the same feelings. With her by my side, I would have everything, I would feel like the king of the world!

———————

After an afternoon of talking, kissing and hugging we decided to head home. Since it was Wednesday, my mom would have come to my house to clean it and she always brought a large pan of lasagna, or stuffed shells, or manicotti and she would have put in my refrigerator. So, on the ride back I asked my new girlfriend if she would like to join me for a special home-cooked Italian dinner. Of course, she would.

So, when we got back to my house about 6:00 pm, I asked my new girlfriend to set the table, light the candles and to select a bottle of wine for dinner. I was drinking a beer; the beach always makes me thirsty. Mom had left me a pan with sausages, peppers and onions, smothered in her homemade tomato sauce. All I had to do was put the pan in the oven and make a couple of side salads and VOILA! Dinner was served.

During dinner, my new girlfriend announced that she could not sleep over that night because she had to work the next day, Thursday. I told her that I had to work as well but we could meet up for dinner if she would like. I showed her where I hid a key to the front door and told her to let herself in, if I wasn't home when she got there.

It so happened that I got home a little late from the Grand Opening of my new pharmacy. My new girlfriend was sitting on the floor in front of the fireplace, which was not on. She was reading the evening newspaper and had removed the Grand Opening flyer for the new and older pharmacies. When I came in, she poured me a glass of Champagne. I asked what the occasion was and she replied, "This is the drink of Kings … I have found out that you, are, the King of Tony's empire of stores!"

"Really, why would you say that?" I inquired.

"Well," she said, "there is an article about your new pharmacy and your myriad of other stores and business … and it shows your picture … the most handsome man I have ever seen!"

All I could say is, "Wow!"

Then she said, "Follow me." She led me into my office and said, "Tell me about this wall!" The one with a picture of me in front of each business that I bought.

Actually, I was very proud of my accomplishments, so, I started with my first grocery store and as quickly as I could, I explained how and why I acquired each business.

"So, you have 15 apartment buildings, with three apartments per building or a total of 45 apartments, that you rent out?"

"Yes, but I have an additional six rental units, since I have two units above each pharmacy … so, technically, I have 51 total rental units."

"And how do you manage to control all of these businesses?" she asked.

"I have grocery store managers, pharmacy managers and a Gas & Go manager. I manage all of them and take care of the rental properties," I replied.

"I'm impressed, and I am surprised that with this much success that you didn't tell me right away who you were … you just said, 'I work in a grocery store'," she said as she wrapped her arms tenderly around my mid-section.

I looked down and told her that I was extremely proud of my accomplishments but I was looking for a girl that was more interested in me than in my accomplishments. Then I kissed her.

She replied, "Well, you found your girl!"

"I know … and she is soooooo beautiful!" I said, as I kissed her again. Then I asked, "It is getting late, what do you want to do for dinner?"

She twisted up her face and replied, "Anything."

I asked, "How about Fish & Chips?"

"Sounds good."

So, I called my original grocery store and placed my order. Then, as I was leaving to go to the store to pick up our dinner, I asked my girlfriend to set the table and select a bottle of wine.

When I returned the table was set, candles lit and two glasses of wine were poured. Perfect!

I quickly plated our meals and we sat down to eat. The food was excellent! So was the conversation.

At one point, she said, "You just showed me how you run all of these businesses … you had the grocery store cooking our dinner, you had me setting the table and you were running in between, to pick up the food."

I said, "Exactly!"

When we finished our meals, our dessert was in the bedroom … we couldn't take too long since she had to go home, for we both had to work the next day.

———————

Friday night we went to the movies and after the movie I popped the question … would she like to go to church with me Sunday morning and then accompany me to my parents' home for our weekly family dinner … without any hesitation she agreed!

So, when she showed up to my house on Saturday, she brought a clothes bag with her outfit for Sunday. Saturday night we went bowling with my buddies A and B, and their present girlfriends. My girl and I won because I believe that the other two guys couldn't take their eyes off of my girlfriend.

———————

I snuck home Saturday afternoon to ask my parents if it would be okay to bring my girlfriend to our family dinner Sunday afternoon … of course, it was okay my folks were always very supportive … but this would be the first time that I ever brought a girlfriend home to meet my parents.

On Sunday, when she got dressed, my mind was blown … she wore off-white slacks that fit snuggly at the waist and thighs, but tapered, widely at the bottom, with cuffs … the top was made of matching material, and looked like a military uniform jacket, with long sleeves, to tight cuffs, but to my surprise, the sleeves were cut open on the inside of the sleeve and on the outside of the sleeve and at times it didn't show but as she moved her naked arms showed …

very, very nice! She wore black low heel shoes and she carried a black handbag.

I wore black Burberry slacks (my most expensive slacks), a black silk, long sleeve shirt, open collar, a black suede sport coat and shiny black wing tipped shoes.

Together we made a striking couple as we walked all the way down the center aisle of the church to the empty front row (I always sat in the front row because we sang in church and I liked to sing, but I had a horrible voice and if I sat behind anyone in church, they would turn around to see where such guttural sounds were coming from … so I sat in the front to avoid the embarrassment). Shortly after we sat down, my sister and her husband joined us and I introduced my girlfriend.

When we arrived at my parent's home, they could not have been more pleasant or more congenial toward my new girlfriend (you have to know that my mom was always concerned that girls would be after me for my money). My sister and brother-in-law came in right behind us. Mom had invited Uncle T and my aunt as well.

During our lasagna dinner I explained that my date worked as a hair dresser locally. She laughed and explained that when we met, she noticed the Tony's on my shirt and when she asked me about it, I just said that I worked in the grocery store … everyone laughed! Then, she continued to explain that she fell in love with me … thinking I was a grocery boy! Yes, she said the 'L' word … that shocked everyone around the table … **including me**! I think it was exactly what my mom wanted to hear … the girl fell for me before finding out about my businesses.

When Mom brought the dessert to the table, my sister said she had an announcement to make … she was pregnant … WOW! … the room exploded with cheers and clapping … Mom asked when she was due and she replied, the end of November … then she looked at me and said, "Don't worry … I will have coverage for my time off."

I said, "I am not worrying about coverage … I am soooo happy for you guys and I am going to be an UNCLE!" Yippee!

So, the afternoon was a complete success for everyone.

Over the next several weeks my beautiful, blonde girlfriend and I spent every free minute together. I met her folks … Mom was a professor at the college (very pretty … blonde of course) … the father was an aeronautical engineer and the manager of engineering at the local aircraft company. Both parents appeared to like me and treated me like a son.

So, in the middle of May on a Saturday afternoon, I cornered the blonde's father alone in the corner of his garage and I asked him for his blessing that I may marry his daughter … he smiled broadly and said I had both his wife's and his blessing and that he would ask that I always treat her well and that I protect her from harm for life!

That evening I brought her to the flower garden in a park and when we reached the fountain, I got down on one knee and I asked my beautiful blonde girlfriend to be my wife, I said, "The day I met you was the best day of my life … if you agree to marry me … this will be the second, best day of my life," and I showed her the gorgeous ring.

She immediately started to cry … then stopped … then said, "YES … YES … YES!" I put the ring on her finger (it fit!) … she couldn't stop looking at it … then she couldn't stop kissing me more and more and more aggressively as it sunk in … WE WERE ENGAGED!!!!!

Finally, she said, "I have to show my parents … they will be soooo surprised!"

So, we drove over to her parents' home and they made a big, BIG deal of it … looking at the ring and taking turns hugging her and hugging me. Neither one of her parents mentioned that I had spoken to her father that afternoon.

We invited her parents to join us for dinner. They accepted and we were off to the Falls of Napoli for our engagement dinner.

As soon as we walked in the door the owner came over and gave me a big hug and kisses on both cheeks (he was actually making a scene) … I introduced my fiancé and her parents … he hugged my fiancé and congratulated her parents … then I told him we had just gotten engaged and this was our engagement dinner … he said he appreciated that I chose his restaurant for the celebration and he told us he had the perfect table for us.

When we were seated, he told my fiancé and her parents that they were lucky … that I was a genius … that he would never have built this beautiful restaurant if it wasn't for me … then he said, "You must-a … have-a you recep-a-tion … in-a my ban-a-quet room!"

I hadn't thought of that or mentioned that to my fiancé's parents, so I said in Italian, "Okay, let's show my fiancé the banquet room after our dinner …"

He agreed and said he would send out a waitress from the kitchen. She arrived with an ice-cold bottle of champagne and four glasses. Without saying a word, she opened the champagne and poured each of us a glass.

My fiancé's dad raised his glass and said, "To a long and happy marriage!"

We all clinked glasses and drank our champagne.

Our waitress disappeared but when she reappeared, she brought us a bowl, of just from the oven, Italian bread and a huge plate of fried Mozzarella Cheese cut into pie shaped pieces, next came green salad my fiancé and I had gobs of Blue Cheese dressing while her folks had the house Italian dressing, next came an enormous bowl of Ziti and Meatballs all covered with sauce … I had to explain to my company that they should limit their portions or they would never be able to finish their meal … next, came the main dish; Veal Parmesan, pounded thin, breaded and cooked to perfection … and for dessert we each got a plate with a cannoli … then the waitress came back out with a Bucci Naught (a small pie shaped Italian dessert) with a candle in the middle and the entire staff sang, "Happy Engagement to You!"

How nice … but we never had a chance to order anything … I thought it was one of the best meals of my life … when we were done the owner came back out and told us that they had just served us the meal he would make for our wedding reception … we were impressed.

Next, we went for a tour of the banquet room where there was a function but without intrusion, he showed us the room … the back wall of which was tons of water cascading into a huge pool … when we got close, it took our breaths away … very nice and very impressive.

The owner informed us that they could seat up to 250 guests, when are you getting married … I couldn't wait … we hadn't discussed it … but I blurted out … the middle of September … the owner checked it was open and he penciled us in.

Over and over each of us told the owner how much we enjoyed the meal. When we were ready to leave, I asked for the bill (in Italian) … the owner replied that I didn't owe him anything, rather, he still owed me. So, I left a big tip for the waitress and we headed home.

On the way home, the father asked me what I had done for the restaurant owner to earn so much of his gratitude. I explained that when I met him, he operated a pizza shop, next door to where the restaurant sits … he told me his dream was to build a beautiful restaurant with a banquet room in the back … I purchased his building diagonally across the street to build a grocery store … I introduced him to my Uncle T, whose architect designed everything that he dreamed of … then when he closed the pizza shop and moved his kitchen to his new facility, I purchased the old pizza shop and converted it into a pharmacy. The money I paid for his two buildings paid for the construction of his restaurant … so, we know each other intimately!

Of greater concern to my fiancé was where did I come up with the date to get married? My answer was that it was the longest that I could wait to get married and still give her the chance to plan everything … and if she would like we could change the date … no, she and her mom both liked the date … Great!

––––––––––––

The next morning in church I noticed my sister looking at my fiancé's ring. Her eyes became as big as saucers … I whispered in her ear, "We just got engaged, last night."

She reached over put her hand on top of mine and whispered, "Congratulations!"

Then I noticed her poking her husband to get his attention so she could break the news to him. He looked at me, smiled and nodded his head to indicate his approval.

When we reached my parents' home, I always go in the door and yell that I'm there and my mom always comes running to give me a warm hug and a kiss … this day I yelled for Dad as well … when they were both there in front of me, I said, "I have big news!"

I am sure they were thinking I had just bought another business, instead I announced, "I just got engaged last night!"

Then I raised up my fiancé's hand up to show her diamond ring off.

Mom let out a very loud yelp and started to cry, I immediately put my arms around my mom to console her … my dad took one of my hands to shake and said, "Congratulations!"

Then he hugged, kissed and congratulated my fiancé.

Mom composed herself wiped away her tears reached up and put one hand on each side of my face, then gave me a kiss and with a big smile, "Congratulations!"

Then she did the very same thing, to my fiancé.

Mom said, "You surprised me … I was wondering how long it would take you to propose … I could see the love in both of your eyes when you look at each other!" Then she asked, "Who knows and have you set the date?"

I told her that only her parents and my sister and her husband knew … my sister noticed the ring in church (my parents went to church every week, but they went to an earlier service to give my mom time to get home and prepare the meal). Then I told her about the date in mid-September at the Falls of Napoli restaurant.

Next, she ran into the study to call all of my aunts and uncles to give them the good news. Mom was very excited!!!

In the meantime, my sister and brother-in-law came in from church and my dad said, "Today's meal will be slightly delayed," and he offered all of us a congratulatory drink, except for my sister, who drank ginger ale.

Mom and my sister wanted to know what plans were made and they wanted to take closer looks at the diamond. I had to explain that we were engaged for less than 24 hours and had not made more plans than setting the date and the venue.

On the ride home, I apologized, again, for picking the date and the venue for the reception. My fiancé in her delicate manor said she was happy with both the date and the venue. Great!

She said she planned to have the four girls that work with her in the wedding. One as her maid of honor and the other three as bridesmaids. Who did I plan to have for groomsmen? I laughed I have no plan but I would ask my three best buddies to be groomsmen but I would have to think of who would be my best man.

I told my fiancé that I would let her and her mom decide on all of the other details … she told me that I was going to have to make a list of reception attendees … no problem I'll tell Mom. Actually, Mom had a list from my sister's wedding and I added all of my managers and my lead bookkeeper to the list.

When I got home, I called my Uncle T. He said he heard the good news from my mom.

I asked him to be my best man, he said that he was surprised and thankful … but he felt that I should pick someone younger … I said, "No … you have been by my side, and you have had my back … since I was very young … I want you there when I get married."

With that said, he agreed. Great!

The next day I went to each store and informed the managers of my wedding plans. I didn't need to go to my sister's or my brother-in-law's stores but I needed to go to my South-end pharmacy and tell the beautiful pharmacist … she was delighted for me and wished me a long happy marriage with plenty of children … she said I was the nicest man she had ever met … I asked how she was doing and she told me that the boyfriend that she had for a while had moved in with her … I asked if this guy treated her right and didn't hurt her … she told me he better not hurt her or the Italian guy next door would tear him apart … Great!

Chapter 5

For my birthday, my mom decided to surprise me with an engagement party! All of my aunts and uncles and even my fiancé's parents were invited.

It was an outstanding party ... it was the first time for my fiancé to meet my relatives and the first time for my folks to meet my fiancé's parents ... fortunately they all got along wonderfully ... and I heard over and over and over again just how beautiful my fiancé was ... and I had to say over and over and over again that my fiancé was just as beautiful on the inside as she was on the outside.

———————

One day at my South-end grocery store, the Italian bakery guy stopped me and said that he had heard that I was getting married ... I said, "Yes, in the middle of September," ... he said, "I'm-a gonna make-a you, the best-a wedding-a cake, you ever see! And its-a gonna be from my wife-a an-a me!"

I thanked him and told him how nice that would be. Then, I ran to the nearest phone to notify my fiancé that my bakery would supply the wedding cake ... she said, "Great!"

I left all of the details to my fiancé and her mom who was delighted to plan her daughter's wedding. My buddies, my uncle and I just had to get fitted for our tuxedos (morning suits), and I went with my fiancé to the florist to select flowers and a bouquet.

We decided we would take four days and go to Niagara Falls for our honeymoon ... so I made the reservations.

All I needed to do was to come up with a wedding gift. What could I get her that would be a surprise?

The night before our wedding we had a rehearsal at the church. My Uncle T sponsored a rehearsal party at his favorite Italian restaurant for all of us! We had our own area of the restaurant and everything went smoothly (in other words … everyone drank too much … but enjoyed themselves).

The weather could not have been nicer the day I got married. The service was beautiful, the singer was magnificent … but the beauty of my bride stole the show! I wasn't the only one that said, "WOW!"

Then we went for pictures in the park next to the fountain where we got engaged.

In the car headed to the reception, my wife gave me a beautiful gold bracelet which she put on me. I couldn't wait until we got to the reception to give my wife her wedding gift. I took an envelope out of my inside breast pocket and handed it to her … inside was the deed to the building and land for the beauty salon where she worked along with the Purchase and Sale agreement for the business … from this day forward **her** salon would be known as … Eve's Beauty Salon, Inc.

My wife almost jumped out of her gown with excitement, she said, "You mean that old bitch will be gone, when we get back?"

"Yep … all gone!" Let the party begin … I didn't think she would stop kissing me … I was almost embarrassed.

Of course, the maid of honor and all of the bridesmaids were in the limo with us and they were almost as excited as my wife … so when they all settled down … I told the four of them that I would purchase a salon of their choosing for each of them, pay them for running it and give them 15% of the profits each year! It would be up to them to select a salon and show that it would be profitable. They were very excited. I asked the maid of honor to run the Eve's Salon while my wife and I were away on our honeymoon.

When we arrived at the reception, the girls had all calmed down. By then, the 200 or so guests had arrived and were inside. The owner came out to meet us. He spoke to the photographer and asked him to enter first and wait for the band leader to announce each of the bridesmaids/groomsmen, as they walked down the short hallway and out past the end of the waterfall into the ballroom … while this was going on I noticed the owner pull my uncle aside and whisper something in Italian … my uncle said, "I know."

Then my uncle and the maid of honor went down the hallway. I could hear their names announced and applause … the owner followed right behind my uncle and told us to follow him … once my uncle left the hallway the Owner closed the door to the banquet room and opened a side door behind the falls … he had us follow him down the narrow hallway behind the falls … then he stopped us while he turned some knobs and levers … next he lowered a big heavy stone covered door (which formed a bridge) and said, "Watch-a you step!"

Then he encouraged us to walk through the doorway through the middle of the falls (he had stopped the water where we were walking) and out into the thundering applause of our guests and relatives as the amazed guests heard the band leader announce, "For the first time in public let me introduce, Mr. and Mrs. Antoine Ferducci"

It was pandemonium as the surprised guests watched us come out of the middle of the waterfall … what an entrance.

When we reached the middle of the dance floor, I raised my wife's arm up high and spun her around before taking her back into my arms for a kiss. Again, the crowd continued to cheer and clap into a crescendo!

The priest gave the blessing, my Uncle T gave the toast and the meal was outstanding.

The band played melo tunes while we ate then ramped up the music for dancing. My bride and I kicked off the dancing then everyone danced at one time or another.

When we got to the cake, I had to laugh … first, let me say it was beautiful … it was a large, 9" deep rectangular cake, decorated with pink and white flowers with a 'tower' in the middle, consisting of the layers ornately decorated, with a bride and groom at the top. The reason I laughed was because the baker gave me two small Italian cakes, as samples to take home and try … to decide which cake we would like for our wedding cake … one sample was Italian rum cake, my absolute all-time favorite … the other sample consisted of white cake, whip cream, strawberries and peaches (my wife's favorite) … I told the baker this and he said, "No problem" … so he made the bottom layer a rum cake, then made the three round layers with the white cake, whip cream, strawberries and peaches … making everyone happy!

My wife and I made sure that we visited each table and spoke to each guest. In between tables, we would fit in a dance here of there. One time while we were dancing slowly, my wife told me that her parents had saved up a lot of money over the years to put toward her wedding and since her parents didn't have to spend much for this wedding, they decided to put it toward a very nice car for me. So, she said for me to act surprised and make a big deal out of the car (since it was sooo expensive) … I asked what color it was … she told me black … I said, "Then I will love it!"

About an hour before the reception was scheduled to end, my wife and I decided to leave to get started on our honeymoon.

The restaurant owner gave us an ice-cold magnum of champagne to leave with. I asked my Uncle T to carry it for me while I hugged and kissed my mom and dad (dad told me they would load all of our wedding presents into the back of my truck and drive it over to my house and park it in the garage … when the festivities were over), then I kissed and hugged her mom and dad … my wife's dad said, "We have a surprise for you!" As he led my wife and I into the parking lot … I expected to see my truck decorated for the occasion … instead I found a gorgeous brand-new black Cadillac sedan with a big JUST MARRIED sign on the back and about six rows of beer cans tied with strings trailing the car from the back bumper … WOW! What a car … what a present! … I was more than delighted … I said, "This is the nicest car I have ever seen!" And I meant it.

After thanking her mom and dad a thousand times … we finally got into the car and drove away … with the embarrassing beer cans banging around behind us.

We drove directly to my house to change into something more appropriate for the trip. I just put on a silk long sleeve shirt and jeans … I had pre-packed my go bag … then I put my tux back in the bag that it came with and hung it over the railing by the front entrance for my dad to return, along with his tux. While my wife was still primping, I took the big sign and all of the noisy beer cans off my shiny new car. Fortunately, my uncle had put the map that we needed for our trip and the magnum of champagne in the back seat. When my wife was ready, we headed out to the highway on out trip to the Falls.

As we drove along, I didn't have a care in the world … my new car seemed to float over the road and my wife was snuggled up against my side. After I drove for about 100 miles, I looked for an exit sign showing food and a motel.

After registering at the front desk, we drove around to our room. I carried in our luggage, put the champagne on ice and we headed across the street for some dinner.

Interestingly they offered breakfast as well as dinner. My wife ordered the Belgian waffle and I ordered chicken fried steak, mashed potatoes and gravy … we both ordered ice tea to drink.

The food came quickly, it tasted great (I had to finish my wife's huge waffle) and then we returned to our room … for dessert!

In the room, I popped open the champagne and we poured it into water glasses … we each guzzled down several glasses as we undressed and jumped into the bed to consummate our union … Outstanding!

The next morning, we checked out and drove across the street for breakfast … then off to the Falls!

When we reached the Falls, we had to go over the bridge, through Customs to the Canadian side which is where everything about the Falls was.

We found our motel which was literally steps from the observation area for the Falls.

We spent the next several days and nights checking out the Falls from every angle day and night, even in a boat that went under the Falls. We went up and down the side streets into many different exhibits and we ate in all types of restaurants … we had a wonderful time … we just enjoyed being with each other.

On Tuesday, after checking out of our room we drove all the way home, arriving in time for dinner at the bar where we originally met … I introduced my wife to the owner/bartender and reminded him of the night that I met her … we devoured two steak dinners and headed home.

Fortunately, we both had Wednesday off … we unloaded all of our presents from the back of our truck, into our family room … sitting on the floor we unwrapped and opened each present or envelope and wrote what it was next to the giver's name on the list we used for invitations (so we could write them a thank you note) … when we unwrapped the present from my parents' it was really special … there were two beautiful yellow gold watches, him and hers, with the date that we were married engraved on the back … I called my folks immediately and thanked them for such a thoughtful and beautiful present.

When we were done opening everything, we had a big wad of money. So, after lunch we went to the bank and added my wife to my personal accounts and we deposited the wedding present money. Then we went home to fill out all of the 'thank you' notes … I sent some special notes to my Uncle T, the owner of the banquet hall and my wife's parents.

Interestingly, on our ride home from the Falls, I noticed that there were not many places on the highway to gas up … I decided that it would make sense to build some Gas & Goes on the highway. I talked it over with my gas manager and we agreed on three stations, 15 to 20 miles apart … we found three closed garages that fit the bill … I hired the company that specialized in renovating gas stations and a little over a month later construction began (following the design of our other five stations). We had our Grand Opening on the first of the year … we didn't advertise or have a special sale because we were catering to transients … but we were open 24 hours a day, seven days a week. My wife could not believe how an idea that I had while driving in the car could come to fruition so quickly.

Personally, I had to scramble to get my head back into what I had missed over the past week. My lead bookkeeper was super helpful reviewing how each business had done while I was gone.

I went to my moms for lunch to thank her personally for the watches and she told me how nice the wedding and reception were and how everyone told her how beautiful my wife was and how good the food and the cake were …

but my mom said the highlight was when my wife and I came out through the middle of those falls … it was a show stopper!

Over the next several days, I visited each of my stores to do a walk through and to speak with each manager … at my South-end store I had to make a big deal out of the Italian bakery guy. Telling him what a wonderful cake he had made. He told me they had gotten several orders at each store already for wedding cakes. One of the fellas that attended the wedding and reception brought his girlfriend who was a newspaper reporter. She wrote a front-page article in the Sunday paper expounding on what a beautiful bride and how beautiful and how good the wedding cake from Tony's Super Market Bakery was and what a phenomenal venue the Falls of Napoli where!

I went across the street to the Italian restaurant for lunch … the owner picked me up in a gigantic hug when I walked in … he told me that he had gotten a number of reservations from people who attended my reception and some from the newspaper article that said how good and how beautiful his venue was! Well, I told him that I had to give him accolades as well, for a wonderful reception from beginning to the end!

After eating lunch, I touched base with my bookkeeper. She informed me that the kid that normally made their deliveries had twisted his ankle carrying out some groceries and that he was sent home and wasn't available to deliver groceries to the homes of our customers. I said, "No problem, I will swing by and make the deliveries myself."

I did not recognize the majority of the names or addresses that I needed to deliver to, except for one name it was close to my house so I made it my last delivery.

When I made my last delivery, the lady now was an old woman. She told me that her husband died the previous year and she was all alone in this large home. Her plan was to sell her home, hopefully, quickly and to move close to her daughters in Florida. She told me that she knew a man that owned apartment buildings in the area she was moving into. The man had been very close to her husband and he said he would rent an apartment to her on a month-to-month basis. She had liquidated all of their investments and had put it all in her checking/savings accounts … this way when she passes her daughters could give her furniture to the Salvation Army and all of her assets would be in the bank. Her problem was what to do with the remainder of her furniture which she adored. Also, how quickly could she sell her home.

I asked how much she was planning on selling the home for and if she could give me a tour … I explained that my sister and brother-in-law had been looking for a home in this area and they may be interested … she asked me if my sister was the lovely girl that ran the pharmacy across the street from my grocery store … the very same one and she is very pregnant.

I had always liked the house, it sat on the corner of the street and was always very well-manicured and well taken care of. The inside was no different. It had four good sized bedrooms and was in pristine condition from top to bottom. I told the lady that I would mention it to my sister.

Sunday, at my parents' family dinner, I asked my sister how their house hunting had been going. She informed me poorly. Either the houses they looked at were trashed or they were way over-priced. I said I had seen a gorgeous house the other day and the lady was asking a very reasonable price. It was a lady I knew well since I had been delivering there for years. I explained the circumstances of why she was selling and said she was looking for a quick sale. My sister and brother-in-law were very interested … so I called the lady and asked if we could come over in an hour and show her house to my sister.

"Of course, dear," was her answer.

On the way over, I dropped my wife off at our home since it was only three blocks away. My sister immediately recognized the old lady and they gave each other a warm hug and a kiss on the cheek. My sister introduced her husband and then told the lady that her house was absolutely beautiful on the outside, the landscaping, the flowers, the way the grass was mowed and trimmed … exquisite! She went on to tell the lady that she couldn't wait to see the inside … my sister continued to compliment the lady as we went from room to room … when the tour was complete my sister told the lady that she wanted to go home and talk it over with her husband but she would get back to the lady quickly … of course the lady agreed.

The three of us went back to my house to have a drink and discuss what they had seen.

My sister said, "What is there to discuss … the place is perfect!"

She went on to say, "We don't have enough furniture to fill up that house."

They only had a two-bedroom apartment at the time. I asked if they would be interested in the lady's furniture since she was moving into a two-bedroom apartment … my sister said she loved the lady's furniture but it looked very expensive. We finished the discussion with my brother-in-law saying that they would need to go to the bank during the week and look into a mortgage. I wondered if they could go through the mortgage approval process and get the loan before the baby was born.

So, the next day I called the lady and asked if I could stop over …

"Of course, dear."

I met with the lady and told her how much my sister liked her home … she said she could see that my sister loved her house during the tour. She said she was looking to move as quickly as possible but it would take forever for her to pack everything that she was moving (dishes, figurines, etc.). I told her that I wanted to make an offer, that I would pay her what she was looking for … she was delighted … I told her that I could come over on Sunday afternoon with my wife, sister, brother-in-law, Mom and Dad and we would make quick work of it. I told her that I could bring all of the supplies that we would need to do the packing and I could line up the mover to move her to Florida the following Monday. She was shocked but delighted. She asked about the furniture that she was leaving … I told her my sister would love to have it … for the right price. The lady told me that she would throw in the furniture since she would like to see my sister and her new baby enjoy her furniture and her house.

When I left, I called my attorney to write a quick Purchase & Sale agreement for the house, including the furniture. He told me he would research the deed as well to make sure there were no liens. I didn't think so but you never know … it was clean.

I called my Uncle T to ask if he knew any Intra-state movers … he did and we met with the guy later that afternoon. The guy had a truck, a crew and a driver available to make the move for the upcoming Monday. He loaded my truck with way too many boxes and packing materials … telling me his guys would pick-up what was left over.

The next day my bookkeeper and I pulled together the money for the purchase of the house … the old lady did not have a mortgage to pay off, so I called her to say that I had lined up a mover for Monday and that she needed to make sure that she had an apartment to move into in Florida. Also, I wanted to get together with her and her attorney to pay her for her house hopefully Thursday afternoon. I would have my attorney contact her attorney in the interim.

On Sunday during our family dinner, I presented my sister and brother-in-law with the deed to the old lady's house and when all the yelling, thanking and screaming was done, I explained that we all needed to go to the lady's house and pack-up everything because she was moving out the next day! I had called a service to come on Tuesday to clean the entire house and my sister could move in after that, when she was ready. My sister kept babbling to my mom what a beautiful house it was.

As I expected my wife, Mom and sister packed the breakables while my brother-in-law and I went through the attic and the basement. Dad took down pictures and wrapped and packed them accordingly. Finally, Dad walked into the garage where there were all kinds of tools and cabinets with little drawers of screws and washers and what not, all stored very neatly over and under workbenches. Asked about all of this … the lady said she had no use for any of it … give it to my brother-in-law … WOW!

On Wednesday, my mom, my wife, my sister, my brother-in-law and me, all were at my sister's apartment to pack-up the breakables and help her move, since we all had the day off. While the women packed the dishes and figurines, my brother-in-law and I took armfuls of their clothes out of their closets and laid them on the backseat of their car. When we were done with the clothes, we took the drawers from my sister's bureau and my brother-in-law's bureau out with everything in them and put them in the back of my truck. Finally, the girls took all the lamps out and stuffed them in with the clothes in the back seat of my sister's car, while my brother-in-law and I took everything off the beds, rolled it into big balls and put it on top of the pile in the back seat.

The girls then went to the new house, to line shelves while my brother-in-law and I waited for the movers to arrive. All they had to do was pick-up furniture or boxes and take it to the truck. It went quickly, both moving from the apartment and moving into my sister's new home.

By dinner time, the move was complete … everything seemed to go fairly easy … except for my sister who was exhausted (mostly from carrying the baby) … so we decided to go out for dinner at my Uncle T's favorite Italian restaurant.

———————

Two Sundays later, my mom threw a combination, Open House/Baby Shower, for my sister and brother-in-law … at my sister's new house … my wife volunteered to help setting the tables and helping my mom in the kitchen.

All of my aunts, uncles and cousins were invited, as well as my wife's parents. It was a great success … everyone commented on how nice my sister's new house was and on how big my sister had gotten.

My mother had bought my sister the baby crib and my wife and I bought the basinet … just about everything else and much more were found in the gifts from the relatives. Great!

Surprisingly, the following Sunday my sister's maid of honor held another baby shower for my sister and she got loads more baby gifts.

———————

My sister left for maternity leave about one week before the baby was born. My lead bookkeeper asked how she should handle her pay … I told her to continue to pay her … the bookkeeper asked if I intended to continue to pay all the employees when they went out on maternity leave … I said no … she said once you start paying one employee then by law you have to pay all future gals on maternity leave. Good to know! Then pay her from my personal account each week … everyone was paid via direct deposit … and don't tell her or anyone. Problem solved.

Several weeks later, my sister contacted the lead bookkeeper to ask where her pay stubs were and the bookkeeper had to tell her there weren't any pay stubs since she was getting paid out of my personal account.

At our Thanksgiving Day feast at my mom's house, my sister thanked me profusely!

The day after Thanksgiving, Antoine James was born (little Tony) … just over seven pounds of pure, cuddly joy.

My sister named the baby after me because she said that she wanted him to be kind, generous and loving … like I was. The ultimate compliment!

———————

In March, my Uncle T who was on the Board of Directors of a very large local bank came to me with an investment he thought I would like. A fairly good size developer had passed away in his early 50s and there was no one to complete his present venture. It consisted of three parallel roads, running between two other existing roads. The concept was to build four buildings on each side of each road. Each building consisting of four deluxe townhouses. When the complex was complete, there would be a total of 96 townhouses. Great!

Evidently, the fella owned the land and the bank had financed all of the infrastructure improvements … the grading, the sewers, water, gas installations and several foundations were installed before the man died.

The bank had foreclosed and was only looking for the money they had lent. It appeared to be a great deal. Since the bank was familiar with the concept, they were interested in financing me, while I completed the development. I talked it over with my wife and we both felt it would be a great investment!

My uncle suggested that we pour foundations and build the exterior structures for eight of the buildings, put on the roofs, the windows and install the heating systems … then his crews could work indoors all winter long to complete the interiors of the units.

The overall concept was that we would complete one street each year … that way we would receive income from the completed apartments while we were building the remaining apartments.

By the end of May, all the paperwork and loans were in place and my uncle's crews got busy working on the project.

Chapter 6

This year, the focus at my birthday party was, little Tony! My mom, dad, wife and I, all took turns holding the little guy … they had to pry him out of my arms when I was holding him … and even though my mom took care of little Tony when my sister was at work, she still had to hold and cuddle the little guy.

My wife had her own savings account which kept growing and growing since I paid for just about everything … so she liked to pay for our vacations. So, for my birthday she gave me an all-expenses paid cruise to the Caribbean in mid-January … she figured we would need a get-a-way from work and the cold.

———————

On Labor Day weekend, my wife and I decided to install a swimming pool in our backyard since it was so difficult for us to actually get away. It was a godsend … it was our oasis away from everything!

———————

Early in September, one of the girls that worked for my wife came to us with a request for me to purchase a salon owned by an older woman that she wanted to purchase. She had three years of financials and she knew what the lady was asking for the business, building and property. I reviewed the financials with my accountant and we both felt it could be a sound investment.

So, I met with the woman selling the salon and we negotiated a fair price for the business, building and property.

The bank agreed with me and by November we owned our second salon!

My wife and I went on the cruise in January and it couldn't have been better … each day we did so much that each day felt like three days. We couldn't have enjoyed the vacation any more than we did … in particular I enjoyed each and every minute I spent with my wife!

In the spring, when the first several apartments were complete, we furnished one unit to act as my showroom and I ran advertisements (because these apartments were nicer and more deluxe, I was charging a premium rental fee). The second person to contact me was this attractive real estate gal that I met when she represented a couple wanting to rent one of my original apartments. At the time, she was married but when I met with her, I found that she was very pregnant, had gotten a divorce and was looking for an apartment for herself. I asked what she was going to do once the baby was born … she said it would be difficult to show houses. She seemed like a great sales person … so I asked if she would be interested in working for me … renting the apartments and managing the development … she jumped at the offer … Great, I could get back to my regular job!

In no time at all, she had rented all of the units. She even had some people waiting to move in while we were completing the last couple of apartments.

In the interim, my uncle was starting on the second street pouring foundations and framing the next apartment buildings.

My other businesses were all doing well especially the Gas & Goes on the highway … each station was selling more fuel and more groceries than any of the other five stations … terrific!

I was content with the businesses that I had.

Often people approached me with business ideas, which I would consider, but for the most part I would pass. Two of my best friends, B and C bugged me, whenever we got together to go into business with them. Of course, B wanted to start up some liquor stores and C, the used car salesman, wanted to open a used car business … neither business was in my wheel house … which was grocery. My wife who I would usually listen to, often told me she felt I should join my friends in business … of course, I was the one that they expected to bankroll the businesses … and if I wasn't really into it, I tended to stay away from that type of investment. So, I would come up with some way to say … no!

Chapter 7

At my birthday party, this year my wife gave me another cruise for a week in January. Knowing how much we enjoyed the last cruise my parents gave me a four-day cruise over Labor Day weekend. I am sure that my wife lined the cruise up for my folks through her travel agent friend and my parents paid for it.

It was a very nice day and my parents had purchased a croquet game which we had a blast playing in the backyard while little Tony ran around chasing and picking up the balls.

We really enjoyed the pool in our backyard … having get togethers throughout the summer with family and friends.

When we got together with my wife's four bridesmaids, I would ask the three that hadn't found a salon how their searches were coming along. One, the one with short light brown hair said that she had an idea for putting in a salon across the street from the high school … the rest of us thought that would be a great idea … she said that there had been a photography studio directly across the street from the school … for some reason the studio had gone out of business … I told her I would investigate the purchase of the building and what it would cost to convert the building into a salon.

My uncle's bank had foreclosed on the property and when I spoke with the loan officer we came up with a very fair price over the phone. So, I got my uncle and the architect over to tour the building to see what had to be done to convert the studio into a salon. The roof was fairly new and the parking lot was very large and in good shape.

My uncle quickly noted that we could convert the second-floor offices into two, two-bedroom apartments. The main floor consisted of a showroom in the middle and photography studios on each side. Usually, we would have six stations and a lounge for those waiting to get their hair done, but in this location, I thought we would install eight stations for when it gets really busy, around prom night for example.

Over the next several days, the architect sketched out what we had mentioned and my uncle estimated the re-construction costs.

When my accountant ran the numbers, it looked feasible … so my wife and I met with the girl with the light brown hair and went over the numbers and our ideas. We showed her that the salon she was thinking about was very feasible, especially when you consider the income from the two apartments on the second floor.

The girl was excited and wanted to get going ASAP. I told her that we wouldn't be done with the renovation until the end of the year … she said no problem … she needed to hire a full staff … her idea was to hire young, girls that had recently graduated from cosmetology school … so they would be closer in age to the majority of her clientele.

I called my lawyer with the details and he finalized the deal with the bank … including the construction loan.

―――――――――

My uncle, as usual, couldn't wait to get started … actually completing the two apartments for December 1 occupancy … which I had no problem filling. The salon was completed by mid-December and we had our Grand Opening the week of New Year's … it was an astounding success!

Again, my wife was astounded that once I had an idea, at how fast I would bring it to fruition!

―――――――――

In the meantime, we went on our Labor Day cruise … we flew to Florida on Friday afternoon so we would be there to board the boat on Saturday morning … that way there wasn't any rushing to fly down and get to the boat before it leaves the dock … I knew of friends that had missed their trip because of flight delays.

Well, we got up at 6:00 am had breakfast then we went on some sort of excursion … if we were in a town at lunch time, we would look for an interesting place to get a bite to eat, if not we would enjoy lunch on the boat … the boat food was always fabulous.

After lunch, we would go on another excursion, then get back to the boat for dinner, followed by dancing in one of their bars until 10:00 pm or so … at which time we would rush back to our room for some, generally, intense loving!

On the last day of our cruise, we left the ship by noon and we were back home in our house by 11:00 pm. WOW! The four-day cruise felt like we were gone for a week! We were somehow rested and refreshed.

———————

The time around the holidays really flies by since it is so busy with customers preparing for large get-togethers and with us decorating the stores and preparing for the on slot of customers.

Fortunately, soon after New Year's we had our next cruise scheduled. My wife's maid of honor filed in running my wife's salon and supervising the other two salons. All I really needed was my lead bookkeeper since she kept everyone, including me, in line.

Again, our cruise was spectacular … but on reflection I realized it was because I enjoyed every minute being with my wife … she made my life spectacular!

———————

We rented all of the next 32 apartments quickly. It seemed like most of the new tenants were just waiting for us to complete the units and put them up for rent.

Spring came early and so did my Uncle T's construction crews to complete the final third of this project.

The bank was very happy. Instead of borrowing more money to build the last section I started to pay the construction loan back with the rental income.

———————

Then in March, I was in my original grocery store when my lead bookkeeper took a telephone call, ran out onto the floor and told me to get to the front door … the chief of police was going to pick me up!

When he arrived, I got onto the car and the chief took off flying with lights flashing and sirens blasting … I asked what the rush was for … he said, "Your wife has been in a car accident … and we are headed to the hospital!"

The chief took several calls on his two-way radio, all in code numbers on the way and when we got to the hospital, he drove around to the back, to a door marked mortuary … I said to the chief, "No this has to be the wrong door!"

The chief escorted me in to the doctor-in-charge.

He explained that my wife had been driving in the city and when she drove through an intersection her car was struck from the side by a large dump truck going about 45 miles per hour through a red light. It crushed the entire driver's side of the car, killing the driver, immediately. My knees went weak … the chief held me up … it couldn't be my wife!

They brought me in to identify the body … OH MY GOD! As the doctor had said, the left side of her body was crushed, half of her beautiful face was gone … GONE … I noticed her watch … the one my folks had given her for our wedding present … then her wedding and engagement ring … it … was … her! I almost fainted … the chief helped me, both of us sobbing back to his car … he asked me where I wanted him to bring me … I said to my house.

When we arrived at my house, the chief helped me get inside, then he asked me who he would like me to notify, someone to come and to be with me … I said my mom … she was at my sister's home and came over in minutes … I asked where little Tony was and she told me he was playing with a little boy his age, across the street from my sister's house. I thanked the chief for all of his help and then he left.

I poured a stiff drink and took a sip … it didn't help. Then I had to try to get the words out of my mouth, to tell my mom what had happened to my wife … my beautiful wife … she was crushed to death … my mom drank my drink! She held me while we both cried and cried. Then she called my dad and my sister at their work and told them to come to my house, immediately … I asked her to call my Uncle T as well.

I was in the living room so as each relative showed up Mom would take them into the kitchen to explain what had happened … my sister let out a screaming loud, "OH NO!"

I had forgotten my in-laws. Mom called them and told them to come right over to my house … when they arrived, my mom and dad took them both into the kitchen to break the news that their precious daughter was dead … my dad caught my mother-in-law as she fainted … my dad carried her over to the sofa across from me, her husband, staggered over to the sofa with a handkerchief held over his nose and eyes … to say the least everyone was emotional … I had my uncle call my original grocery store and order, Fish & Chip dinners for everyone and have the delivery boy bring them over to my house.

My uncle called my lawyer at home and asked him to find out what had happened from the police.

An hour or so later, my attorney called back to talk with my uncle … first he told my uncle, he had called the best accident re-constructionist in the state … second, he called the number one attorney in the country, a real expert at suing the insurance companies … a real purana! When my uncle got off the telephone his olive skin was white. As he reiterated what the attorney had told him there was loud sobbing even my uncle cried and he was the toughest guy I had ever known.

A 10 wheeled dump truck, loaded with sand, ran the red light and T-boned my wife's little car … pushing the drivers-side-door, all the way to the middle of the car … instantly killing and crushing my wife … my uncle paused for a while to compose himself … then he went on to say that the driver was extremely drunk … they found an empty six pack of beer cans on the floor of the cab along with a bottle of bourbon that was almost all consumed … the driver didn't have a current driver's license … he had lost his license for drunk driving!

Then he said almost in a whisper … the autopsy showed she was pregnant … they suspect she was coming from the gynecologist since they found an ultrasound picture on the passenger seat (I carry that picture in my wallet to this day).

I was inconsolable. The light of my life had been extinguished; I didn't know how I would go on. My mom couldn't reach the doctor so my brother-in-law went to my sister's pharmacy and got a bottle of Valium … to calm my nerves … it did dull the pain some, but not enough!

Everyone but my mom went home by 10:00 pm. I laid in bed but I got very little sleep … neither did my mom.

The next day, my father-in-law picked me up and we went to the funeral home to make the arrangements … it had to be a closed casket affair … we picked the prettiest casket on display … the funeral director asked for a good picture of my wife … yes, we had plenty. Then he asked about the cemetery … we both just assumed she would be buried in the cemetery in the center of the town … the funeral director called over to the cemetery and made an appointment for us. Finally, we had to select the date and time for the wake and the funeral … the funeral director called the church and lined up an 11:00 am mass. I told the funeral director to send me an invoice and I would pay it promptly. At certain points in the funeral home, I would break down and at other points my father-in-law broke down.

Next, we went to the cemetery to select a plot for two (on the top of the hill, overlooking my grocery store).

They suggested where we could order a stone and said there was no hurry to do so but we decided we wanted to get everything done that day.

We selected a beautiful, dainty granite headstone that had three arms that rose up and met about five feet up, then it was topped with a fancy cross. My father-in-law wanted to pay for it but it was expensive so I decided we would both pay half.

It would take about six weeks to get the stone in and to engrave it … they would contact us when they planned on installing the headstone.

Before the wake, I took some Valium, it took the edge off … at the wake the line of well-wishers, wrapped around the building … they all meant well … many of them trying to console me but they just made my sorrow deepen. I personally thanked each and every attendee … breaking down the most when my wife's, I should say ex-wife's, maid of honor came in … and also, when the bartender that basically introduced us, came through the line to tell me how sorry he was to hear of my loss. The owner of the Falls of Napoli came to me and offered his restaurant for after the funeral at no charge to me … how generous … I said, "No, I have too many great memories there … I wouldn't be able to keep it together … but thank you, soooo much!"

The following morning, I took some Valium and I felt that I had a little better composure. After the ceremonies, we invited everyone over to my Uncle

T's favorite Italian restaurant for a meal and drinks (my uncle paid for the whole affair). When it was over, I went home and collapsed in my bed.

I just stayed in seclusion with the shades down … not eating much … not drinking much … barely existing. The light of my life was gone … the light inside of me, the light that had always driven me, was close to extinguished. I didn't know or care what was next.

My mom asked the priest to pay me a visit. He told me that life must go on when you lose a loved one … that my wife in heaven would want me to continue my life … that she would be watching me … she would be rooting for me … that made me feel significantly better … I told the priest that.

The next day I went to work with my Valium in my pocket, just in case. It was difficult because everyone in the store, employees and customers wanted to tell me how sorry they were … it hurt but I learned to thank them with a smile. It was the same reception in every store that I went to.

As the days wore on, I became less and less sensitive concerning my loss.

I took my ex-wife's maid of honor to lunch and told her how much I appreciated her filling in and taking charge. I told her that I was making her the permanent manager of the salon … she would get a raise and 20% of the profits … retroactive to the day my ex-wife died. She was delighted!

In order to keep my finger on the pulse of how the salons were doing, I decided we would have a dinner meeting the last Tuesday of the month, each month, to discuss how they were doing and if there were any issues. I would suggest a different restaurant each month and I expected all four bridesmaids to attend. Even the one that did not have her own salon yet.

———————

Chapter 8

My birthday party was fairly solemn … if it wasn't for little Tony making everyone laugh it would have been pretty glum. My sister and parents purchased me a cruise in January … because they knew how much I enjoyed it … it was very thoughtful … what they didn't understand was that I enjoyed the cruise because of my ex-wife.

———

As fall approached, my uncle had all eight buildings framed, sided, roofed, windowed, electrified and heated. Ready to be completed on the inside. My uncle and I would order the components for the apartments in bulk for the entire street, we got a significant discount for ordering such large quantities … like 64 toilets at once, since each townhouse required two toilets. We stored everything at my uncle's warehouse until it was needed.

———

I also started to meet with the three brothers again after several months of me not wanting to get together. I called Mr. X and told him I wanted to meet with him and his brothers again but I needed him to ask them not to console me … I thought it was very kind but I was trying to avoid the sadness and the memories.

We got together and had a very nice meeting.

———

In addition to meeting with the brothers, I was meeting monthly with the four bridesmaids. The three salons were all doing well. Interestingly, we thought the salon across from the high school would do very well at prom time but the student council sponsored dances for the whole school every month and tons of girls would get their hair done for those dances. GREAT!

Over the next several months I went to work every day and fortunately my businesses were doing well … although, if I listened to my Uncle T, when someone asked how is business, I should bellyache about how poor business was and how difficult it was to make a dollar … that way, they would be reluctant to ask for some money … versus, if you brag about how well you are doing … then it is difficult to say no when someone asks you for money.

I didn't partake in many festivities over the holidays, generally staying home and watching TV and laying low.

When it got to January, I would have liked to cancel my cruise but my sister and parents had spent a lot of money on my trip. So, I packed my bag and off I went.

The first day or two I kept to myself. The second night I went to the singles bar. I sat in the back watching the goings on. There were way more gals than guys! The girls in general were attractive and ran in age from 20 to 60 years old, the majority were 25 to 35 … just my age. Although the dance band was excellent, I couldn't motivate myself to ask anyone to dance … I left early and returned to my room.

The next day I put on my bathing suit, grabbed a book and I was headed down to the adult pool area to soak up some sun. On the way out of my room, I ran into the concierge for my area. I told him that I would like him to put a bottle of champagne in an ice bucket, in my room, each time I left my room … just in case … and I gave him a very large tip!

As it worked out, when I arrived at the pool area there were very few people and a plethora of lounges. I selected one, well away from other people in the sum and I began to read.

I hadn't been there long when two very attractive young ladies, wearing tiny bikinis and large brimmed hats came over and asked me if the lounges next to me were taken.

I said, "Yes, almost every lounge is taken … except, for the one on each side of me … which are available."

The girls both smiled and laid down on each side of me. Both girls had great tans. The one to my left had black hair, a black hat and a tiny red, white and blue striped bikini. The one to my right, had light brown hair, a white hat and a tiny yellow bikini.

Once they were settled in, the girl on my left said, "We came for the four-day cruise package … today is day three."

I couldn't ignore them so I asked, "Well, how has your trip been so far?"

Both girls laughed, then the one on my left said, "The weather has been great, the food has been outstanding … but there are very few single men and neither one of us have had any sex and we are headed home tomorrow!"

WOW! Maybe I shouldn't have asked, I did not reply, I just looked directly at her and smiled.

She said, "We were thinking that you are the perfect candidate."

How can a guy turn down an invitation like that?

I said, "I have a bottle of champagne on ice in my room."

Both girls sprung out of their chairs and said simultaneously, "Let's go!"

When I got up, each girl took one of my arms, snuggled up to me and it felt good. I hadn't felt anything for soooo long but this felt good. So, I led the girls to my room which really impressed them since I always get a balcony room one step down from the best room on the ship.

The champagne was in the ice bucket as I mentioned and the girls were impressed.

The girl with the light brown hair asked, "We saw you at the bar last night but you left without talking or dancing with anyone … why?"

I really couldn't answer that question honestly so with a smile, I said, "I was saving myself, for the two of you girls, for today."

She must have liked my answer because she put her glass down, took her hat off and she snuggled up to my side purposely brushing one breast against my front chest and the other against my back … it felt very, very good. Then she turned my head, with both of her hands and started to kiss me as passionately as I had ever been kissed … tongues, lips, suction, everything!

The other girl wasn't going to be denied. She came up to my other side, rubbed her breast against me, rubbed one hand around on the front of my bathing suit while she kissed and nibbled at my ear. WOW! I had never felt anything like that!

We somehow made it to the bed and tumbled into it. While I undressed one girl at a time, both girls helped me off with my bathing suit … from there it was a free-for-all! I was glad (and so were the girls) that I had brought a nine pack of ribbed condoms. By lunch time, the three of us were exhausted … I went to take a shower and revive myself … and when I came out of the bathroom, I found the girls in an interesting embrace, satisfying each other.

For lunch, the girls mainly ate fruit and salads … I had a double cheese burger, with battered French fries and an ice cream cone, with pistachio ice cream. Great!

The two girls were evidently not done with me! So, they escorted me back to my room … amazed that there was a fresh, ice-cold bottle of champagne in the ice bucket. After a few drinks, we were back at it in the bed for the next several hours.

Finally, I said, "That's enough!"

I went into the bathroom took a shower, came out and got dressed for dinner. The girls put on their suits and went back to their room to get dressed for dinner.

When they showed up for dinner, the two girls were dressed for the nightclub; they had fixed their hair, put on earrings and make-up, with fancy dresses and high, high heels … they had to be two of the hottest girls on the ship … and they were with me!

We enjoyed a lobster and steak dinner with all the fixings. Then, we headed to the bar for a nighttime of dancing. Only after a few dances they wanted to go back to my room.

Again, they were amazed that there was a brand-new bottle of champagne in the ice bucket. I was amazed at their thirst for sex … by the end of the night I had used all of my condoms … that never happened before … so I sent the girls back to their room and for the first time, in a long time, I went to sleep and I slept very well!

I didn't run into the two girls the next day which was good … it gave me time to purchase more condoms from the pharmacy and to actually lay by the pool and read … and rest.

That night at the bar. I saw a very attractive girl, with long red hair, fair skin and luscious body. All wrapped up in a little black dress. I strolled over to her and slipped in between her and another girl at the bar.

The redhead turned to look at me and said, "Where are your two girlfriends?"

I replied, "They went home today … they only had a four-day package."

"And now you're on the prowl?" she said as she finished her drink.

I flashed the two more signal to the bartender, looked her in the eye and said, "No … I have found my prey."

She looked impressed.

She asked, "What do you do for work?"

"I am a grocer … I work in a grocery store." After a pause, I asked, "What do you do?"

Her reply was, "I am a lawyer."

"You are the prettiest damn lawyer that I have ever seen."

She blushed.

I noticed, she was looking at my ring finger on my left hand, it wasn't very tan where my ring used to be, she asked, "Married?"

"No … my wife was killed in a car accident … last year."

Then, I asked her, "How about you?"

She said, "No … I fell in love and got married during my last year in college and two years later my husband fell out of love with me and we divorced."

The bartender brought our drinks and we both took a drink. Enough for the small talk, I asked her to dance. She was very light on her feet; her perfume was intoxicating and her body was fit from what I could feel. The conversation was light but continuous. After several drinks, she asked me where my room was. I explained that it was concierge level, an outside balcony room, toward the back of the ship.

She said, "I thought those rooms were reserved for couples."

I chuckled and said, "They are … if you would be so kind to accompany me … we will be a couple."

With that said, we left for my room.

She was very surprised with my room … how large and deluxe. She was also impressed with the champagne and after several drinks she stood up straight, took hold of the thin shoulder straps and lifted the little black dress all the way up and over her head … exposing only skin, lovely skin with tons of freckles and fit as a fiddle. I stood up, took her into my arms and kissed her passionately. Starting with her lips, then her neck (she moaned), then her lovely breasts (she kept moaning), then her belly button … but before I could go any further, I had to have her lay on the bed. She was passionate and so was I … several times. Finally, I didn't think I had any energy left so we took a shower … and guess what, I did!

We slept nude in my bed entangled in each other's arms. The next morning, I gave her my robe to wear to her room to get dressed. We spent the next several days (and nights) together … at the end of the cruise we gave each other telephone numbers and addresses and wished each other a wonderful life.

Once I got back home, I was refreshed and renewed and ready to get back to work … like the old days … *FINALLY*!

First of all, we needed to run the ads for the last 32 new townhouse apartments, which were coming to completion quicker than we expected. My real estate girl handled the showings and the leases, effortlessly!

I mentioned to her that if she would like, she could rent the townhouses on this last street, as of the 15th of the month, since the original townhouses were rented as of the 1st of the month. That way she would only have to handle 32 rental payments/deposits in the middle of the month. She liked the idea.

The bank was impressed with how promptly we completed the project and how quickly I was paying them back.

I was on the road, almost continually. I liked to make sure that each business ran the way I had envisioned it … carrying out customer's groceries, delivering customer's groceries and taking their orders, via fax or telephone, shopping for the order and delivering the order.

Our lunch crowd had really expanded in each grocery store specializing in made-to-order grinders, chicken and fish sandwiches.

I also toured each store to make sure my employees kept my stores as clean as I would expect.

I liked to talk to each of my employees to make sure there weren't any issues … and to get to know them better.

I was finally back to loving my job! Great!

One night as I was coming back home from checking on my highway Gas & Goes, I stopped at a small Oriental restaurant. I had driven by it a number of times but this night I had a taste for General's Chicken. Inside I found a very nice restaurant starched white table clothes and a candle on each table. A tall, thin, oriental girl, with shoulder length jet black hair, wearing a long, silk, pencil dress, escorted me to my table, she left me with a menu and as she walked away, I noticed that everything under her dress moved with every step … how nice!

The waitress came over, with a pot of tea and took my order. General's Chicken with a side order of Crab Rangoon's … and a beer. The food came quickly and was excellent. I was impressed! When I was done, I went to the front counter to pay for my meal. The tall girl that brought me to the table smiled and asked how my meal was … I felt like she really cared and I had the sense that she was flirting with me. In any event, I enjoyed the restaurant.

Chapter 9

This year on my birthday I was much happier. Little Tony was a real handful, running all over constantly. My sister and my parents bought me another January cruise … I protested that they had spent too much on me … they said, based on how I came back from the cruise last year … it was worth every penny.

As we came to the end of the month, I asked the bridesmaids if they would like to try somewhere different … they did, so I suggested the real nice oriental restaurant that I had visited. I called early afternoon to make a reservation for 5 at 6:30 pm … no problem, I didn't think there would be a problem on a Tuesday night.

I arrived a little after 6:00 pm and the tall girl smiled at me when I walked in. She escorted me to our large table which was on the other side of a divider … good for privacy, good for quietness, but bad for seeing who was walking through the door … so I asked the tall girl to send the girls looking for Tony to my table. Then I asked her to tell my waitress that I would like an Old Fashion.

The tall girl returned with my drink … walking as sexy as could be … she smiled, winked and placed my drink on top of a coaster on the table … she asked, "How is that!"

She waited as I stirred the drink with the plastic stirrer then I took a drink, swirled it around in my mouth and swallowed it, looking her straight into her eyes I said, "It's excellent … you must have made it."

She smiled back and replied, "I did … I made it special for you."

"Thanks," I said and then she turned to welcome more customers … I loved to watch her when she walked, especially when she walked away!

The girls all showed up together. The tall girl escorted them to my table and gave me an odd look.

We all ordered a drink and our meals. Then we started to discuss how each salon was doing, problems, issues, whatever. The fourth girl still did not find a salon or a place for one although she was still interested in finding one. Everything seemed to be going well in general. Great!

When the girls left, I was just starting my third drink so I sat at the table while the waitress cleared away the dishes and silverware. Then to my surprise came the tall girl with another drink for me and the register tape showing my bill. She sat in the chair right next to me, put my new drink on a coaster and handed me the register tape.

She asked, "How did you and your girlfriends enjoy your meals?"

"Outstanding … everything including the hostess has been … outstanding!"

She seemed more than pleased with my answer.

She said, "I made you another drink."

I shook my head and replied, "That drink may just push me over my limit."

"What happens then?"

I said, smiling, "I start to get romantic and I will ask my date to come home with me!"

"What date?"

My reply, "In this case it would be you!"

We were both sort of giggling and looking into each other's eyes when the waitress returned with a brown paper bag, turned down and stapled and placed on the table next to the tall girl … they had a quick exchange in their original language and then the waitress left.

"What's in the bag?" I asked.

"My dinner," she replied. "I get off early on Tuesday night"

"Where do you eat it?" I asked.

"Upstairs, in my bedroom, sitting on my bed," she said shyly.

"I've got a great idea … why don't we swing over to my house which is only a few miles away and you can eat your dinner on proper plates at a dining room table."

She smiled and said, "You're right … you are drinking your fourth drink and you have asked me to go home with you."

I hadn't realized it but she was right … I started to laugh loudly. I gulped down the remainder of my drink, I got up and said, "Let's go!"

I went directly to the cash register and paid my bill. The tall girl followed me out the door. We got into my truck and I drove home.

When we got to my house, the tall girl asked, "Who's home?"

"No one. I have timers to turn on my lights so I don't come home to a dark house," I replied.

When we got inside the house, in the kitchen, the tall girl said, "This is a nice house … you live here alone?"

"Yes!"

In the bag was Sweet and Sour Soup, an Egg Roll and a plate of some stuff her mother in the kitchen had made specially for her. I put the soup in a bowl and everything else on a dish and brought it into the dining room. I lit the two candles on the table for ambiance. Then I went back to the kitchen, grabbed a cold bottle of Pino Grigio from the frig, got two glasses and returned to the table to pour the wine. The tall girl was chowing down using her chopsticks … very interesting. We made small talk as she ate. She asked me if I was married … I explained that I had been, but my wife was in a terrible auto accident and was killed. Last year!

When she took her first drink of the wine, she said, "That is very good!"

She drank several glasses with her meal.

When she was done eating, she asked if I would show her the rest of my house … certainly!

As we left the dining room, I showed her the living room, then my office, the guest bathroom, my workout room and finally, the master bedroom, with the electric candle lights … I could tell she was impressed. As I started toward the master bath, the tall girl reached up grabbed my shoulder and turned me around, stood on her toes and kissed me, gently. I reached around her tiny body, pulled her against my chest and kissed her more passionately … next thing you know we were in the bed … she reached behind her and pulled down the strap that was attached to her zipper … voila, the dress was gone and all that was left was her white underpants … not for long!

She was naked and even more beautiful … I was naked in a New York minute … and an hour later the two of us were in the shower together … she bathed me, then I bathed her, over and over … we ended up in the shower for over 30 minutes … WOW!

The tall girl spent the night. I had the next day off and I found out later so did she. So, the next morning I got up early and made bacon and omelets. By the time I was done cooking, my girl called to me, "What can I put on?"

I told her to try my bathrobe that was on the chair. When she came into the kitchen, I asked if she would like coffee but she chose tea.

As we ate our breakfast, I asked her if she wanted to go directly home or if she would like to do something with me.

She inquired, "What can we do?" I suggested several options but when I mentioned the beach she perked right up and asked, "The ocean!"

"Yes," I said.

"I have never seen the ocean in my life!" she said excitedly.

"Then it's settled … the ocean it is! We will have to get you a bathing suit and an outfit to wear to the beach," I explained.

The girl could not have been more excited … when we were done with our breakfast I went into my ex-wife's bureau (for the first time since she died) looking for a bathing suit … there were two brand new suits with the tags still on them … I asked her to pick one to try on, she picked the black one (a girl after my heart) … I had the sense that she was similar in size to my ex-wife. The bikini fit and looked outstanding!

Then in the closet we found a black short sleeve silk blouse, which she tied the ends in a knot, exposing her midriff … HOT, HOT, HOT!

She picked a pair of jean shorts and I found a brand new three-pack of underpants, with the tags still on them … for the ride home. Then, I found some short, white, socks and a pair of slip-on white canvas sneakers … everything fit. Great!

On the way out, I grabbed my 'Go' bag filled with a beach umbrella, a beach blanket, two sand chairs and two beach towels. I tossed the bag in the back of the truck and we got in to go to the BEACH! YAHOO!

My girl slid right over and sat next to me in the truck. It was a long ride but we found a lot to talk about. For example, she explained that in her country her parents had a dry-Cleaning business and because she was intelligent the government sent her to college to become a dentist. Her sister was getting ready to attend college as well, when a wealthy countryman from the USA picked them and offered to pay passage for the four of them to the United States and to put them up in an apartment and to provide an automobile but they would have to work in one of his restaurants in the US for 10 years. It sounded like a great deal at the time. She had just completed her third year in college but she decided that they would all do better in the United States and they came over about five years ago.

I told her the story of my mom sending me to the grocery store for a job and the manager putting my name on a long list. Then, when my mom heard about that she took me to the store, chewed the manager out and I started the next day. When I asked my mom why the guy gave me the job so quickly, she explained that they were next door neighbors and very good friends. When they both came to this country from Italy … so I got the job in the grocery and I love it … I'm a grocer and will always be a grocer! I did not expound any further.

On the drive down, it came to me that this day was unfolding very similar to the one I had with my ex-wife, déjà vu so I drove to a completely different beach from the one I took my ex-wife to!

Next thing you know we arrived at the beach … she was straining to see the water from the truck … she was soooo excited … I told her not to worry we would be in the water very soon. She bounced up eyes as wide as saucers, and said, "NO! NO! What about the undertow?"

I laughed heartily and said, "Don't worry, I will protect you!"

Then, I pulled her over against me and kissed her … she was very cute!

We walked, hand in hand out onto the beach, we both kicked off out sneakers and socks and walked directly down to the water's edge … it was low tide and there were 3 to 4-feet waves … as we walked into the water, the water was cold, she ran back out screaming, "It's cold!"

I laughed.

She said, "How do people swim in it?"

I explained that the water warms up in the summer … you can stay in it all day … but if she would come back in to me, she would get used to the cold water in a few minutes … she came back in but I don't think she ever got accustomed to the cold water … I turned my foot sideways and kicked water onto her … she responded by kicking water at me and we ran around splashing each other for a while … she must have gotten some water in her mouth and she said, "Wow, this water is salty!"

Then we went back to my go-bag and I set up the umbrella, the blanket and the sand chairs. I rolled up the towels and used them for pillows … we both stripped down to our bathing suits and laid on the beach … it was all new and exciting for her … she was excited … how cute!

It was about 80 degrees on the beach and sunny. A perfect day!

After cooking in the sun for about an hour, we took a walk down the beach to a stand that sold hotdogs on-a-stick … I got two, she got one and we both got a cup of soda. We sat at a table on the beach and laughed about how she reacted to the cold water.

When we got back to our blanket, I said, "Watch this!"

And I ran as fast as I could down the beach and into the water finally diving into a wave as it broke over the top of me … I swam underwater as far out as I could go then popped my head up out of the water … my girlfriend had come down to the water's edge looking for me … I waved, ducked under and started to swim back toward her under water, then in the shallower water I stood up … I could see that she would have liked to walk out to where I was but the water was too cold … so I walked toward her on the beach. When I got to her, I wrapped my ice-cold arms around her very hot body … she yelped and I gave her a kiss.

"How can you swim around in that cold water?" she asked.

"Once you get completely submerged … it doesn't feel so cold," I replied.

She asked, "Can you bring me again when the water is warmer?"

I said, "I'd love to," and I kissed her again.

Then we walked back to our blanket hand in hand.

Later in the afternoon, we strolled over to a bar on the beach and changed back into our street clothes, in the men's/ladies' room and we drank a couple of beers. I always like the taste of a beer after I have been swimming in the ocean … my girl mentioned how good the beer tasted as well.

On the drive back to my house, I asked her what her plan for the future was. She told me in detail that she would like to have her own restaurant … a Polynesian restaurant so that she could offer something different from the myriad of Oriental Restaurants. Very interesting!

When we arrived home my mom had been there to clean (she stopped coming over to clean once I was married but started to come over to clean a week after my ex-wife died), so I knew we would have some sort of delicacy in the frig.

So, I said, "How would you like a homemade Italian dinner tonight?"

She said, "That sounds great!"

Fortunately, Mom left a big pan of her lasagna, my favorite. While I warmed up the lasagna and some Italian bread, I asked my girlfriend to set the table. She had to explore through the cabinets and drawers to find what she needed. I picked a fine bottle of Chianti from my stash. I also made a nice green salad with cucumbers and cherry tomatoes.

As I prepared the meal my girl seemed to hang all over me … indicating that she was interested in something other than dinner. So, I asked her if she would like to sleep over again. She said she would but she didn't have anything clean to wear for the next day … so she would need to go home.

She told me that my lasagna meal was superb! And then we headed for the bedroom for dessert.

When we got into the bedroom, we found her pencil dress ironed and hung up on a hanger, on the outside of the closet … and my mom had also washed her little white underpants; folded them and left them on the dresser. So, we decided she could stay for the night. Great!

The next morning, I drove my girl home to her restaurant wearing her freshly pressed pencil dress and looking beautiful … she gave me a passionate kiss and asked, "When will I see you again?"

"I will pick you up after work," I said.

She replied, "How about 9:00 pm?"

"I'll be here."

As I drove away, I noticed she lived 10.5 miles from my house … also I noticed that I was starting to develop very strong feelings for her!

My new girlfriend and I spent the next several nights together. I realized that I had fallen completely in love with her in a very short time!

So, on Saturday I stopped by my sister's pharmacy to ask her opinion regarding me bringing my girlfriend to Mom's house for our family dinner on Sunday.

My sister said, "You have only brought one girl home to meet Mom and Dad and you married that girl … are you that serious about this girl?"

My answer was, "Yes … she completes a part of me that has been lost for the past year."

My sister, with a tear in her eye, hugged me tightly and said, "Great!"

Then I went to my parents' home. I asked them if they would mind if I brought my new girlfriend to our weekly family lunch.

My mom asked, "You mean the Oriental girl?"

I said, "Yes … how did you know?"

Mom replied, "I ironed her dress the other day!"

I went on to explain that we went to the beach the other day. I find that this girl fills a part of me that has been missing. Both of my parents looked happy when I told them and both hugged and kissed me when I left.

That night after I picked her up, I asked my girlfriend if she would like to go to church with me the next morning and then go to my parent's home for our weekly family dinner.

She smiled and asked, "But what will I wear?"

I said, "Look through the closet, I'm sure you will find something."

Sure enough, the next morning my girlfriend picked an outfit out of the closet which still had the tags on it. It was black and white stripped. She also, found black heels, a black hand bag and a big black hat, with a white band around it. She looked FANTASTIC!

I wore the same thing every week; a black silk shirt, with an open collar, black slacks and a black linen sport coat.

When we walked into the church, the organist was playing very softly and as we walked further down the aisle there arose a murmur which continued to get louder as we walked to the front pew. My sense was that people were saying, "Look who Tony is with!"

Just before the mass was about to start my sister and brother-in-law came in and sat beside us.

I whispered to my girlfriend, "This is my sister."

My girlfriend looked at my sister and smiled.

My sister smiled and said, "Hi!"

When we got to my parent's home, they could not have been more congenial … my mom and sister peppered my girlfriend with questions; where did we meet, where did she come from, where did she work, on and on. My girlfriend seemed to fit in fine. Great!

———————

Over the next several weeks my new girlfriend spent every night and every spare minute we could together. During that time, I had to explain about the various businesses that I owned. She was more than impressed … almost scared that I might be too important for her. I had to comfort her by telling her in this country everyone is equal!

I measured her finger by tracing our hands on a piece of paper. When I went to buy her an engagement ring, I brought the piece of paper to the jewelry store and they sized the ring from the paper.

I picked up the ring on a Friday afternoon and had to decide when to give it to her. Since the ring was burning a hole in my pocket, I decided that I would give it to her that night. I called and asked if she could leave work a little early and I made a reservation at a real nice restaurant.

When we arrived at the restaurant, it wasn't very busy but it was very romantic. The lights were turned down low, there were candles on all of the tables and we could hear the sounds of a piano playing softly from the cocktail lounge.

We ordered our drinks, appetizers and dinner all together and after the waitress returned with our drinks, we both took a sip then I slid off my chair and onto one knee, I simply said, "You fill a void in my life … I love you and I want you to be my wife!"

My girlfriend immediately said, "YES!"

And the entire restaurant started to clap.

I stood up and she stood up … I put the ring on her finger and I gave her a big kiss. The entire restaurant all clapped again. It was embarrassing, but I was pumped!

My fiancé was sooooo excited … she had a huge smile and her cheeks were bright red from blushing … she looked beautiful!

My fiancé could not wait to tell her family. She finished eating her meal quickly and passed on dessert.

We went back to the oriental restaurant, where she told her family. They were overjoyed, babbling in their home language … even though they could all speak English. The father, mother and sister all shook my hand and kissed me. Everyone was happy!

Come Sunday morning we went to church. My sister did not come down to the first row of the church because they had little Tony with them. He was so rambunctious that they sat in the last row so they wouldn't distract others.

When everyone arrived at my parent's home after church, I couldn't wait … I said, "I have an announcement to make … we have gotten engaged!" And I held up my fiancé's hand!

My sister yelled, my mom covered her mouth, my brother-in-law said great and my dad hugged me and whispered in my ear, "Good for you son!"

Everyone seemed happy!

Dinner was later than normal, since Mom had to go into the study and call all of the relatives.

During dinner Mom asked, "Have you picked a date, yet?"

I replied, "Early in October."

Mom got right up went to her calendar and told us what day the first Saturday in October was. I went on to tell them that we hadn't picked a venue or anything else …

Mom said, "You have to go to the Falls … I can't wait to see you both come through that waterfall!"

Tears started to run down my checks, as I said, "I don't know if I could do that again."

The mood became very somber … my fiancé hugged me and asked, "Are you okay?" I nodded.

I pulled myself together and said, "I don't expect this to be a large wedding or reception … just a bridesmaid and best man … only our relatives and her family … probably 40 people or so."

Everyone nodded their head and started to ask about our honeymoon. I told them that we could only get away for a few days and where we were going was going to be a big surprise for my fiancé!

Since my fiancé's folks were not privy to how we do things in the States, I asked my mom and sister, if they would make all of the arrangements … there wasn't a lot of time. They were ecstatic!

The following Sunday, my mom invited my fiancé's folks over for dinner. It wasn't easy for them, they had to find others to fill in for them.

Well, Mom actually threw an engagement party for us! It was outstanding … all of my aunts and uncles and my fiancé's sister and parents. I told my mom that I really appreciated the gesture, and this is basically all of the people we would invite to the wedding. A great time was had by all!

When we were all outside, it was a very warm day ... I pulled my Uncle T aside to ask him if he would be my Best Man again. Of course, he would! GREAT!

I asked my uncle if he was available to have lunch with me the next afternoon and he was available ... we decided to meet at the steak house for lunch.

At lunch, I told my Uncle T that my plan was to buy out my fiancé's contract and those of her sister and parents from the guy that they owed for paying their way to the US. My uncle asked how much longer that they were under contract ... I told him five years ... he winced. Uncle T told me that these people were the guy's employees and they ran one of the guy's restaurants ... my Uncle T told me that he didn't think the guy would agree to letting me buyout the four contracts. I told my Uncle T that I wanted to go to New York and try to buyout the contracts on the Thursday, two days before I was to get married. My uncle said he would look into it.

I asked my uncle why we didn't meet at his favorite Italian restaurant. He told me it had just closed. The owner's father-in-law owned an ice cream factory in Italy and the man was just diagnosed with inoperable brain cancer and only had a short time to live. So, the restaurant owner gave his keys to my uncle and asked him to explain to the bank that he had left the country so he could run his father-in-law's company.

My uncle laughed when he asked me if I had any interest in the building!

As a matter of fact, I was very interested. Since my fiancé informed me that they will not have a job when I buy their contracts out and my fiancé's dream is to run her very own restaurant. So, I asked my uncle if we could show my fiancé the restaurant on Wednesday her day off. Sure, my uncle would meet us there at 8:00 am.

My fiancé was very interested. So, I took the liberty of asking my architect to join us.

When we met at the closed restaurant, my fiancé liked the look of the restaurant and the size of the parking lot … very good. Inside was pretty much ideal as well … the kitchen would have to be modified (her dad could tell us exactly how) but the biggest thing was that a much larger stage needed to be built where the present band stand was and it needed a gathering room, with dressing rooms attached. Other than that, and the walls being painted another color, it was perfect!

Upstairs was a three-bedroom apartment which still had food in the frig and kitchen cabinets.

My Uncle T told me that all I needed to do was to assume the present mortgage. That was about 20% of the appraised value and to pay or negotiate payments with the vendors … it was a no brainer!

I said, "Let's do it!"

I asked my architect to rush the redesign (he had to meet with my fiancé's father to get the kitchen layout), and I asked my Uncle T to line up a meeting with the bank. He told me to plan for Friday afternoon.

My fiancé was giddy but everything relied on me buying out her and her family's contracts.

When I got to the office on Thursday, the lead bookkeeper had a message for me to call my big-time attorney.

He told me that he felt that he had hammered out the best deal that we were going to get from the company that was responsible for my ex-wife's death.

We had spoken about four months earlier, he thought he had a pretty good deal and I told him that it was not even close to what I expected. I reminded him that two people were killed in that accident. He informed me that companies buy insurance for these types of things and generally the most that gets paid out is the maximum of the insurance policy … and this agreement was equal to the maximum of their policy. I told my lawyer it's not enough … they need to hurt … how about the Beer Manufacturer and the Liquor Distiller and the Liquor Store … how much are they paying? He said he would go back and lay into them.

Now he was back with what he felt was the best and final offer. IT WAS OUTSTANDING!!!

I couldn't believe my ears … I told my lawyer to finalize the deal!

I set up a new savings and checking account just for the money … this money wasn't for arbitrary spending … it would be spent how my ex-wife would have liked it. It was an embarrassingly large amount!

The bank manager told me that there were better places to put my money than in a savings account but since I didn't know where I wanted to use it, I decided to leave it in the savings account.

The following week I got the approval from the bank to assume the Italian restaurant guy's mortgage. I called my attorney to set-up a corporation for, Tony's Restaurant, Inc.

The prints were all set so my uncle got started and figured it would take about three weeks.

On my fiancé's day off, my mom took her, her sister and her mom to pick out a wedding dress, a bridesmaid dress and a mother-of-the-brides dress. Evidently, it went very easily … my fiancé wanted a white pencil dress … my mom talked her into a removable train. They also went to the flower store and selected the flowers.

My Uncle T, my fiancé's dad, my dad and I, all got fitted for just regular black tuxedos.

My sister lined up a DJ and the church.

Mom and my sister sent out the invitations, reception at the Falls of Napoli … and at our Sunday family dinner Mom told me, "You are walking through those falls … so just suck it up!"

It was unusual, Mom was never that forceful … so I better suck it up!

I needed to pull together the cash that I planned on using for the buyout.

It was unclear how much I would need but I couldn't be short. I had to estimate what was owed and I had to overestimate what it could be. Then I tripled that amount. I accumulated the cash and stored it in my original store's safe.

My Uncle T requested a meeting on the Monday prior to my trip to New York to do the buyout. My uncle was very inquisitive. He knew I would be carrying a huge amount of money. So, he wanted to know who I was meeting with, where we were meeting and when we were meeting …

He was very serious. I asked why. He told me that these were very dangerous people that I was going to meet. He felt that I should have some back-up protection. My uncle went on to say that he was going to have the owner of the Falls restaurant and one of his muscle-bound buddies travel with us on the train and he would have a friend in New York pick us up at the train station in a limo, to take us to and from the meeting. There was no dissuading my uncle.

For our trip on Thursday to New York, I put one and a half of what I thought was owed in a brief case. I stuffed my sport coat inside vest pockets, with bundles of cash and I carried my rain coat with a removable liner. Inside the bottom of the liner, I put the remainder of the cash.

We took the train to New York. I wore a black silk shirt, black slacks and a black sport coat. My fiancé wore a pretty silk flowered pencil dress. Our two bodyguards wore black V-neck T-shirts, with black slacks and black sports coats. We looked like we were going to a funeral … I hoped not!

When we got to New York, we were met by the limo driver. He took us to his car. Which had great big men all dressed in black standing at attention, at each corner of the limo. Once we were in the limo, two of the four guards outside got into the car in front of us and two got into the car behind us.

All three cars drove to Chinatown to a big restaurant. Before we got out, the four bodyguards got out of their cars and resumed their positions on the four corners of the limo. Then the limo driver got out and opened our door. The four of us, me, my fiancé, the owner of the Falls and his buddy got out and went into the restaurant and asked for the man we were there to meet.

We were escorted through the restaurant down a long hallway to a very large ornate office.

There was a large, bald, oriental man with a long fu-man-chu moustache sitting behind a large fancy carved wooden desk. There were four other oriental men standing in each corner … I suppose they were his bodyguards.

The man behind the desk asked in pretty good English, "Why do you bother me today?"

I told the man that I was planning on marrying my fiancé and I wanted to buyout her contract and those of her sister, mother and father.

He spoke in his original language and asked one of the men in the room to get the four contracts that I was talking about.

He looked over the contracts then he snarled at my fiancé and spoke to her in their language (she interpreted for me; "Why do you bring these men to me … you know I do not cut short a contract").

I said, "It is me you should be talking to."

There was a great deal of tension in the room.

The man looked at me and said, "I spoke to your uncle on the telephone last night. He has some very powerful friends in this city … it is best for my health that we make an agreement … I will ask (and it was a large number of dollars)."

I said, "For all four contracts?"

"No … for each one."

I just stared in the man's eyes and said, "That is far more than what they owe … I am a reasonable man … give me a reasonable amount."

The man looked down at the contracts once more. Then he gave me a much lower number close to what I felt it should be. I said, "I will pay you that amount, now, in cash for each of these people and I will take their contracts."

He agreed. I opened my briefcase and counted out the exact amount that he requested. Fortunately, I didn't need to go into my raincoat lining, it would have been embarrassing.

The man stood, handed me the four files containing the contracts and said, "These four must be completely out of my restaurant and apartments by midnight tonight … and they cannot start or work in another oriental restaurant within 10 miles of where they are now … or it will be bad for their health."

I stood and said, "Agreed!"

We turned and walked out to our waiting limo. The limo took us to a terrific big-time restaurant in the city. The restaurant was loaded with big time actors and older actors and on the walls were pictures of the owner and many different presidents that had dined there. The owner came over, introduced himself and said he knew my uncle and had spoken to him … the owner said I have a special lunch made just for you!

My bodyguard, the owner of the Falls restaurant, paid very close attention to how the meal was prepared and how the waiters did their work.

The meal was exquisite! I told the owner that and he said my uncle had paid for everything, including the tip. Fantastic!

We went out to our limo and back to the train station for our trip home. As we were waiting, my fiancé called her sister and explained that they had to be out of the restaurant and their apartment by midnight and we would pick them up and move them, just be prepared. Then I called my Uncle T. I told him that everything went amazingly well. Thank you very much … and that my fiancé's family had to be out of their apartment by midnight, so could he prepare the apartment over the new restaurant for them … I told him I would send my mom over with groceries, meats and drinks. I would pick up the family later when we get back. I called my mom and explained what I needed for her to do and she said she would get right on it.

On our trip back, the owner of the Falls of Napoli Restaurant went over the menu for our reception on Saturday. I asked for two things; chopsticks for four people and one dish of something oriental … he said he could make Chop Sui … and my fiancé agreed! Great!

———————

When we got off the train, we went directly to my house to unpack my truck and to get my big sedan. Then, I drove the truck and my fiancé drove my sedan over to pick up my fiancé's family.

They were all giddy about being free to do whatever they wanted. They kept hugging and kissing me and my fiancé as gestures of their gratitude … it was greatly appreciated by both of us!

I loaded their stuff in the back of my truck and my fiancé loaded her family into the sedan.

When we arrived at their new restaurant, there were plenty of lights on and several cars in the parking lot. My mom and dad, sister, brother-in-law and my Uncle T all came out to meet us. When my fiancé's family stepped out of the car, my uncle started an extremely loud and long uproar … everyone was clapping and yelling and kissing and hugging … it was a heart-warming scene. Once the hoopla settled down my mom led the way to their new apartment while all the men carried the family's stuff up to the apartment.

It didn't take long to get them settled in. My mom and my sister had washed all of the sheets, pillow cases and blankets and remade the beds. There was food in the cabinets and drinks in the frig. My Uncle T took a cold bottle of champagne out of the frig and poured everyone a glass of bubbly … he gave a toast and the hoopla all started up again … the relief and pleasure to be free was evident on my fiancé and her family's faces. Hip! Hip! Hurrah!

At one point, I explained that this apartment was only a temporary fix … I had a couple that was moving out of one of my original, two-bedroom apartments at the end of the month and my fiancé's family could move over there.

––––––––––

The next day, Friday, I had a number of loose ends to tie up at work.

My dad picked up and delivered all of the tuxes.

Mom picked up and delivered all of the dresses.

That night we had probably the shortest rehearsal ever! Then, my Uncle T took us all (Mom, Dad, my aunt, sister, brother-in-law, my fiancé's mom, dad, sister, my fiancé and me) to the Steak House for dinner. It was great everyone got along so well!

At one point, I cornered my uncle and told him how appreciative I was for what he had done to protect us and to help secure the release of my fiancé's family from their contract of servitude.

Then, I said, "You must have some very powerful friends in the city."

My uncle smiled and said, "We do favors for each other … some day they may need us to do them a favor out this way … all that's important is that you are safe and your fiancé and her family are free of their contracts … what did it cost you?"

I just said, "You don't want to know!"

––––––––––

On Saturday morning, my fiancé and I had waffles for breakfast then my mom and dad drove my fiancé over to the new restaurant to help everyone get dressed … my sister did my fiancé's hair, putting it up for the occasion.

Ultimately, the limousine showed up and took them all to the church.

I thought the ceremony went very well. The highlight being my beautiful wife, in her white pencil dress, with the long flowing train, being escorted down the aisle by her father.

When the ceremony was finished, the bridal party loaded into the limo and we headed to the flower garden in the park for pictures. Then off to The Falls of Napoli for the reception.

When we got there, the owner was in the parking lot to meet us. The two sets of parents walked through the hallway and into the ballroom, we could hear the applause as they were announced. Next was my uncle and sister-in-law … louder applause. Then, the owner took my wife and I down the corridor behind the massive falls … he turned some knobs and levers … then he lowered the heavy field stone door … and encouraged us to walk through the falls (where he had shut off the water) … which is what we did and as we walked out of the middle of the falls the DJ announced, "For the first time in public … I give you Tony and Mei Ferducci!" The applause and cheering were deafening!

I looked directly at my mom … she was jumping up and down and clapping and crying … all at once. My sister came over to take my wife's bouquet and we did our first dance as man and wife.

The owner had remembered to make the Chop Sui for my in-laws and he had the wait staff ask everyone if they would like some as well. Plus, he remembered to have chop sticks for my wife and her family which my wife's family greatly appreciated.

At one point, I met my buddies at the bar for a drink. I told B and C that I was interested in starting a business with them if we could work out the logistics. B was always bugging me to open up several liquor stores. I told him to find the locations and the price to purchase them. C sold cars and wanted me to finance a used car lot with him … this was not a business that I was familiar with except that people looked down at used car salesmen and I didn't know if I wanted to be associated with that type of business. I told C to look for locations and get pricing. If my friends were not interested in putting forth the effort to do some due diligence, then I wasn't interested either …

understand that the only reason I was motivated to get into these businesses, is that my ex-wife always pushed me to do it and now, due to unfortunate circumstances the money had been provided.

Prior to heading for the church, I had driven my sedan over to the restaurant and my uncle picked me up and drove to the church.

Well, when we left the reception, my buddies had attached a Just Married sign to the back of my car, along with strings of beer cans. We drove away to the clamoring of the cans and the chuckles of the crowd.

At home, we quickly changed into our street clothes, grabbed our pre-packed luggage and headed for the airport to go on a surprise location honeymoon for my wife!

The surprise only lasted until we checked in and she found out that our destination was … Miami Beach! I told my wife that we had a hotel room overlooking the beach and that the water would be warm enough for her to swim in it … she was over the moon excited!

When we arrived at the hotel, you could not tell that it was so close to the beach. When we got to our room, we opened the slider and went out onto the balcony overlooking the beach and the crashing waves.

We quickly unpacked. We put on short pants and sandals and headed down to the beach. We walked past the beautiful very large inground pool, lighted for the evening, then a small grove of Palm trees onto a white sand beach down to the water's edge. We took off our sandals and walked into the water over our ankles … it was warm … the waves were four to five feet high and I think they scared my wife, for she held onto me for dear life!

We kissed and hugged and slowly decompressed from the activities of the day … standing in the ankle-deep water. I promised my wife we would go swimming in the ocean in the morning … she didn't seem very enthusiastic.

Then we went back to our room, went to bed and consummated our marriage (several times).

In the morning, we put our bathing suits and sandals on, we sprayed each other with sun tan lotion, she put on a cover-up and I wore a polo shirt. We went to breakfast in the hotel restaurant. She got an omelet and I got an omelet and a small stack of pancakes.

Outside the temperature was headed for 90 degrees. A beach attendant had put out lounge chairs in pairs. As he saw us come out onto the beach, he snagged a couple of cushions and put them on the chairs we had chosen. Then he asked if we wanted an umbrella, which we did.

There were a number of people already out on the beach, some with children, some in the water and some out of the water. The waves had grown to about six feet.

My wife looked at those in the water and asked, "Aren't they afraid of the undertow?"

I laughed and said, "Don't worry about the undertow … it is insignificant, at the moment."

We walked hand and hand down to the water's edge … it felt cooler than it had the night before … I explained that the water was the same temperature as the night before but the air was a lot warmer … I had to encourage my wife to go into the water … I told her to look at all of the children in the water, they were not complaining! Then, I told her that the slower you go in, the colder the water feels … the best way is to run in and to dive into a wave … I told her to watch me as I ran into the oncoming waves and dove head first into one (the water was actually pretty warm) … then, I walked back to get her but when I got to her, she took off running into the water and dove into a wave and when she came up, she had the biggest smile on her face … I ran out to her, picked her up, kissed and hugged her (it was a very salty kiss).

We stood in what was chest high water for my wife and when a wave came through, we had to jump up or the wave would go over our heads. My wife was an excellent swimmer so I wasn't too concerned for her in the water. I tried to show her how to body surf … which is difficult without a board but we would catch one right every now and then and travel from the deeper water to the very shallow water (probably 40 to 50 feet) … it seemed like a long way … then we would stand up and run back out to catch the next wave.

We must have been in the water for a couple of hours when I saw a young waitress walking across the beach holding a tray with several drinks on it … I yelled out, "I'll take two of those!"

The waitress laughed and gestured for me to join her. I ran out of the water with my wife on my heels and asked what kind of drinks she was carrying but before she answered I asked, "Are those, Frozen Mud Slides?" She nodded her head. I took two drinks and asked her to charge them to my room. My wife and I took our drinks to our lounge chairs sat and relaxed, we were both physically tired from wrestling with the water.

When the waitress came back with an empty tray, I stopped her and asked for two more Mud Slides but with bananas mulched up in them. When she came back, she had what she called Special Banana Mud Slides … I slipped her a 20-dollar bill.

We drank and swam all through lunch time … it was okay since the drinks were very filling. My wife loved the beach, loved the water, loved the waves, loved the drinks and above all she appeared to love me … we had a blast!

When we got back to our room the first thing, we did was take a shower … together … it must have taken 30 minutes but we were very thorough. When we finally toweled off, we noticed that we had gotten more sun than we should have. So, I went down to the little store in the hotel and bought Aloe Vera crème to apply over our sunburn.

We had a late dinner in the hotel restaurant then we went into the bar where there was dancing. We didn't last long after playing in the ocean and baking in the sun, we were exhausted!

The next day and the following morning were pretty much a carbon copy of our first day on the beach only we were a little more careful to reapply the sun screen.

Tuesday afternoon we were both sad that we had to pack-up and head home … our short honeymoon could not have been better … we both did not have a care in the world … but we had to head back to reality!

We both had the next day off (Wednesday). So, I suggested that we take all of the wedding presents that my father had put in the back of my pick-up truck and spread them out on the family room floor. As we opened the gifts, we made a note on our guest list (in red pen), what was received. Then at lunch time I sat at my desk and wrote thank you notes (which I mailed the next day).

While I was writing, my wife called her folks and told them we were back safely and that we had a great time. She asked how they were getting by and her sister said that they were doing fine but they needed a vehicle. When she got off the phone, she told me that her parents needed a vehicle.

I called C. I told him I needed a family van for my in-laws. He told me he would meet me at the auto auction in 30 minutes.

We found a great van with low mileage and a super price … I bought it and my wife drove it to our new restaurant with a temporary plate. I called my agent and had the vehicle insured in my sisters-in-law's name.

The next day I registered the van and got the plates which I put on the van before lunch. My sister-in-law and her folks were delighted … now back to work.

The work on the new restaurant was almost complete except for a few critical items in the kitchen which were not due until the first week in November. In the meantime, my wife had to finalize and print the menus, find an entertainment group, hire a complete kitchen and waitstaff with the exception of her sister, mother and father. We had plenty of cutlery and glass ware from the previous restaurant. My wife had to decide if she wanted plain white dishes, which we had a mountain of, or order something special more appropriate for a Polynesian Restaurant.

Fortunately, my wife called an Oriental Placement Agency to order the type of employees that she needed. She happened to ask if they knew of any available Island Bands and the lady said she had. There was a band that came to the US to play at a restaurant but the restaurant burned to the ground before they could get started. The lady said she hoped the band had not left to go home yet. So, she hung-up and called them. Then she had the band manager (the father) call my wife. Yes, they were available. Yes, they would be interested in playing for us.

There were six people in the group, all related: father plays the organ and sings, oldest son plays drums, youngest son plays electric guitar and performs, wife and two daughters dance in grass skirts to genuine island music. Fantastic, that is exactly what she wanted for entertainment. My wife asked if they had a demo tape … they did. She asked if they could send the tape, next day air, to us to review and she asked what they planned to get paid … the guy said he would include a copy of their contract with the tape. Great!

Then my wife called the agency girl back to line up the staff … the lady had already found a number of interested and available people that fit the description that my wife requested. My wife thanked the girl for having the band contact us. It sounded on the telephone like they would be perfect!

Next, we had to order the alcohol for the bar and all of the meats and ingredients to make the dishes on the menu.

I worked with our advertising expert (professor). We … she came up with a multi-media campaign sort of a blitz for TV, radio and newspaper. To start two days before we open and run for a full week.

I went to the sign shop and we/they designed a real pretty illuminated, Polynesian sign, which would be installed where the present sign was. It would be ready in one week. Great!

We received the tape of the band. They were not good … actually, they were outstanding … better than we could ever have expected of: three grown men, with long shoulder length hair and three attractive female dancers.

The band was looking to get paid a reasonable amount, but they also needed a three-bedroom apartment. Fortunately, the only three-bedroom apartment we had was above the restaurant. Unfortunately, it was inhabited by my in-laws.

My wife called the band manager and explained that we were not going to open until the first week in November but we were very interested in hiring them. We would like to see/hear them play in person on our stage. The manager said they could come up on Tuesday, my wife gave them our address and directions.

I faxed the contract they had sent us to my attorney with the appropriate modifications. I requested it be complete by the next Tuesday. I also checked to make sure there were spotlights, etc. for the stage … there were.

The next day I took my in-laws and sister-in-law, to the furniture store, since they were going to move into one of my 2-bedroom apartments at the end of the month. They were easy to satisfy, we picked out two-bedroom sets of furniture, a living room set, a kitchen table and chairs. Then, we went TV shopping and selected a TV and a TV stand.

I asked my wife to take her mom and her sister to buy towels and linens, on the weekend.

Everything seemed to be falling into place. My wife had contacted, interviewed and hired, tons of wait staff, kitchen and bar staff … then she needed to train them.

———

When Tuesday came around, the band arrived late morning, in a large van with all of their equipment. They just looked like island people. Perfect!

After introductions, I showed the band where the stage and dressing rooms where … they carried in and set up lots of equipment. The ladies went into the dressing room and changed (into coconut halter tops and green grass skirts). The father hooked up his keyboard to the speakers, one son hooked up his electric guitar and the other son set up some drums and then stacked what looked like several logs together. They each did mike checks and volume checks. The father checked on the girls in the dressing area and when they were ready. The father told me that they were going to do what they called a regular show.

My wife and I and her family were sitting at several tables so I said, "Let's see it!"

They started to play island music then the father in a very deep voice, said into his microphone, "Now for your listening and watching pleasure we present our island dancers," and at that moment the older son started to bang loudly on the logs thump, thump, thump and the door to the dressing room opened and out came the three women dancers, one by one, with their hips pulsating to the drummers, thump, thump, thump, and their arms moving and their hands gesturing. The father explained that the dancers were doing a welcome to the island dance. When they were done with the dance, the dancers went back into the dressing room … hips never stopping.

Next came the youngest son, slapping his body, making various sounds to the music the father was playing … it seemed corny but it was very entertaining.

While the son was slapping the women changed costumes … and when he was done slapping himself, the three dancers came back out with red grass skirts and red coconut halter tops to do a variety of dances, while the father described what the hand gestures meant.

As soon as the women went back into the dressing room the other son ran out to the middle of the stage. He was carrying a double ended sword with a hand grip in the middle. There was a sponge (which had been soaked in some type of flammable liquid) impaled on each end of the sword. The son lit the sponges on fire … we were 15 feet away and the heat felt intense. The son did an incredible dance, spinning the sword in front, behind, above and then he straddled the sword with fire just inches in front of his chest and his back …

he looked out at the audience (even though it was meager), and he gestured with his hands for applause … everyone clapped enthusiastically. Then, he started throwing the spinning, fiery sword up in the air and catching it. He finished his performance by sticking the sword in a block of wood, to show it was sharp. We all stood and applauded again!

Then the music volume went down low and as the door to the dressing room opened, the father in his very deepest voice announced. The girls are now going to perform … The Dance of Desire!

The logs started to thump, thump, thump again and the dancers took the stage with black grass skirts and black coconut halter tops. The ladies did a wonderful dance and at the end the father said, "That concludes our presentation," all of us stood and clapped, he then said, "we will play dance music for your dancing pleasure for the next hour."

Then he came to the front of the stage and asked, "What did you think?"

My wife smiled and said, "That is exactly what we were looking for!" Great!

We sat at a table with the band and hammered out the contract and the lodging. We showed them the three-bedroom apartment on the second floor and explained it would not be available until the first of the month … they said no problem they had brought everything that they owned with them … so they would get a local motel room or two for the next week and a half, then move in upstairs.

I asked them about the lighting which was fair to poor during their demonstration. I asked if we needed to get someone to operate the lights. The band manager said if we gave him the light board (which controls all of the lights), he would learn how to operate it and he could control it during the show. Perfect!

The couple moved out of my two-room apartment a few days before the end of the month and my in-laws and sister-in-law cleaned the apartment until it was spotless. The furniture and the TV were delivered the next day. They set the entire apartment up and moved in the next day. My wife contacted the band and they moved right in over the restaurant.

As planned the kitchen equipment showed up and was installed on the second of the month and we were ready to go.

Our Grand Gala Opening was scheduled for Friday, so for a dress rehearsal we invited my entire family; aunts, uncles, mom and dad and my sister and her husband for dinner and a show. We had a little cocktail party (to test the bar), then we all ordered off the menu (to test the wait staff), a wide variety of meals were ordered (to check the cooks) and finally a show (to test the band) … we received rave reviews from all … everyone felt the food was outstanding … but the band was pheromonal! Great!

I had to tell the band manager what a difference the proper lighting made.

The Grand Opening went off without a hitch and through word-of-mouth and advertising we were booked solid, every night! Lunches, also, did very well. My wife was ecstatic!

As I was getting back into my businesses, my buddy B called to ask when I was available to go and look at the possible locations for our liquor stores. He had five locations for three stores. I said to line up all five owners and we would visit the stores the next day. B then said that we had not discussed what he would get paid or what percent he would get of the profits … I asked what he wanted and what he asked for, I felt was fair, so I agreed. Then, I called my Uncle T to explain what I wanted to do and to ask if he would come with me the next day. He agreed.

All of the locations were at least several blocks from my existing stores. Great!

I felt that the first location was perfect. I made the owner an offer … he laughed … I told him I would pay him in full by the end of the week … we had several more locations to look at and I could always change my mind … the owner agreed to take my offer. I called my attorney and asked him to draw up the papers … I would be paying from my new account (my ex-wife's account) … and I planned on buying two more places. I asked my lawyer to create a new corporation; Tony's Liquors, Inc.

The next place my uncle shook his head as we walked through, nope not interested. The next two locations were ideal, so I bought them, startling my uncle and my buddy. My Uncle T told me I was becoming an expert in negotiating. I told him that I would never be as good as he was.

When I got back to work, I called my attorney with the info for the second and third locations and I asked him if we could use his offices for the closings, no problem.

Then I called the architect to explain that I was buying three buildings and I wanted to turn them into liquor stores. I asked him to meet; my Uncle T, my partner B and myself at the first store that I bought at 1:00 pm the following Monday, he agreed.

Then I called my insurance guy to insure my three new buildings. Next, I called the sign shop and asked them to design the signs for each of my three new buildings … TONY'S LIQUORS.

When I got back to my office, my lead bookkeeper told me that C had called. I asked her to call C and tell him I was very busy and I would call him the following Tuesday.

Each of my existing stores had decorated for Halloween and were now changing over to Thanksgiving.

The closings went smoothly, all of the deeds were clear of any liens and on Monday we toured the three buildings with my architect and pointed out where we wanted coolers, counters and registers.

The following day, I called my buddy C. He said that he had identified several excellent locations for our used car business. We decided to go and take a look that afternoon. Once we got together, I mentioned to C, my concern over the haggling that people do with used car salesmen … what I suggested was we post the price for each car on our lot, right on the front window (we would determine that price by adding up what we paid for the car, how much we put into it and then our mark-up, determined by my accountant), and then no haggling, that would be the price. Take it or leave it. Just like everything in my grocery stores … when you picked up a can of beans the price was marked on it. If you didn't like the price, you didn't buy it … there was no haggling over the price. C thought it was a good idea. Great!

My other idea was to only offer the top selling cars (the top two or three models, from the top two or three companies), for quick turnover. C agreed and said that there were tons of cars coming off three-year leases. Great!

The first place C took me to was at the intersection of a major route and the highway … right next to one of my Gas and Goes. Perfect location, three buildings; a showroom building, with a glass front, a garage style building, with several bays to work on cars and a smaller two-story building, maybe for storage. Perfect!

Who owns it and how much do they want for it? C didn't know. There weren't any signs. So, we took a ride to the Town Hall. We found that the town had taken the property for taxes. The city assessor said that what was owed was about 60% of the value … I asked the building inspector to take us along for a quick tour of the buildings on the property, which he did … the buildings appeared to be in good condition … so when we returned to the Town Hall, I asked the mayor how much they wanted for the property … he said he just wanted the taxes paid in full and he wanted to see the property fixed up and operating again … I gave him my word that he would be pleased with what we planned on doing. We left the Town Hall and went straight to the bank to get a bank check for what the mayor said they wanted for the property. Then we went back to the Town Hall to pay-off the taxes and take ownership of the property.

C was impressed. I told him what my uncle had told me that if we were to wait a day or two the word would get out and someone else would have paid the taxes and would want us to pay a lot more for the property.

From my office, I called my attorney and had him create a new corporation, Tony's Used Cars, Inc. I asked him to contact the Town Hall and finalize any paperwork. Then I called my insurance agent to cover my new property.

After withdrawing the money for the liquor stores and the used car lot, I noticed it barely made a dent in what I had in my ex-wife's account. GREAT!

While my architect was drawing the first liquor store, I took my Uncle T for a tour of the buildings for my new used car lot. He agreed with me that it was a great location. Not a lot had to be done in the showroom but the garage was completely empty. My uncle suggested that I contact the company that remodeled my Gas and Goes. My uncle noted that the third building would make a great warehouse. There was a garage door opening on the second floor, where I could move everything that I was paying to be storied to. Great!

My uncle and I went to lunch at my new restaurant and later stopped by the car dealership that my uncle used to see his buddy the owner. My Uncle T told the guy about my new used car lot and the guy said there is only one thing to worry about … that is the titles for the cars … you must have someone you trust implicitly to control them. It is easy for someone to sell a car and keep all the money if they can get their hands on the titles! Good to know!

I shared this information with my lead bookkeeper. I asked if one of her girls could be trusted to run the used car office and keep tract of the titles. The answer was yes, she had just the right girl. We asked her if she was interested and she was excited for the opportunity!

I lined up my Gas and Go Manager, C and I to tour the buildings with the top guy from the company that did my Gas and Go remodels. He felt that there wasn't anything major that they needed except for an alignment machine. Fortunately, he knew where a used alignment machine was available. Also, he felt that we had everything we needed to outfit the garages in storage. We had plenty of lifts and compressors for example to choose from … the rest could be stored on the second floor of the third building. Great!

My Gas and Go manager said that he knew a great mechanic that was now working in one of the Gas and Goes but would love to get back into the garage. I told my manager to ask the fellow if he was interested … he was. Great!

All we needed was another salesman and a detail guy. I left that up to C.

In a blink, it was Thanksgiving Day.

We invited my in-laws and my sister-in-law over to my moms for a traditional Thanksgiving Day dinner. It was great, my wife's family thoroughly enjoyed the meal!

Then it was back to our restaurant to help with the onslaught of customers for the holyday. The restaurant was almost always packed to capacity which was great! Maybe we should have built a larger restaurant.

———————

My Uncle T had gotten started right away on the first liquor store and soon after, on the other two stores. The three buildings were slightly different but the designs were very similar. It would take until the first of the year to get the coolers, racks and registers delivered.

We planned to be open by the end of January. I left it up to B to hire and train all of the help.

I wanted to open all three stores simultaneously.

———————

My Uncle A painted the exterior of all three buildings bright white at my used car lot and I had a crew empty the showroom so my uncle could paint it as well. Then we had the floors polished, before we put the desks, etc. back into the showroom and offices.

There was a good fence all around the lot but we needed to have a very wide gate on wheels installed for security.

It didn't take much to put the garage together.

Throughout the month of December C and I would go to the auto auction to buy the kind of cars that we agreed on. Once we brought the cars to our lot each car was checked out by our mechanic and then detailed by our guy … then we would write the price on the front window and it was ready to be put up for sale.

I talked with the owner of the dealership that I bought my trucks from and I asked, what they did with the cars coming off lease … he said that it went through the service manager … they would keep some, but the others went to some guy that would give them a price and then get the car because there was no competition … and the service manager felt the guy was screwing them with the price. The owner told me that the next time they had a lease car for sale he would find out what the other guy offered. My mechanic or C would checkout the car and if we wanted it, we would bid $100 more than the other guy, if we didn't want it, we didn't bid on it. I would give the owner another $50 (on the side) for each car we got … and it was a lot of cars!

We had our new sign installed, TONY'S USED CARS, and beneath was printed, One Price – No Haggling.

We had our Grand Opening the day after New Year's … lots of people tried to haggle but we said we are sorry but the price on the car is what we will sell it for. We sold all the cars on the lot in four days and we took orders for more! I found this business exciting!

We had to buy a lot more cars at the auction and as I had time, I went to dealerships to line-up ways we could buy their excess previously leased cars. Our business went very well … most cars came and went fairly quickly.

Fortunately, back in October I added my wife to my mid-January cruise and we changed it from a singles cruise to a family cruise in the Caribbean.

On the first night of our cruise after dinner, cocktails and dancing, my wife and I headed back to our room. After a little foreplay, as I was reaching over my wife, to get a condom from the drawer … my face was directly over my wife's face when her face went serious … she looked me directly in the eyes from inches away and asked, "Why don't we make a baby on this cruise?" WOW!

I said, "What a great idea … I love children!"

And for the remainder of our cruise whenever we made love (and we made love a lot), we tried to make a baby!

Then during the day while we laid out in the sun we would ask each other, "Do you think we made the baby yet? Do you think it will be a boy or a girl?"

We went to shore each evening to look for island bands for backup. We found several … introduced ourselves and got their contact information.

As always, each day seemed like three days and by the end of our cruise we were totally relaxed and ready to get back to our daily activities.

When we returned from our vacation, it was time for the Grand Opening of our three … TONY'S LIQUOR stores. As usual, our advertising lady did an excellent job. We had a ton of customers from day one!

Just as B had always said … the liquor store business was very profitable!

Every evening, my wife and I would have dinner together. Either at our home or at our restaurant. When we dine together in our restaurant, we generally eat at a table in a corner out of the way. But this Thursday my wife wanted to eat at a table in front of the stage. She said that the band was going to try something new, so she also asked her folks and her sister to join us. My wife took my order and hers and then as usual she went into the kitchen to place our orders. A short time later it was time for the dancers to come out and do the dance of desire, instead the band manager announced that they were going to do something new, darn, my wife was still in the kitchen and going to miss it … the lights got brighter … the music started and my wife came out with a black coconut halter, a black grass skirt and a huge … fake … belly bump … she danced out to the middle of the stage and picked up a large sign for all to see. It said … HONEY WE ARE GOING TO HAVE A BABY!

The audience exploded with clapping and gave her a standing ovation … I climbed up onto the stage and we kissed and hugged … the audience clapped more … by then my wife's mom, dad and sister had come up the stairs onto the stage and they were as excited as me … they were jumping up and down kissing and hugging my wife. The word spread fast and the entire staff came out and stood around the stage all excited for my wife … they continued the hollering and clapping, it was pandemonium!

It took a while to get everyone calmed down and for my wife to put her normal clothes back on. When she came back to our table, she brought our dinners. As we ate, she told me that she went to her gynecologist at lunch time and couldn't wait to tell everyone … until she thought of how to surprise me. I told her that it was a great surprise and I could not be happier!

Next, we had to plan a surprise for my folks on Sunday.

What we did was, we put the belly bump in a grocery bag and covered it with a big bag of potato chips, the other bag was actually filled with groceries. When we arrived, I brought both bags into the kitchen. When my wife took off her raincoat, she went to put it in the closet, but then hightailed herself into the kitchen to get the belly bump. Then she went into the bathroom to put it on.

When she came out wearing the belly bump, she started to say and repeat, "Look what Tony did to me!"

My mother ran like a track star toward her to kiss and hug and congratulate her … my dad shook my hand and put his arm around my shoulders until my mom came to hug and kiss me … my sister and brother-in-law were whooping and hollering congratulations and little Tony was just running around laughing!

Of course, the big question was always when are you due! Mid-October. GREAT!

Mom had to run in the other room and call all of our relatives with the big news!

———————

Chapter 10

At my family birthday party, my wife appeared to be the center attraction. How she was feeling, what she needed for the baby and how long would she work? My sister said she would have a baby shower for her in a few months.

I thought it was great … the way my wife assimilated with my family!!

As the months progressed, it was amazing to see all of the changes my wife went through.

We painted our second bedroom and redecorated it with furniture and presents she received from my mom, my sister, her mom, her sister and from the myriad of presents that she received from the baby showers that her sister and my sister had for her!

Including a bassinet which we had in our bedroom.

The months flew by … finally our little present from heaven arrived.

My wife and I went around and around trying to come up with a name that was Italian and Oriental. We decided on Ava! It was perfect for our little bundle of joy!

My folks and my wife's parents couldn't get enough of our little girl. When they were around, I could hardly get her back!

My wife stayed home with Ava for the first six weeks but had a burning need to get back to work. Fortunately, one of the waitresses had a daughter who decided to take a year off from college and she was looking for a job. We interviewed her and hired her on the spot … she was perfect!

Before you knew it, it was time for the christening. At the christening party which was at our restaurant, my Uncle T pulled me aside and told me that he had a huge opportunity for me if I was interested. He asked if I could go and take a look first thing on Monday morning. Of course, I agreed.

My uncle picked me up at 8:00 am, Monday and he drove to the mall. When we arrived, he pulled into a partially completed development across the street from the main entrance to the mall.

It appeared to be a shopping center with a large store in the middle, several storefronts to either side and large storefronts on each end. The buildings (shells) looked complete, the parking lot was complete and my uncle informed me that the developer had gotten permits for the two pad sites on each side of the entrance to the parking lot.

My uncle explained that the developer was just about to finish the buildout of the stores when he got arrested for being a pedophile, he was sent to jail for a minimum of eight years. His construction company was closed and his wife was divorcing him.

Meanwhile, the bank was owed a lot of money and they were looking to unload the property for what they were owed, and something for the wife.

I was very interested. I asked my uncle how much the property was appraised for. He said it was a little over double what the bank wanted. I told my uncle we can put one of my grocery stores at one end, one of my liquor stores at the other end and a huge restaurant in the middle. In one of the smaller storefronts, I could put one of my salons and on the pad sites I could build a Gas and Go on one side and a pharmacy on the other. As I was explaining what I could do with the property I was getting more and more excited … and it rubbed off on my uncle.

Then he said, "It's going to take a big bundle of money to do this."

Only the bank manager and I knew how much money was in my ex-wife's account. So, I told my uncle … I was somewhat embarrassed to tell him how much I had … and with tears running down my cheeks I told him that I felt my ex-wife had sent me to this opportunity. My uncle felt I had much more money than what I would need to complete the project and asked if I wanted to go to the bank and finalize the deal.

I said, "No, I want to pass it by my wife first."

—————————

After lunch, my uncle went back to work and I went to our restaurant to pick up my wife. I told her I needed to show her something, and it would only take about an hour.

So, we drove over to the mall and I showed her the building and I explained what my plans were for the site. My wife became as excited as I was. She had to see what the restaurant area looked like. My uncle had given me the keys so we drove up in front of the building and went in. It looked expansive since it was wide open … it had a high ceiling and a second floor. There was an elevator but no electricity so we had to take the stairs. Of course, the second floor was almost identical to the first floor … massive!

My wife loooooved it! She said we could have a private room for weddings or parties which was difficult and next to impossible to do in our present restaurant.

On the way back to our restaurant, I asked my wife what she would do with our present restaurant. She said that she would have her sister run it, she was more than qualified. I asked if she could still be a good momma for our little Ava and she said Ava would always come first! Great!

So, when I got back to work, I called my uncle and asked him to set up an appointment with the bank on Tuesday.

Then I went over to see the bank manager. I told him my plans to purchase and buildout all of the stores. I explained that my plan was to wire the money the next day and I wanted him to know that it was alright to process the transfer. He said he would watch for it and make sure that the transfer went smoothly. Great!

When I got back to my office, I spoke with my attorney. We setup a new corporation for Tony's Shopping Center, Inc. My attorney checked for liens on the property and found only the bank and the property tax liens.

The next day, my uncle and I met with the vice president of commercial loans, regarding my purchasing the partially built shopping center. The first thing that I asked for was a copy of their latest appraisal. It confirmed what my uncle had told me. Next, we haggled over the price they were looking for … just a bit. I held to my guns and said I would wire in full what I was offering immediately. That seemed to finalize the deal … it was a large amount of money and the vice president questioned if my bank could cover it. I said it should not be a problem and he could call the bank manager to confirm.

I showed the VP the Purchase and Sale agreement my attorney had prepared and we closed the deal. The money was transferred before my uncle and I left the bank.

On Wednesday, my day off, my wife, Ava and I met my architect and my Uncle T at our shopping center for a walk through of each storefront. We concentrated on the ones that I had plans for first.

The first building we went through was for the grocery store. It was a little longer than my original store and a little wider. Fine, we can just about duplicate my first store.

Next, as we were walking over to what we were calling the restaurant storefront, my architect said that he felt a dry cleaner would be a good idea for that storefront.

My wife's head spun around when she heard that, she said, "My dad owned a dry-cleaning business in the old country."

"Terrific, we will have to talk to your dad," I replied.

As we toured the new restaurant building, my wife told the architect exactly how she wanted it laid out. A larger cocktail lounge, a larger kitchen since the room was much longer than the width, my wife suggested that the stage be placed in the middle to the right side. Then, we toured the second floor. My wife explained we needed a large storage room in the back. Leaving quite a large room for banquets. My uncle said we should have two dumbwaiter elevators for getting the food up to the room. When the meals were ready, the kitchen would place the dishes on the dumbwaiter and send them up to the second floor wait staff.

I called B and he met up with us to go over how we wanted to layout the liquor store on the end. It was much larger than the other three stores.

When we were done, my architect could get started.

We still needed to talk to my wife's dad regarding the dry-cleaning store and the one gal that hadn't come up with a location for a salon. Did she really want her own salon?

My wife's dad was excited when he heard about the prospect of a dry cleaners … that is what he loved to do! We told him we would take him over to see the storefront on Sunday late afternoon.

The next day, I called my ex-wife's first salon and invited the salon manager and the girl that didn't have a salon to go to lunch. We went for a quick lunch where I asked the girl directly, if she was still interested in having her own salon.

Her answer was, "Yes."

I drove them to the mall to show them the storefront next to the proposed liquor store … they were both impressed. The unit was much deeper than what was required for a salon … not to worry, we can come up with a use down the road. I think it scared the girl with no salon … she said she thought it was a lot for her to handle creating a new big salon.

The salon manager was bubbling over with enthusiasm for this salon.

I suggested, "Why don't you two switch salons?"

They both loved the idea and I think it was a good decision since the salon manager had a lot more experience running a salon. Therefore, we ultimately made the switch.

On the way back to their existing salon, I asked the salon manager to meet me on Monday, at 8:00 am to go over the layout with my architect.

On Sunday, at our family dinner I sprung the news that I had bought a partially built shopping center and what my ideas were to develop it. I asked everyone to come over and see it when we were done eating.

My wife and my sister helped my mom clean up. Then, we were off to meet up with my wife's dad.

My sister-in-law and my wife's mom and dad were waiting for us. Her dad could not wait to get inside.

I asked, "Do you think this will be large enough?"

He felt that given the depth of the building it would work out well. He had brought a pad of paper and was sketching how he would like to see it laid out.

I then took my family on a tour of the other storefronts, my proposed grocery store, a huge restaurant, a liquor store and a hair salon. Also, I pointed out where I planned to build a new Gas and Go and a new pharmacy, my brother-in-law yelled, "First dibs on managing it!"

"Of course," I said, "it's much closer to your house."

My mom pulled me aside and told me that she felt that I was out of control … that I was spending too much and creating more and more work for myself … she was worried about my health. I told my mother that I really appreciated her concerns but I do not work any more hours than I did when I had just one store … and I really enjoy what I am doing!

When everyone had enough of looking at empty buildings, my wife took the sketch her dad made and we packed the baby and all of her other paraphernalia into my car and we headed home.

Monday at 8:00 am, I met with the original salon manager, my architect and my Uncle T at my new shopping center. Initially, we toured the proposed salon storefront. We decided to set it up with a large customer waiting area, a central counter for checking in customers, setting appointments, and checking out customers, eight hair dressing stations, four hair washing basins and eight hair drying stations. The salon would not use up more than half of the unit, so we decided to put up a wall, with a door in the center. Behind the door to the right would be customer restrooms, to the left would be employee restrooms. Beyond that my uncle suggested tanning beds … where did my uncle get that idea … but we loved it! So, we decided to add ten tanning beds and ten shower stalls.

When we left the storefront, it was time for the salon manager to head off to work.

I showed my architect the sketch that my father-in-law had made of the proposed dry cleaners.

Immediately, my uncle said, "Hold on, I was speaking to my friends in New York and they told me about this guy to get the equipment from, he is a young oriental guy from the city. He has the most state-of-the-art equipment and the best prices … I asked him to stop over on Wednesday at 1:00 pm."

We decided to reconvene then.

Before he left, I asked my architect how he was doing with the blueprints for my new grocery store and my new restaurant … he told me that he may have them completed by our Wednesday meeting. Great!

When I got back to my office, there was a note requesting that I stop in and see the bank manager. After lunch with Mom, I went to the bank to see what the issue was. The bank manager asked if I had any room in my new shopping center to put a branch of his bank?

"Of course, we do," I said.

He told me he happened to take a ride by my new shopping center over the weekend and decided it would be an excellent location for a branch. He went on to inform me that he needed a storefront and a half … that would probably be okay, if he was next to the dry cleaners, since the dry cleaners would probably require more space than they would get in a single storefront.

On Wednesday, my Uncle T, my architect, my wife, Ava, my father-in-law and myself, all met the young fella from the city. He was very professional saying exactly how he would layout the store. He described what we needed for an entry, the counter and the in-take area and the electronic conveyor for the cleaned clothes. All of which he drew with chalk on the floor. Then he started to layout where all of the machinery would go … he decided we needed more space to adequately have the proper spacing between equipment. I offered half of the next storefront.

"Perfect," the fella said and we went into the adjoining storefront for the fella to complete his layout.

When he was done, he went to his car and returned with an order pad and a pricing booklet. As he walked around the storefront, he wrote down each machine that was required and added several racks. Also, we would need a skid of the plastic bags to cover the clean clothes and two skids of hangers.

Next, he priced each item then added it up to get a final price.

When the fella said how much it would come to my Uncle T shouted out, "Bullshit!"

My great big uncle put his great big arm around the tiny shoulder of this demure fella and they took a walk toward the back of the building … my uncle was speaking in a very low volume almost a whisper. When they came back, the guy said that the price he had given us did not include our discount which came to about 25%. WOW! Thank you, Uncle T, the best negotiator I ever met!

Before he left, the equipment salesman told us that he would put the order in when he got home to the city and it wouldn't take very long for the order to be ready. My Uncle T gave him his card and told him when the order was

100% ready, to have it delivered to him and he would store the equipment in his warehouse until it was needed.

My father-in-law walked out to the fella's car with him speaking in their original language and when he returned, my father-in-law was laughing heartily.

He said, "That guy is afraid of Uncle T."

My architect took pictures of the floor and also measured where the fella said each piece of equipment should go since the entire floor would need to be tiled (for cleanliness), before the equipment could be installed.

Also, my architect gave me and my Uncle The blueprints for my new grocery store and the new restaurant. WOW! I asked my Uncle T to go and pull the permits so his guys could get started on the construction phase.

When we got home, my wife could not wait to look at the blueprints of her new restaurant. She was delighted to see how it would look when it was completed! Almost twice the seating capacity, of our existing restaurant, in the main dining room and room for 250 people on the second floor. Outstanding!

The next few days were devoted to the Thanksgiving holiday. I made my rounds to my various businesses. On Saturday afternoon, I stopped in at my new used car dealership and my buddy C, told me that everything was going great. When they get really busy even the girl from the office comes out and sells cars (because the price is on the windshield and there is no haggling).

C took me aside and said that he would like to add a foreign car lot. Same idea as our present lot … we would offer cars coming off lease … the two or three most popular models … from the two or three largest manufacturers. He went on to say that there was a perfect place a mile down the highway, on the opposite side of the road.

We took a ride down to what formerly appeared to be a new car dealership. Vacant for a number of years. A nice sized showroom and a vacant eight bay garage.

I asked, "Who owns it?"

C said, "I think it is still owned by the company that owned the dealership."
I said that I would look into it.

On Monday, I went to the Town Hall to see who owned the property. It was the company that had a number of dealerships in our general area. The building inspector told me that the company consolidated all of their dealerships into one area and closed the location I was interested in.

That night, I called my Uncle T and I told him about the property I was looking at and why I was interested in it. I asked him if he knew anyone in the group that owns the property and went on to say that I felt I could use someone with his superior negotiating skills to hammer out a deal with a real car salesman. My uncle said he was always happy to help out and he would make a few calls to find out who to talk to … and he would get back to me, probably Monday or Tuesday afternoon.

My Uncle T called me on Wednesday morning to inform me that I now owned the vacant dealership on the highway. He told me that it was ultimately owned by one of his friends in New York. The guy was looking to unload it and sold it to my uncle for even less than the appraised value. My uncle received the bill of sale early that morning.

I asked how my uncle could have gotten the money to the guy so quickly and my uncle laughed and said that the guy owed my uncle and they are even now!

My uncle went to the Town Hall paid the back taxes and transferred ownership of the property. Then he told me that we could settle up down the road.

I asked my uncle if he and the architect could meet me at the lot the next day. No problem.

The next morning, my architect, my uncle, C and me, all met at our new foreign car lot. We went through the showroom which was in excellent condition it just needed a thorough cleaning. The garage building had eight bays, we only needed four bays, three with lifts and one for detailing. The garage building was empty except for the office which wasn't required. The asphalt lot was in good condition as were the roofs.

When I got back to my office, I called the cleaning company to schedule a total cleaning, including waxing the floors. I called the company that modified my Gas and Goes to have them come and outfit three garage bays. They told me that we still had a number of good lifts that they could use.

Next, I called my Gas and Go manager, to see if he knew of any foreign car mechanics. He did, he said the guy was terrific with foreign cars and he would contact him. I told him that I could use another mechanic and a detail guy ... he said he would keep an eye out for them.

Then I had a talk with my lead bookkeeper, I told her we would need to find someone to work in the office at our new foreign car dealership. She said we could have one of the girls that was working for her in the office ... she went on to say that all of her girls wanted to work in the used car office since they heard how much the girl in our present used car office liked it! Great!

In the meantime, C went to work, buying the type of foreign cars we had agreed on and we stockpiled them behind the garage in our new lot. C was also in charge of finding two more salesmen, scheduling the installation of the telephones, electric and water.

Early December, I went to the sign shop to order a sign, for my new car lot ... TONY'S USED FORIGN CARS, and beneath was; One Price – No Haggling.

We received a CO (Certificate of Occupancy) late in December and had our Grand Opening the first week in January. It was a terrific success because we were offering low mileage, popular vehicles at a reasonable price.

The following week, my wife and I went on our annual cruise vacation. It was such a pleasure to get away from the everyday challenge of juggling all of our different duties. I especially enjoyed my wife; she was fun, interesting and very sexual!

We traveled in the Caribbean and explored the various islands. On one island that sold gold and gold jewelry at exceptionally low prices, I bought my daughter her first birthday present … tiny gold earrings! I told my wife that we had to keep this a secret from Ava until her birthday in October!

We generally found time to lay out on chaise lounges in the sun each day.

One day my wife turned to me and asked, "When will it be enough?"

I knew exactly where she was going, so I said, "You sound like my mother … she has asked me that exact question, a number of times … my answer is, I had enough after I bought my first grocery store … since then I have been offered some fantastic deals … too good to ignore … some have been emotional, but I think each decision has been good … I have turned down tons of requests … I do not plan on making any more purchases of property in the future."

My wife started laughing, she said, "You are an enterpreneur-aholic … you cannot stop yourself from buying and developing companies."

I replied, "Since we have gotten married, I have passed all of my ideas past you … and you have agreed with me … you are an enabler!"

The two of us laughed, kissed and ordered two more chocolate-banana, frozen mudslides. We weren't too worried about our waistlines while we were on vacation.

I have to say that my wife had done a phenomenal job of getting her shape back after having our child. She turned our rec room in the basement into a workout room. She got up early every morning, seven days a week and she busted her butt working out to get back her core strength and to lose the excess weight she had gained. I have to say she looked great!

One night after a day that seemed like four days, as we were playing around in the bed, I had to reach over her to get a condom from the bedside drawer … it was like de ja view … I looked down into her face as she was looking straight up into my eyes and I said, "We make no babies on this cruise … maybe next year!"

She replied, "You must be reading my mind!"

As usual we couldn't have been more relaxed and refreshed and ready for the everyday pressures of our jobs when we returned.

Interestingly when we got back to work and I stopped by my shopping center to see how everything was going I noticed a yellow note stuck to the door of one of the vacant storefronts.

It read, "I am looking for a storefront to put in a jewelry store … if you have one available, please call me," and he left his telephone number.

When I got back to my office, I called the fella to tell him that I had two storefronts available. I told him that I felt a jewelry store would be an excellent addition to my shopping center. I went on to say that we planned an April first Grand Opening and we could have his store ready by then as well. I said that I would have my attorney fax him our lease agreement in the morning.

He asked if there were other storefronts available. I told him there was one more next to the one he planned to put his jewelry store in. He said his brother (who had a chain of shoe stores) was also interested. I said, "Great, I will have my attorney fax over a lease agreement for a shoe store as well."

I called my attorney and asked him to prepare and fax lease agreements for the jewelry store and the shoe store in the morning. He said that he felt that we should have lease agreements in place for all of the stores in my shopping center (we only had a lease agreement with the bank). I told him that we had been recalcitrant in not getting lease agreements with all of the principal owners of the other storefronts!

So, I asked my attorney to create the lease agreements for each of the other storefronts and I would pick them up the next afternoon and get them signed.

Well, the grocery store, dry cleaner and liquor store all had to be signed by me and the restaurant lease had to be signed by my wife. We did all of the signing after dinner.

When all of the dry-cleaning equipment was installed. The young fella that had sold it to us, came to show my father-in-law how to run, maintain and repair the equipment.

So, the dry-cleaning crew could get experience, I went around to all of my relatives to collect clothing to be cleaned. I got rave reviews from everyone that they were happy and impressed with what a good job the cleaners had done!

On the first week in April, all of the stores were complete and we had our Grand Opening of my shopping center and it was OUTSTANDING!

It was like these customers were coming out of the woodwork!

Our new restaurant opened with a BANG! Based on the success of our first restaurant, our customers flocked to our new fancy restaurant!

Our first restaurant was still open and run by my sister-in-law. We had hired one of the island bands that we saw on our cruise. They were a little different from our original band but they were excellent in their own right.

Meanwhile, my new pharmacy, the biggest yet and my new Gas and Go were not scheduled to be complete until June. My Uncle T was building the pharmacy and the gas station reno guys were building the Gas and Go. They were taking a bit longer because they were built from scratch, plus we had to wait for permits.

Chapter 11

This year at my birthday party my little girl was the center of attraction. At times, it was like a tug-of-war trying to get to hold her. Little Tony was a bit jealous but he got plenty of attention from each of us as well.

At the table, my mom asked, "I hope there are no more announcements today!"

We all laughed!

Early in June, we had the Grand Opening for my new pharmacy and my new Gas and Go. There were lines at the gas pumps and packed aisles in the pharmacy as well.

It takes time to build the pharmacy business because you need to have customers have their prescriptions sent to your new pharmacy. Fortunately, as the days passed, we seemed to get lots of prescription orders.

I promised! I promised! I promised my wife and my mom that I would not spend any more money on my ideas … that was it … I am done … I am not buying any more businesses!

Fortunately, my new dry-cleaners business was very successful. Women liked dropping off their dry cleaning on the way to the grocery store. I even got requests from a lot of customers at my other grocery stores for dry cleaning services.

So, I had an idea to add an area in my other existing grocery stores where customers could drop-off their dry cleaning and pick up the cleaned clothes. I discussed it with my wife and she felt it was an outstanding idea. I also asked my father-in-law if he liked the idea (which he did) and he felt that he had plenty of capacity.

I called the young salesman in New York city and we made an appointment to meet at my original grocery store.

When he arrived, I explained that many of my customers told me that they would like to be able to drop off their dry cleaning when they come to shop and pick up the cleaned clothes the following week as they were leaving.

The way the store was laid out, there was 20 feet from the entry door to the butcher's coolers. The salesman felt that was more than adequate to have a drop-off and pick up area.

He recommended an L-shaped counter which would start at the wall, adjacent to the doorway and end at the coolers. He continued by saying that I needed a clothes carousel, which he suggested would start by the coolers, run toward the back wall and make a right turn toward the doorway. There would be a three-foot section of counter top which could be lifted up so employees could enter or exit the area.

The salesman took dimensions for the carousel and although the three grocery stores were laid out similarly, we still went to each store to confirm the layout and the dimensions.

Additionally, the salesman felt I should order the cloth bags to put the incoming clothes in. He said the bags should be color coded for each store so that the clothes always get returned to the correct store.

So, the salesman wrote up the order for three carousels and a large number of cloth bags, color coded.

When I looked at the price, I asked, "Does this include my 25% discount?"

"Oh yeah," the young salesman replied. He took the order pad and subtracted 25%. Then he said that he would call the next day with delivery information.

The next day the salesman called to say that it would take three to four weeks and that they would deliver everything to my Uncle T's warehouse. Great!

Later, I called my Uncle T and asked him to stop over when he had a chance. He suggested 8:00 am the next day.

I told my uncle what my plan was and showed him a sketch of how I planned to lay out the area. I said that I would like all three stores to be complete in three weeks. My uncle asked what I wanted the counter top to be made of. I said Formica would be fine. Then, my uncle reminded me that we needed the architect to make blueprints so we could show the building inspector what we planned to do. My Uncle T told me that he would give my sketch to the architect and get him going on the prints.

The next day, I went to the sign store and had them print three identical signs reading;

The future home of
Tony's Dry Cleaning
Three-day turnaround
coming in July

When the signs were completed, I picked them up and taped them to the walls in my three grocery stores.

In the interim, C and I looked for a good used van at the auto mall. We were fortunate to find a low mileage, four-year-old, panel van that was perfect for our use. My father-in-law had a young fella that could drive it around to the stores each afternoon to pick-up dirty laundry and drop off cleaned laundry.

At our Sunday family lunch, my mom said, "I see you are at it again … adding dry cleaning to the grocery store!"

My reply was, "So what do you think about it?"

My mom said, "It's a great idea … I can't believe someone didn't think to do it earlier!"

By the time the carousels showed up, my uncle's guys had the counters complete and they built a dividing wall between the coolers and the drop-off area. They also ran the electrical power to the cash register (on the counter) and ran power overhead for the carousels.

The assembly of each carousel took one day and then we were ready for customers. During slower times we had a cashier go back and forth to the drop-off counter but during busier times we needed a dedicated girl.

It was amazing how easy this new service was to provide and how lucrative it was!

———————

My wife and I were kept very busy by our businesses. My new shopping center added a lot of work since it wasn't like opening one business it was more like opening five new businesses, which is what it was!

The new restaurant was so much larger and more difficult to run than our first restaurant, it really kept my wife busy.

Then our little bundle of joy required more and more of our time as she grew.

But what a wonderful life … my wife and I loved what we were doing for work … we loved each other so much … and we loved our little girl, watching her grow and learn was amazing!

In October, we threw a huge backyard one-year-old party for my daughter. We invited all of my relatives and all of my in-laws. It was fun … we set up tables on the back lawn and we had it catered. Of course, we had plenty of wine and beer. Everyone got along very well! It was an outstanding day!

———————

The rest of the year just flew by and before we knew it, it was mid-January and time for our annual cruise.

On the flight south, my wife slid over against me in our seats and asked, "Are we going to make another baby on this cruise?"

I said, "That is entirely up to you … when and if you feel it is the time to make babies, then I am in!"

She smiled as she looked up into my eyes, and said, "I think it is time to make another baby."

My reply was, "Great but you'll have to wait until we get to the cruise ship!"

We hugged and kissed on the plane and when we got to our room on the ship we didn't even stop to unpack before we tried to make another baby.

We tried to make a baby every night, most mornings and often in the afternoon. Practice makes perfect!

As in the past, we had a wonderful relaxing vacation!

Back at work it was important for us to keep our finger on the pulse of what was happening. Each month I would ask my wife if she was pregnant yet. Not yet. So, we kept trying.

In May, my wife informed me that her home pregnancy test showed positive, so she made an appointment with her doctor. Guess what … she was pregnant … YIPEE!

Chapter 12

On Sunday at our family dinner, at my birthday party, I stood up and announced that we were pregnant. Just like the last time my mom started to scream and jumped out of her chair to hug and kiss my wife … my sister was right behind her … then my mom attacked me with warm kisses and hugs … my dad, my brother-in-law and my sister, all congratulated me. It was like we were the first ones to ever have a child!

Of course, as soon as dinner was over my mom made a beeline for the telephone to call all of our relatives with the big news. My sister and my wife cleaned up the dishes and the kitchen.

Later, we went to my in-law's apartment to spring the great news on them. They were just as excited as my family! Great!

––––––––––––

Monday, first thing my Uncle T called to see if I was free … he wanted to show me something, I said, "Sure."

We met at 9:00 am at my new shopping center … as my uncle drove up into the hills, he told me that now that I had a second child on the way, I needed a larger home and he had the perfect home for me and my family!

We drove to the richest neighborhood in the state and then onto the richest road in that area. As he drove up the hill the mansions became larger and larger. WOW! What a beautiful area. At the very top of the hill at the end of the cul-de-sac, was what appeared to me to be a castle! It was huge, all gray granite, with a round section (a turret) to one side of the imposing front door. It had a circular driveway in the front and fantastic landscaping as far as the eye could see!

My uncle pulled into the driveway up near the front door turned in his seat toward me and with a huge smile said, "Welcome to your new home!"

I laughed at the idea, and said, "No way!"

My uncle explained that the guy who owned and built the home was brought over from England to be the president of the local aircraft company, by far the largest employer in our state. They paid him millions of dollars per year and he did a poor job over the past three years so they fired him and he went directly back to England. Leaving his mansion and furniture behind and an extremely large loan.

As we walked up to the front door, I noticed that my uncle had lost a lot of weight.

I asked, "Have you been on a diet?"

My uncle laughed and replied, "Yes."

My uncle had always been a big, husky, kind of guy, but now the husky part was gone and he looked fit … good for him!

The front door was huge, solid mahogany, with brass hardware, oval at the top to fit the contour of the inset entryway.

As we walked in it was nothing short of magnificent! The foyer was gigantic! It was sort of circular with a wide winding staircase to each side, with a ceiling that was three stories high. The floor consisted of very large, white marble tiles … but the most outstanding feature was that you could look straight through the great room to the back wall of the house which consisted of an entire wall of floor to ceiling glass, divided in the middle by a magnificent granite fireplace with the granite reaching the ceiling … just breathtaking.

These two rooms were so large it would fit two of my houses, one on top of the other, with room to spare. WOW!

The white marble floors extended into the great room but on the floor in the middle was what looked like a ten-foot diameter black compass design … beautiful!

In the great room were several very large, fluffy looking sofas, along with several large, fluffy looking chairs, all shockingly white. Contrasted by a jet black, full size, grand piano, with large gold framed pieces of art on the walls … outstanding! In the right corner of the great room was a beautiful, full-sized carved wooden bar with a black granite top … fully loaded! Behind the bar to one side was a wine refrigerator and on the other side was a half size refrigerator and in the middle were two taps coming from another refrigerator made just for this use! On the wall behind the bar was a large mirror and in front of the mirror were several shelves with every kind of liquor you could think of. Below were cabinets full of a variety of glasses, napkins and small plates.

Between the foyer and the great room to the left was a wing with a large hallway closet for coats and jackets, across from a large powder room. Further down the hall was a massive master bedroom the back wall was all glass looking out over the magnificent Roman style gunite concrete swimming pool. The bed must have been special ordered … what else was new, because it was the largest, four poster super king-sized bed I have ever seen, sitting on a pedestal. Toward the front where two walk-in closets (his and hers), each one big enough to fit my entire family's wardrobes … outstanding! Further toward the front (across the hall) was the largest master bathroom that I could have ever imagined! To the front under the windows was a huge white soaker tub set down into a white marble surround which was three steps up from the white marble floor. To one side was a huge walk-in shower for at least two! There were a variety of shower heads: two on the ceiling (12 feet high), several fixed and several more shower heads with hand held sprayers. Next to the shower was a cabinet with plush, heated, warm towels. Across from the shower was the massive vanity with two inset marble sinks. The walls were all white with gray graining, book matched marble. All of the fixtures were gold plated … of course!

The wing to the other side of the house included a massive kitchen with state-of-the-art appliances, on the back wall was an alcove with a table and a built-in banquette and several Edwardian style high back chairs. In the center was an elliptical shaped island with a sink … to the stove side was seating for four on Edwardian style stools, on the other side. On the wall opposite the stove were all cabinet doors. In the middle was a large cabinet door leading to a big hidden walk-in pantry.

Toward the front of the house was a mammoth dining room! In the center was a massive table. The top was one, four inch thick, four foot wide and 12-foot-long piece of mahogany, supported by big thick round pedestal supports. The table was surrounded by 18 large heavy looking Edwardian style, high back chairs, with white suede cushions on the seat and on the back. On one wall was a 12-foot-long buffet with a matching China closet on top. On the other wall was a large oil painted picture of a king walking in a flower garden surrounded by an ornate gold frame.

Between the kitchen and dining room was a door leading to the humongous mud room and through another door to the spacious four car garage.

On the second floor, over the kitchen wing were four good size ensuite bedrooms each with a queen size four poster bed and very spacious closet.

Over the master bedroom wing was an incredible study with a wall of glass looking out toward the back, with a balcony (from the balcony I could see a lighted tennis court, surrounded by an eight-foot-high fence, the landscaping was breathtaking). The walls of the study consisted of floor to ceiling mahogany book shelves. In the center was an oversized carved mahogany desk, with a super plush looking chair … with white leather seat and back cushions. There were three similar guest chairs facing the desk.

Across the hall was a large bathroom next to a completely fitted out exercise room.

In the center section of the basement was a full-size carved mahogany pool table with white felt top. Since there were no windows, there was an incredible system to filter the air.

To one end of the basement was a full bathroom. At the far end of the basement was a movie theater with plush white leather recliners for twelve. Outstanding!

We entered the back yard through a sliding glass door in the kitchen (there was a matching door in the master bedroom), onto a large half-round gray granite deck with ornate railings. From the deck was a 10-foot wide three step stairway to the huge roman shaped swimming pool with a raised heated spa to the right, a diving board at the end and a very wide patio to the left with a 12 foot by 12-foot pergola in the middle. Beautiful!

On the deck and on the patio, there was a plethora of white chairs and lounges.

The landscaping was fantastic! Behind the diving board was a granite pool house. It consisted of a good-sized living room with a TV and a large refrigerator. In the back were two large bathrooms, with showers and closets, for changing. In the back of the pool house was the equipment room containing the pool pump, filter and natural gas heater.

To the left was a path to the tennis courts and to the right was a path back to where the garages were.

In this area the lots consisted of two, very expensive, acres. This property covered four lots, every inch immaculately landscaped and manicured. Outstanding!

On the way back to his truck, I told my Uncle T that there didn't appear to be any expense spared in building this house. He agreed and he told me that the aircraft company felt that the owner had spent too much time thinking about building this house and not enough time thinking about his job!

When we got back into his truck, my uncle reminded me again that with another child coming, I needed a larger house and this house would be perfect now and if we had more children in the future. I told my Uncle T that this house was fantastic but I couldn't afford it. My uncle disagreed. He asked me what I planned to spend on a larger house. I told him what I planned to spend and he told me that I could own this house for just a little more than I planned to spend. No way!

My uncle said that the bank was pissed at the guy for just leaving the country and leaving them to continue to pay the taxes and for the gardeners to keep up the yard. Each week it was costing the bank more and more on a house that had been abandoned. My Uncle T told me how much to offer the bank and then I would own it. How could I argue with the price? I asked my uncle if I could show my wife the house and get her opinion.

My uncle said, "Sure, why not … but let's do it quickly."

We drove back to our new restaurant and I ran in to tell my wife that I had just found a house that I thought she would love as much as I do, but she had to leave with me right then to go and look at it. She asked one of the servers to fill in for her and then, her, my uncle and I headed back up into the hills to show my pregnant wife the house of my dreams!

As we drove closer and closer to the house, my wife kept commenting on how nice and how beautiful the homes were. When we reached the top of the hill and my uncle pulled into the driveway, my wife exclaimed, "This is a castle!"

I said, "No … this is your castle!"

She started to cry – pregnant girls are very emotional. I hugged her tightly and said, "Come, you haven't seen anything yet!"

When she walked through the front doors, she almost fainted it was a good thing I was holding onto her, she said, "This … is … spectacular!"

We led her through the great room, then into the master bedroom, my wife's little eyes were the size of saucers. When she saw her walk-in closet, she told us that she had lived in apartments that were smaller! As we walked through the house, my wife was amazed at the size, the quality and the beauty of each room. Then we went outside. My wife really appreciated the detail in the gardening and the magnificence of the swimming pool!

Overall, my wife said that it was the most beautiful house she had ever seen or could ever imagine … but we couldn't afford it.

I explained that we could buy the house for just a little bit more than what we planned to spend on a larger house … and I had the money in one of my accounts.

With tears running down her cheeks, she said, "Then let's buy it!"

We were all emotional.

After we dropped my wife off at our restaurant, we went directly to my uncle's bank. We walked straight into the bank president's office. My uncle introduced me and the president told me how much the bank appreciated my helping them out in the past. My uncle said I was there to help out again. He went on to explain how the bank got stiffed by the Englishman and I wanted to make an offer to take the property off their hands for a fair price.

After I made my offer, the president called the bank treasurer to come to his office with the file for the property that I was interested in. The president asked the treasurer what was owed to the bank on the property. It was slightly less than my offer (thanks to my uncle). The bank president smiled and told the treasurer what I had offered. The treasurer felt that my offer was a bit low. The president told him that my offer would make them whole and anything I paid over my present offer would go to the Englishman that was stiffing them. The treasurer acquiesced and my offer was accepted. YIPPEE … HIP HIP HURRAH!

I transferred the money and received a clear letter from the bank. When we got outside, I mentioned to my Uncle T that it appeared that the president of the bank was on our side. My Uncle T told me that the president of the bank was on the Board with him … he then looked straight into my eyes and said, "He is one of my friends!"

Meaning his friend, like the friends from New York, also Board members!

That night, my wife and I celebrated big time with ginger ale floats!

The next day I called my attorney to ensure the paperwork was completed to his satisfaction and I called my insurance agent to fully insure my new house.

Then I started to plan for our move … I wanted to do it so my wife would not need to be involved because of her pregnancy. Really with all the furniture that was in the new house there was little that we needed, other than our clothes and our tooth brushes.

I called a professional mover and scheduled our move for Friday. We needed to set up a baby's room with a monitor back to our bed room and we needed to set up a child's room, with a junior bed for my daughter also with a monitor. Of course, we would have a bassinette in our room for the new baby for the first several months.

The movers told me that they would store the furniture from the existing bedrooms in our basement storage room, until needed.

On Wednesday, my wife and I went out and bought our daughter a child's bed and bureau. We also bought a rocking chair for the new baby's room. Plus, we picked out and purchased two sets of the most expensive monitors that they had. All to be delivered, Friday, to our new home.

On Friday morning, when we got up, I immediately emptied the contents of my bedside drawers into a large plastic bag, which I put in my car trunk. I would have been greatly embarrassed if one of the movers had opened those drawers to find my cache of condoms!

The movers came early, as expected. They took all of our clothes from our closets. Took everything from our drawers. Emptied out all of the food from our kitchen cabinets, we left all of the silverware and dishes. They took all of the wine from my office, using the crates that they were displayed in. They took everything from my daughter's room, plus I got a box and put all of the timers and all of the electric candles in it. They packed all of our workout equipment and everything from the garage. We left everything around the pool, but we took the gas grill.

My wife drove the sedan, I drove my pickup truck and the movers followed me to our new house.

When we arrived, the movers exclaimed what a beautiful house and neighborhood it was.

By mid-afternoon, we were completely moved in and my wife barely had to raise a finger!

I had the idea of how we could show our parents our new house. We would call our parents (and my sister) and invite them over for a special lunch. We told them to meet us at noon on Sunday in front of our new restaurant. Then, I called my Uncle T and invited him and my aunt. I asked him not to tell anyone about my new house. I also asked him to meet up with our families on Sunday and have them follow him to our new house.

It worked perfectly!

In the interim, I hired the Italian bakery lady and her husband to come and cook our meal … they did catering, on the side. They showed up at 10:00 am and brought in everything that they needed. The meal was already cooked, it just needed to be warmed up at the right moment. The couple loved my new house and kept telling me so. When all of their boxes were in the kitchen and unpacked. I took them both on a quick tour of my new home … they loved it … of course!

When the husband noticed the bar in the great room, he volunteered to be the bartender. Great!

My wife and I were on the front stoop as my Uncle T led the caravan into our front driveway. As everyone got out of their cars they were in awe of the grandeur of our new home.

"What's this?" my sister yelled.

"My new house," was my reply.

That was greeted by a chorus of 'No ways!'

My wife and I were beaming with joy (and pride) as my mom and dad came up to us and asked, "Is it true?"

Simultaneously we responded, "Yes!"

My mom and dad hugged and kissed us and congratulated us over and over.

When my mom walked into the house, she turned back to me and said, "When … will you stop spending money?"

I didn't reply, I just smiled and hugged and kissed and welcomed my sister, little Tony and my brother-in-law. Next came my in-laws and sister-in-law, so excited they were talking in their native language at a mile a minute. You could see on her face how proud my wife was … my face was most likely similar. Next, came my Uncle T and my aunt.

As I kissed my aunt she said, "This house, this lot, this neighborhood, is breathtaking!"

I think that summed up what everyone was thinking.

We traveled into the great room, while everyone got a drink of their choice. My mom recognized the bartender and asked about his wife … he called to her and when she came from the kitchen my mom and her kissed and hugged and my mom was surprised to see her at my house. The lady explained that she and her husband had a catering business on the side and I had hired them to help out with dinner.

Next, I took my family into the master bedroom wing as my wife took her family up the stairs to the study. The women kept commenting on how pretty the rooms were and the men kept commenting on how nice and how intricate the wood work was! Mom noticed the bassinette next to our bed and commented that we were ready for the new baby.

In the master bath, the shower was so large, that my mom, dad, sister and her husband, all walked in and there was still room for my aunt and uncle but they didn't choose to go in.

I showed them the heated towel closet and they were further impressed!

We continued up the stairs to the study, everywhere we went I could hear, "Wow … look at that … Oh my god!" (That's exactly how I felt the first time I came through).

My dad pulled me aside to ask, "Are you sure you can afford this place?"

My answer was, "I own it outright, no mortgage … all I have to pay for are the taxes and the upkeep."

My dad smiled, shook his head and said, "Good for you son!"

Next, we crossed over the bridge toward the bedroom wing.

When my mom reached the middle of the bridge, she said, "OH MY GOD … look at the swimming pool!"

My sister said, "Look to the left, there's a full-size tennis court!"

"And it is lighted at night," was my reply.

Mom continued but was shaking her head. I showed them a bedroom and explained that all four bedrooms were exactly alike when I bought the house. Then we went into Ava's room which dwarfed her little furniture, ditto for our expectant baby's room. I explained that the original furniture was stored in our basement storage room. We made our way down to the kitchen which couldn't have smelled better.

The Italian lady said, "Look at these appliances … top of the line!"

Two dishwashers, an eight-burner stove, two sets of double ovens, plus they were amazed with the amount of storage, in the pantry.

As we walked into the dining room, my wife and her family were already seated. The Italian lady asked us to take our seats, dinner was ready. I sat at one end, my uncle and aunt to my left, next to my wife's family … to my right were my mom, dad, sister, little Tony and my brother-in-law … my wife sat at the other end (with Ava next to her).

I stood up with my drink and said, "I want to thank my Uncle T for showing me this house and for showing me how I could afford it!"

My wife and the Italian lady had determined ahead of time what the menu would be. We started with Egg Drop soup, next came a crisp green Cesar salad, with a loaf of hot sliced Italian bread and the main course was Veal Scallopini … everything was outstanding! For dessert, we had a white cake covered with gobs of whip cream, strawberries and peaches. Everyone (especially little Tony) enjoyed the cake!

When we were all done with our meals, I took them outside to see the pool and the pool house. Then I took them down into the basement where they were surprised to see a full-size pool table and another big-time bar! My father, uncle, brother-in-law and myself played a couple of games of pool, while my wife took everyone else into the Theater Room.

I could hear a chorus of 'Oh my god's', coming from the room. My wife put on a TV program but when the guys were finished playing pool, we went into the theater room and I put on a first run spy movie to show off the sound system. Everybody loved the show but by the end they were ready to go home.

Each person told my wife, then me, how lucky we were to have such a beautiful home! My wife and I had to agree … we were fortunate … but we had worked for it!

I noticed several times my mom asking my Uncle T if he was feeling alright, he had lost a lot of weight. Each time she asked, he smiled and said he was on a diet … but he didn't look healthy.

———————

The next day my mom called to invite me to lunch. She told me what a great time they had and what a beautiful house I had. I told my mom that I had to get a larger home with the second baby on the way and my new home had plenty of room for more children.

My mom told me that I should have an open house for all of our relatives and friends. I told my mom that I felt that would be showing off.

Mom looked me in the eye, shrugged her shoulders and said, "Exactly!"

She went on to say, "I am so proud of my son … and what you have accomplished … it's time to show off!"

WOW! Mom was never like that. Mom went on to tell me that my dad had told her that I had no mortgage on my new home. Which was true. That's what really impressed her!

So, I asked my mom when do you plan to have the Open House? Her answer was the next Sunday. She had already scheduled the Italian bakery lady and her husband … she said we can have an open bar and hot hors d'oeuvre passed around. Mom said she would call our relatives and I could call my friends. Schedule the Open House from noon to 5:00 pm, she told me.

I hired a fellow to play the piano during the Open House and I called my buddies; A, B and C and invited them. That night when we got home, I told my wife about the Open House and had her call her family and invite their friends as well.

My wife thought to ask the girl that watches our daughter, during the week to come and watch her during the Open House.

———————

I asked the piano player to start playing before our company arrived so that they would not be coming into a quiet house. His music filled all the rooms of the house. Perfect!

A gang showed up a few minutes after noon. One was my buddy C. He said, "Hey everybody we must have gotten the wrong address!"

Just to bust my chops.

My wife and I welcomed our guests as they came in. We pointed them toward the bar. It was warm but a few ladies had brought their coats which I took and put into the closet in the foyer. As you would expect, a crowd gathered around the bar.

I left my wife at the door and asked the crowd if anyone would like a tour of my house. Most of them followed me toward the Master Bedroom wing. As I led them around the house there were many, "Uwe's and awes," and a few, "oh my god's!"

By the time I had made the circuit, another group had gathered around the bar. I asked my wife if she would like to take the next group on a tour and she said she felt better just sitting by the door, plus she had enlisted my sister to hang up coats in the closet.

So, I took the next group on a tour … with the same reactions as the first group. When we returned, there were several couples dancing in the foyer to the piano music! Everyone seemed to be enjoying themselves, so I paid the piano player and the bartender to work until 7:00 pm.

Come the first of October our baby was born … a six-pound, eight-ounce, baby boy! What a delightful surprise for both my wife and I! We would have been happy with another girl but I think we both were hoping for a boy.

My sister had, had a baby shower for my wife and we were inundated with tons of diapers and duplicates of everything you could ever use for a baby!

I have to say that my wife was the perfect baby making machine, but I think two children was enough … she agreed!

The work involved with having one child isn't bad but the work involved with having two children is all of a sudden equal to having three children!

Fortunately, we had excellent help. From the girl that we hired.

In mid-December, we had a christening for our little baby boy … Antione Ferducci, Jr. … we named him after … ME! We agreed to call him AJ not to confuse him with my sister's son little Tony.

We had the christening party, upstairs in the banquet room of our restaurant … It was great! Except every time I saw my Uncle T, he looked worse … and thinner!

My wife and I decided to move her family into our old house. They loved the idea. So, I had a company go through and give the house a deep cleaning, plus I had my Uncle A repaint the baby's room gray, for my sister-in-law. There wasn't much furniture needed, just my sister-in-law's bedroom set needed to be moved from the apartment. I got a bunch of cardboard boxes from the moving company so that my in-laws could pack up all the stuff in the kitchen and other things.

We moved them in on the last Sunday before year end. My brother-in-law and I went into the clothes closets and took arm loads of clothes and put them in his back seat carefully, so we wouldn't wrinkle them. Then we took all of the drawers from their rooms with clothes, etc. in them and we stacked them in my truck along with all of the boxes they had packed.

We drove to the house, hung the clothes in the closets, unloaded the truck and left the ladies to unpack the boxes and drawers.

We drove back to the apartment to get my sister-in-law's bedroom set which just fit into my pick-up truck. Then back to the house to unload the truck and set up my sister-in-law's bed and bedroom.

The total move only took about three hours. I wanted to take everyone out to dinner but my wife decided it would be easier if we stayed home to eat. So, my wife and her mother prepared dinner while the men watched football on the TV and my sister and sister-in-law played in the family room with the children.

Dinner was excellent sitting around my former dining room table … it still felt like home!

I had the moving company, move everything that was left, to my storage loft at my used car lot.

Mid-January my wife and I were off to take our annual cruise in the warm weather provided by the Caribbean. We always had a terrific time on the boat and the food was great. Off the boat we really enjoyed the excursions, all topped off by top-notch entertainment and dancing. Is there any reason that each day feels like three days?

We came home; tanned, rested and satiated with food!

When we got home, my mother called to welcome us home and to tell me that I better go see my Uncle T … he wasn't doing well.

———————

Monday morning, first thing, I took a ride to my Uncle T's office. He really looked weak. He looked happy to see me and he brought me into his office and he closed the door, which was unusual since he newer closed the door before.

In a low voice just above a whisper, my Uncle T told me that he was dying … he had inoperable cancer … the doctors had given him only 4–6 weeks to live. OH NO! My heart dropped down into my stomach. He was my mentor … my best friend … my confidant.

My uncle went on to tell me there were three important things that I needed to do for him.

The first was that I had to make sure that my aunt would be taken care of. My uncle had 196 rental units all paid off … I was to take care and maintain all of the rental units for my aunt … all of the rent money would go into my aunt's account. Plus, she would get to keep their house and her car.

Second, I would inherit his entire construction company. He said, "And don't take any shit from them!"

This was unusual, since my uncle loved his employees, like they were his children.

Third, he told me his friends from New York would come to me with a request to take his place on the Board of Directors … be sure to accept … he felt it would open new doors for me.

I told my uncle not to worry that I would always look after my aunt and that I would be proud to carry on the tradition of his company and I would accept the offer to become a Board of Director.

At this point, my uncle could hardly speak and needed to rest. I asked the girl in front for a cold bottle of water.

I held his cold hand as I told my uncle with tears running down my face that I loved him, he had been my best friend. I appreciated everything he had done for me and often time just being there for me was important to me.

My Uncle T told me that they couldn't have children, but he always thought of me and treated me as his son. I told him that I felt that love.

When I left, I was saddened to know that I was going to lose my beloved uncle.

I threw my heart and soul back into my work … fortunately there weren't any catastrophic problems while I was on vacation but in business there are always issues here and there that need to be taken care of.

I wasn't interested in starting or buying any new businesses, especially given the fact that I would be soon having to run my uncle's construction company as well as all of the companies that I owned.

When I got home, I hugged and kissed my wife and each of our children.

I told my wife that my uncle only had six weeks to live. I hugged and kissed my wife and children again and sat holding my wife with AJ in her lap, as I said, "Life is short … we need to enjoy every minute of it!"

After dinner, we all went over to my mom's house. We all wept and hugged as I told my folks about my uncle. He had always been such a big strong figure in our family.

The doctors were correct, five weeks later my uncle was admitted to the hospital and given days to live. All of our relatives came to see him and I spent as much time as I could each evening.

Finally, he passed!

OH MY GOD … WHAT A LOSS!

My Uncle T's attorney contacted me almost immediately. He wanted to go over my uncle's last wishes and have me sign some paperwork. My uncle had picked a cemetery and he had paid for a spot for him and my aunt. Also, my uncle had purchased a stone from a company. All we had to do is give them the date of death and the location for the stone (which was a six-foot tall, Eiffel Tower looking head stone).

My dad went with me to the funeral home to make arrangements. My uncle of course, had picked a casket and a lining. He had also requested that they include a regular mattress in the bottom!

We went over the time and day for the wake and the funeral. They said they would contact the church and the cemetery. I said we would have a luncheon in the banquet room of my wife's new restaurant after the funeral. Done!

It looked like every employee my Uncle T ever had, came to the wake … they loved him, no wonder, my uncle always treated them so well! Also, all of our relatives and my uncle's closest friends came.

The next day of the funeral, my uncle's friends from New York came as well.

I gave the eulogy, I spoke of how kind my uncle was, how he would spend his time and money freely to help others and to donate to those less fortunate. How he was my mentor and how much he helped and trained me … I went on to say that I along with everyone there would miss him, greatly!

After the ceremonies when we got back out of the church into the parking lot. I noticed that my uncle's friends from New York had come in their big black limousine, with the four big body guards waiting at attention at each corner of the car … they stood out like a sore thumb!

We all went to the cemetery where the priest said many kind words which made us feel somewhat better.

Then, we headed over to my wife's new restaurant, up to the banquet room. Most everyone that had gone to the cemetery came for the luncheon. Including my uncle's four friends from New York and his fifth friend, the bank president. They sat at a separate table.

We provided an open bar and a nice buffet lunch. As I went from table to table my uncle's friends from New York invited me to join them, which I did.

Each one of these gentlemen introduced himself and they explained how much they liked my uncle and how long and how well they had worked together (I noticed each man was Italian). They told me that they felt as though they had lost a brother and there was now a void on their Board of Directors which they hoped I would fill. I graciously accepted and we all had a drink to seal the agreement. Soon after they left to go back to New York.

When we got home my wife and I were beat. The emotion of the day was exhausting. I told my wife that I had sat with my uncle's friends from New York and how congenial they were. I explained that they had offered me the position vacated by my uncle on the bank's Board of Directors … and I accepted it.

My wife said, "Wasn't that the same limo and the same bodyguards that protected us when we went to New York to meet with that scary man in Chinatown."

I replied, "Yes!"

My wife looked scared when she asked, "If that man in Chinatown was scared of these men, shouldn't we be scared too?"

"No," I said, "now they will protect us every day."

I think that made her feel somewhat better.

———————

The day my uncle died – his company closed. At the wake, I asked the two foremen to organize a meeting for all the employees at 7:00 am on Monday morning.

At the meeting, I addressed almost 100 employees.

I explained that my uncle left the company to me and that I hoped we could all continue on in his tradition. I went on to say that I believed I had met each of them over the years and if they had any questions, they could come to me at any time.

I said that their insurance and other benefits would not be affected and I expected each of them to work as hard for me as they had for my uncle. Then I sent them all back to work.

One of the foremen took me for a ride past each of the projects/jobs that they were currently working on.

By lunch time, I was back on the road checking on my other businesses.

The next day I stopped in the construction office to look at the receivables, something I do with my other businesses weekly. I found that on the largest project that we had, we had not received payment on any of the invoices that we had sent out. In construction, especially on large projects, payments are expected after certain work is performed (per contract).

In this case where the developer was intending to build 176 deluxe town house apartments. We were expected to clear the land (send an invoice), install sewers, gas and underground electric, rough hook-ups (send an invoice), pave the road, sidewalks and parking lots (send an invoice), pour concrete foundations (send an invoice/per four foundations) we had poured and capped all 48 foundations, frame and roof each building of four units (send an invoice) … we had completed all of the above work. Unfortunately, we had not received any payment for any of the invoices which were sent, going back to the middle of the previous year. I asked our office manager, the girl at the front desk why there had not been any payments. She said that my uncle would often cut large customers some slack. This wasn't slack, it was ridiculous.

I called the developer's office and left a voice message for the developer to call me immediately regarding their outstanding invoices!

The office manager told me she had left many similar messages and never got a reply. I took the developer's office and home addresses with me intending to stop by the developer's office or home if I didn't hear from him.

The issue of non-payment was not a problem in my other businesses, since we didn't sell anything on credit even on my rental units, I expected payment on time! So, I didn't have patience for those that didn't pay.

I went about my day touring as many of my stores as I could but it bothered me that someone would take advantage of my uncle like that!

Later that day I checked with my construction office and we had not gotten a call from the developer regarding the past due invoices. I was triple ticked!

So, I went to the developer's office … it was closed, no one there.

I went to the developer's home. The wife a very pretty blonde, who came to the door.

I explained who I was and that I was looking for her husband for payment of too many past due invoices.

Tears came to her eyes. She told me that her husband ran off to Canada with his pregnant secretary.

The wife went on to say that she was so revolted by her husband's actions that she was in the process of divorcing him!

I asked how she planned to pay for the work we had completed. She said she didn't plan on paying anything! I could sue the company but I wouldn't get anything.

I said I could foreclose on the property and that would cost her something for attorney's fees ... or she could sell me the land for the development for expenses incurred. She said that would be fair. I told her I would have my attorney draw up the agreement.

———————

The next day was my day off but I called my attorney and explained the circumstances regarding the developer and the non-payment of invoices. I explained that I needed a Purchase and Sale agreement for the land in leu of expenses incurred to date. Also, I asked my attorney to check to see if there were any outstanding loans or construction liens on the property.

Later we took the kids to the park for a long walk. At the pond, we fed the ducks crackers which Ava loved to do, AJ just watched from his carriage and smiled, he was a very good-natured baby!

I told my wife all about how the developer had not paid so many invoices and how ticked off I was that he didn't even call us back. I explained the agreement that I had made with the developer's wife and my wife agreed that it sounded fair.

———————

The following morning, I drove by the big construction project that we were working on. It appeared that not much was accomplished since we drove by on Monday so I headed to the construction office and I called in my two foremen. I explained what the present deal was with the wife of the developer ... and the story of why the developer left his wife. I was irritated again!

So, when I asked the foremen why it seemed that so little had been done since Monday. Their reply further irritated me.

They told me that all of the men had decided to perform a 'slow down', to request an across-the-board increase in what they get paid! I was off the board … *TICKED!*

I told the foremen to meet me in the office at 9:00 am on Friday.

On Friday morning, I told the foremen to have all of the equipment, trucks and materials that we had in the field, brought back to our yard and stored properly in our buildings, by the end of the day. Then I gave them a box of locks and asked them to lock all of our buildings when they were done … I did not give them any keys.

On Monday at 7:00 am, I stood outside the main gate which was locked and I told everyone including the two foreman and my office manager that the business was closed until further notice! This was a big deal for the two foremen and the office manager since my uncle always paid them and had them work year around.

Over the next several weeks, I finalized the agreement with the developer's wife and I then owned the development which I had put into my Tony's Rental, Inc. Company.

I put together a plan for a construction loan from my bank. I didn't think there would be any opposition given my status with the bank, but I felt that the bank should handle the loan like they would for any other customer.

I spoke to the president of the bank and he passed me off to the vice president of commercial loans. I explained to him that I would put up the land and the improvements as collateral … he approved the loan while I was still in his office!

I met with the girl that handled my rentals. I showed her the development and our plan for when the apartments would be available and I asked if she could handle it. She felt she would need to add another girl to help keep track of all the rents, on my previous properties. She also suggested that she move into the apartment next to the model apartment so that she would be more available for appointments. Great!

As I explained to my rental girl the plan was to complete two buildings every month (eight apartments). We would frame several buildings ahead of time so that we could work inside all winter long. Overall, it should take almost two years to complete all of the 176 units.

––––––––––

Each day going forward I stopped by the construction office to answer any messages that required follow-up and to pay bills.

On Thursday morning of the third week of closure for the construction company, I called in the two foremen and the office manager. I asked them to call all of our employees and have them come in to a meeting Friday morning at 8:00 am.

On Friday morning, I had the main gate to the construction yard open so everyone could get in. I stood in front of our big garage door to address the group.

I said, "I was ashamed of your behavior … my uncle always treated you all very well … and you have the gall to slow down to force me to give you all a pay increase … well … that is not going to happen! You all know me … you know that I do not need the added work of running this company … nor do I need the income from this company to exist … I have agreed to run this company because my uncle asked me to keep it going, so all of you would have a job … and the first chance you get, you try to stick it to me … well you can see that isn't going to work! In each of my other companies if we have someone that cannot keep up or slows down purposely, we fire them … and that is exactly what we are going to do here going forward! If anyone has a problem with that, come and see me individually. My plan is for those of you that want to work for me to start Monday at 7:00 am … come in ready to work and work hard … thank you!"

Then, I went into the office with the two foremen and the office manager. I gave the keys for the locks to the foremen and said not to unlock anything until Monday morning. I went on to say that I expected them to be my eyes and ears and to tell me what is going on if not, I didn't need them.

When the foremen left, the office manager came into my office to say, "You are tough! You are not going to take any shit from these guys … are you!"

"No, I'm not! I do not allow my employees to push me around or dictate to me!"

She said, "You got your point across."

Great!

————————————

Going forward it seemed like we were much more productive than before. Great!

When we needed to quote, I let the foremen calculate what they thought the manpower and materials should cost, then based on the fact that they were generally 20% low on earlier jobs, I added 20%, then I added our mark up. We were not usually the low bidder and certainly not the high bidder. Most of the time we got the job because of our quality and performance … and so we had plenty of work! Great!

————————————

Chapter 13

When it got to my birthday dinner at my mom's house, we had a ball with Ava and little Tony running around kicking a ball and laughing … AJ could almost stand up in his play pen but seemed to enjoy watching the other kids running around having fun.

The meal was outstanding it was one of my favorites, homemade Enoch (a potato-based macaroni the shape of a sea shell) with homemade meatballs and homemade sauce … just before dessert my mom looked at me and said, "I hear you think you're a tough guy now … at the construction company!"

"No," I said, "I am a mommy's boy!"

Everyone around the table broke up laughing.

By July, the first two buildings were complete, including landscaping. The model apartment was furnished and my rental girl had moved into the apartment next door.

So, we ran a full-page ad in the newspaper and we were inundated with interested people. All six available apartments were rented and moved into, by August 1. Terrific!

Plus, we had a waiting list for many of the apartments that wouldn't be available until September.

I had been keeping an eye on my aunt. At first, I stopped by every week then every two weeks.

She had been keeping herself busy by playing bridge with her partner, the divorcee who lived next door.

My aunt seemed to be coping well. I made sure that she always had plenty of cash and plenty of food. She shopped at my grocery store and had it delivered to her house. My wife and I invited my aunt to come to our house for dinner on Wednesday nights and my mom invited my aunt to join us at our family dinner on Sunday … most of the time she came to both dinners.

My travel agent told me about a special bridge players cruise. I didn't think that my aunt would want to fly (since she had never been on an airplane) so, we found a cruise ship that went out of New York city. It was a five-day cruise with a duplicate tournament each day with three meals per day and entertainment at night.

It sounded good to my aunt and her partner. We offered to pay for my aunt's partner as well (my aunt had tons of money in her account). I hired a limousine to drive them from their house to the ship (and I gave my aunt the number for the limousine to call for the ride home).

The two ladies had a blast!

Of course, I got them a large room on the concierge level.

My aunt asked, "Isn't that expensive?"

I told her that she could afford it and it was time that she enjoyed life and her money!

She said they met lots of real nice people on the cruise.

When could they go again? I explained that there was probably a cruise every week, but they would have to fly south to get to the ship and the cruise would probably be for a week.

My aunt's reply was, "No problem!"

My travel agent researched bridge players cruises and suggested several. One in early December had a tournament every other day and was in port for sightseeing on the off days. My aunt liked that and we booked it before it was sold out.

––––––––––

Also, in June I got a call at my construction office from my friends in New York. It was time for our quarterly review meeting (they got together after the close of each quarter of the year. April, July, October and January).

So, the president of the bank and I met at our bank and we took a limousine with a bar in it to New York City for a luncheon meeting.

I just drank iced tea but the president of the bank had a couple of martinis.

On the way, he explained that we get together after the books are closed each quarter to review how the bank is doing. He prepares the presentation, profitability of each branch, unproductive loans and any other issues that come up … and we eat!

I recognized the restaurant as we drove up. It was the same restaurant that my wife and I ate at when she and I were in the city. The limo with the four bodyguards was parked in the front, our friends beat us there.

Inside, our four friends could not have seemed more pleased to see us. They made me feel very welcome. Not sure what I was responsible to do at these meetings.

We were seated in a separate room to avoid any excess noise.

First came the drinks and then the food … a medley of just about every kind of Italian dish imaginable! Exquisite!

For dessert, I had a cannoli!

All through dinner the drinks and wine kept coming … I drank beer … I don't know how they can drink so heavily during the day.

When the table was cleared, it was time for the president of the bank to present his report.

The bank profit was humongous! They asked what we should do? The president was prepared for the question and suggested that we build two new branch offices, along the coastline. That was agreed too rather easily. They all looked at me and said, "We will need to go through the bidding process as usual but Tony's construction company will build them … of course."

Then the president went around the table telling each Board member how many 'credits' they had … I had no idea what a credit was and I was not going to ask. By the way … I had no credits!

Finally, we discussed un-productive loans … loans that were not being paid. This was an issue for the bank. Evidently banks are evaluated poorly by the auditors for having un-producing loans.

The bank president would explain what the property consisted of, where the property was located, how much the remaining loan was for and what the appraised value was. Then a Board Member would speak up and agree to take the loan over, for some number of credits. When everyone agreed, we would go to the next loan.

The last order of business was to pay everyone for attending the Board Meeting, we all received a generous check.

There was a terrific comradery amongst the men … they really seemed to enjoy each other (and the tremendous amount of liquor that they consumed).

The bank president really seemed to relax after he gave his report. He could then pound down the drinks as well.

When we left the restaurant, both of our limousines were out front waiting for us.

On the ride back, I asked the bank president how they could guarantee that my company would get the contract to build the branch banks.

The bank president started to laugh, he said, "It's easy we send out four or five RFQ's (Request for Quotes) and when they are all received, I will tell you what to quote to get the job. Usually, we will go with a number slightly less than the middle quote. If that is not enough for you to build it, then you will put through change orders, which I will approve."

During the ride back the bank president continued to drink martinis. I had one beer.

When we got close to home, the limousine driver politely asked if we would like to be dropped off at our homes.

The bank president said, "Yes!"

I asked the driver to drop me at the bank, so I could pick up my truck.

During the following week, when I stopped into the construction company office, I asked the office manager if we had built any branch banks before. She told me that we had built many branch banks. So, we took out the blueprints, the estimates and the invoices for the last branch that we built so I could review them.

I asked the office manager how we did financially on building the branches. She told me that she felt we made out very well, after the change orders were paid for.

I spoke to the two foremen regarding how they estimated work required for the branches in the past. They told me that my uncle pretty much did the estimates and he generally copied the last estimate/proposal with just a few changes since there was always something different from job to job. They told me not to sweat it!

Pretty much each month we completed another two, four townhouse apartments, which we rented out quickly!

I could not have found a better person to manage my rental properties … this girl was right on top of everything and the renters loved her. GREAT!

We survived the holidays and the New Year's celebrations … it was hectic but we did very well!

It was time again for my wife and I to go on our annual cruise. I look forward to the cruise because it gives my wife and I time to relax and recharge. Just being able to sit somewhere and read a book for two hours without interruption is so relaxing.

On the flight down south, my wife informed me that this would not be a 'make a baby cruise'! We have a boy and a girl both are healthy what else could a parent want?

My wife also informed me that we would need to practice making babies a lot, in case we decide to have more babies in the future. Great!

After the ship left the dock, my wife and I stretched out on lounge chairs by the swimming pool. We each had a frozen chocolate/banana mudslide and a book. My wife informed me that just before we left her sister told her that she wanted to marry one of the guys from the island band that plays at the restaurant, that she manages.

She didn't want a big deal, there were only his band members, my wife's parents and my wife and I. She was thinking of getting married by a Justice of the Peace.

I suggested that we have the ceremony and a small party in the banquet room of our new restaurant and we can get the piano player for the afternoon.

I said, "Your sister can just wear a nice dress and the guy can wear a suit, if he has one … and we will pick up the tab."

My wife said, "That's very generous of you … but her real issue is, where are they going to live?"

"That's her issue … well how soon does she need an apartment?" I asked.

My wife's reply was, "She can wait a month or two."

"Great … I will call my real estate girl and ask her if we have an opening coming up in one of the older units, and I will give them a deal on the rent."

My wife came over to my lounge and kissed me tenderly, "Thank you … you are so generous!" Then she gave me another (juicier) more romantic kiss.

I whispered, "If you would like we could head back to our room and you could work on me to pay for their honeymoon cruise!"

My wife laughed and pulled me up out of my lounge chair.

Finally, the decision was made for us to pay for a cruise that would stop at the island that the husband was from, so that his friends and relatives could meet his wife and she could meet them.

From land, I called my real estate girl to ask her to keep an eye open for an apartment that would be available in the next month or two. She said she would have a vacant apartment in one of my original brick apartment houses at the end of the next month.

"Great … do not fill it … I have two newlyweds that need it."

I told her and thanked her.

So, then my wife called her sister to give her the big news regarding the wedding, reception and the apartment. When my wife got off the telephone with her sister, she told me her sister was delighted, but they do not have any furniture … or anything. Of course, not!

I told my wife to tell her sister that when we got back, we would take her sister and her fiancé to the furniture store and we would get everything she will need. But she will still need dishes and glasses and silverware, and whatever, which we can print on a sheet and distribute to those coming to the wedding, to purchase as wedding presents.

Then, we could resume our restful vacation. Although, I noticed that my wife would write something down every now and then … I am sure it had to do with the wedding.

By the end of our vacation, we were tanned, relaxed and recharged, as usual.

―――――――

Once we got home, my wife and her sister started to make plans. They chose a date, the last Sunday of the month, which was the 30th, they chose a time, 1:00 pm and they chose a venue, our banquet room. Great!

I remembered that we had stored the furniture from my wife's parents' apartment, it was like new and would be free to the sister and her new husband.

I called and scheduled the JP and the piano player.

My wife and her sister made up a list of people to invite, then they split the list up into three sections; one section for the prospective husband (his band members), my sister-in-law (her mom and dad and a few girls from the restaurant that she manages) and my wife (me, my mom, dad, sister and brother-in-law). I was surprised to see that she wanted to invite my relatives but my wife said that my family always made her feel like part of their family. Great!

―――――――

My wife and I ordered flowers to decorate the small alter and at 1:00 pm that Sunday, my sister-in-law and her island band member were married. It was a warm and cozy ceremony. My wife was matron of honor and my sister-in-law's husband, asked his brother to be best man.

Of course, we had an open bar which everyone took advantage of. The meal consisted of roast beef, a pile of oriental vegetables, an eggroll and a scoop of mashed potatoes. Bottles of red and white wine were on the tables and for dessert we had the wedding cake (which was an Italian rum cake, made by the Italian cake lady).

During dinner the pianist played slow tempo, quiet music. Then when the dinner was over, he stepped up the beat and the volume. Most of the guests mingled and danced.

I went over to the pianist to request a few songs, incidentally so did one of the dancers from the island band, the youngest one. She looked spectacular wearing a white harem outfit which really stood out, given her milk chocolate skin. Her outfit consisted of an off the shoulder top, with flimsy (gauze like) see through, puffy sleeves, ending in a white cuff with a gold button. The top consisted of a tube top of the white material, covered by bunches of the flimsy material … the top was almost see-through … you could tell she wasn't wearing a bra, since her young brown nipples protruded through the fabric. The bottom consisted of a white elastic band around the top (which was, well below the navel), a white bikini like bottom and the pant was made of the flimsy gauze like material, puffy around each leg, ending in a white cuff around each ankle, with a gold button. She wore shinny white high heels and had a pretty white flower in her waist length jet black hair!

She told the piano player to play 'Unforgettable' and she asked me to dance.

I took her hand and led her to the middle of the dance floor.

When I took her in my arms to dance, she looked up into my eyes and said, "I have been waiting a long time to get you alone!"

As she said that she pressed her entire body up against mine. Her pert nipples poked through my thin silk shirt and her lower extremities pressed against my crotch. WOW!

She caught me off guard.

I could hardly say the word, "Why?"

As she continued to gyrate against my body, she said, "Because I want to go to bed with you!"

Let me say that what she was doing with her body against mine was highly distracting, but I uttered, "If I were single, I would take you up on that offer immediately but … I am happily married and I don't think my wife would go for it."

She kept smiling and she kept gyrating and she said, "You can invite her as well!"

My reply was, "I am sorry … I have to decline your offer … but I have to tell you that I am flattered!"

Fortunately, the song was coming to an end. I thanked my dance partner for the dance and given my aroused condition danced over closely to our table and when the music stopped, I sat right down with the table cloth covering my lap. My partner was laughing given the effect she had on me!

My wife came over and asked if I had enjoyed my dance and I said, "Yes! I will tell you about it later."

I waited a few dances then I danced with my wife, the bride, my mother and my mother-in-law.

My brother-in-law and I put a Just Married sign on the back of their car and we tied several strings of beer cans to the back bumper of their car.

Late-afternoon the bride and groom left for the airport stopping home to change into something more comfortable to travel in.

––––––––––

When we were going to bed, I told my wife about the proposition the beautiful island dancer proposed to me during our dance and how seductively she moved against me as we danced (I was getting aroused again). I told my wife that I turned the girl down, I told the girl that I was happily married. We were cuddling but when I looked in her face, I could see she was mad. I went on to say that the girl said we could invite my wife as well! Then my wife's face changed, she became exuberant. I think she liked the idea of a menage a trois with the young island girl, but I didn't think it was a good idea.

So, we started to play around with each other saying, "I think I would do this … or that." To the young girl (while we did, this or that to each other). It was very stimulating and we used it as inspiration over the next several weeks during foreplay.

––––––––––

On Monday morning, I had the moving company come and pick up the furniture for the apartment, which was stored on the second floor of one of the buildings in my car lot.

My father-in-law came and picked up all of the material type items to take back to the laundry and clean them (towels, sheets, and curtains).

On Wednesday, my wife and I, met my mom, my dad, my sister, her husband and my in-laws at the apartment to set it up.

While my sister and my mom cleaned the cabinets and put shelving paper down, my brother-in-law and I unpacked and loaded the dishwasher with the glassware, dishes and silverware. Then he washed the counter and I washed the sink. We put all of the figurines and other choochkies in the sink to be cleaned.

While we waited for the first load in the dishwasher to finish, I vacuumed the carpets and my brother-in-law dusted all of the furniture. My in-laws scrubbed the entire bathroom and put in fresh clean towels. Then, they made the bed and when they got to the pillows my mother-in-law decided that the pillows smelled from storage.

So, my wife took her mother to buy new pillows.

While they were gone, my brother-in-law and I, helped my father-in-law to hang all of the cleaned curtains.

My mom and sister washed all of the pots and pans by hand and put them away. When the dishwasher stopped, my wife and sister put all of the cleaned dishes, silverware and glasses away. My mom cleaned the refrigerator.

My dad found all of the table lamps … he dusted them, plugged them in and made sure they worked. He hooked up the TV and he dusted/cleaned all of the ceiling lights and put new bulbs in them.

My wife and her mother were gone a long time to just buy two new pillows but when they returned, they both were carrying two bags of groceries.

We were done setting up the entire apartment by mid-afternoon. My mom invited us all over to her house for a homemade ravioli dinner. It was terrific!

On Friday night, my wife and I went over to my in-law's house (my old raised ranch) and we got my wife's sister's clothes and brought them over to the new apartment. NO WAY were we going over to the groom's apartment to get his clothes (I didn't want to run into his sister) … he could do it for himself!

My sister-in-law and her husband could not have been more thankful for the wedding reception and the cruise which they said was out of this world! They really thanked us for picking a cruise that stopped at the groom's home island. They had a wonderful time seeing his close friends and relatives and introducing his wife to them all!

Also, they could not believe their apartment and how it was all set up. We explained that it took our entire families.

It was back to work on Monday. My wife had loaned her second in command to her sister's restaurant while the sister was on her honeymoon but now, she was back to my wife's restaurant.

My shopping center and my original businesses were doing very well. I met regularly with my construction company to make sure we were quoting on time, are we collecting on our invoices on time, and the men are working at an expected pace.

In the interim, the prints for the new branch banks had come in and I had the foremen compare them to the prints of the last branch that we built. There were a few changes here and there. So, I modified our quote, proposal, to exclude what was not in the new branch and add what was new.

I did that for each branch and had the office manager re-type the proposals (leaving out the sheet with our quote).

When they were complete, I took the proposals for the new branches over to the bank, to show the president of the bank. All of the RFQ's were sent to the bank president for his review. The president was impressed that I was done so early, the quotes were not due for two more weeks and mine looked great. All I had to do was wait for the other companies to send in their quotes, so I would know how much to quote. RELAX!

After the initial surge of car sales due to our new car lots, the sales seemed to fall into a predictable routine. More sales in the spring when people are getting back their tax refunds and less at Christmas time as people are spending their money on Christmas presents. I really like the car business! Instead of making pennies on a can of beans we make thousands on the sale of one car. Great!

The liquor store business was another home run! As my buddy B had told me many, many times, "When times are good … people drink … when times are bad … people drink!" And the business is very profitable!

The dry-cleaning business just for the clothes dropped off at the shopping center was making a slight profit but with the clothes from the other three grocery store drop-off's it was doing great and my father-in-law was delighted!

I stopped in to the jewelry store in my shopping center to buy a 'no special event' present for my wife. The jeweler remembered me. I asked the jeweler how he was doing. He said, he was doing very well, better than expected! Since I had no idea what I wanted I just looked around to see what caught my eye. The store was exquisite, I told the jeweler. He thanked me. I saw a number of things that I liked but what really caught my attention was a watch. The watch itself was in the shape of a heart with a red face mounted in a gold bezel, the band consisted of small gold hearts linked together … beautiful!

"I'll take it!"

The jeweler put the watch in its box and gave it to one of his girls to gift wrap it. Then, he started to write up a sales receipt for it. I had seen the price tag and it was expensive but understand I do not look at what items cost when I shop … I buy what I like! In any event the jeweler wrote up the sale for significantly less than what was on the price tag. I asked him if there was a sale going on. He told me there weren't any sales at that time. Therefore, I asked him why he was charging me less than the price tag amount.

He said, "Aren't you one of the Board of Directors of the big bank?"

I replied, "Yes, I am."

He said that he was indebted to us because the bank helped him out in hard times and he wanted to thank me by discounting my purchase.

"Well, thank you so much!" I replied.

When my package came, it could not have been wrapped any nicer!

That night, I snuck into the kitchen and put the gift on my wife's empty plate and when she saw it, she was amazed at how pretty the box was wrapped. When we sat down, she couldn't wait to open it and when she saw the watch inside, she screamed, because she liked it so much! She said she had never seen a prettier watch in her life!

My wife asked why I had bought her such a nice gift? I told her that she was an outstanding mother and wife and I just felt like buying her a 'no special event present'.

From that day forward, my wife has worn that watch!

———

Chapter 14

As I have gotten older, my birthdays are not such a big deal any more.

Don't tell my mom, she makes a real big deal out of all of our birthdays.

My brother-in-law and I kicked a ball around in the backyard with little Tony and Ava, while the women prepared the meal.

Later, when we arrived home, it was time for the kids to go to bed. Then, my wife wanted to go to bed early as well. She always made a big deal in bed that it was my birthday and this year she was as exuberant as ever … culminating in two magnificent, 'Happy Endings' for both of us!

While my wife was in the shower, I laid on my back with my hands beneath my head reflecting on what a wonderful life I have had to this point.

I have come to the conclusion, upon reflecting, that I am no longer just a grocer but given the number and diversity of the businesses that I own, I am really an Entrepreneur. So, in future writings I will be The Entrepreneur.

Who knows what's to come down the road … life is a magnificent journey!

THE END